GM

IN MINIATURE

• RANDALL OLSON •

Also from Veloce Publishing:

SpeedPro Series
4-Cylinder Engine – How to Blueprint & Build a Short Block for High Performance (Hammill)
Alfa Romeo DOHC High-Performance Manual (Kartalamakis)
Alfa Romeo V6 Engine High-Performance Manual (Kartalamakis)
BMC 998cc A-Series Engine – How to Power Tune (Hammill)
1275cc A-Series High-Performance Manual (Hammill)
Camshafts – How to Choose & Time them for Maximum Power (Hammill)
Cylinder Heads – How to Build, Modify & Power Tune Updated & Revised Edition (Burgess & Gollan)
Distributor-type Ignition Systems – How to Build & Power Tune (Hammill)
Fast Road Car – How to Plan and Build Revised & Updated Color New Edition (Stapleton)
Ford SOHC 'Pinto' & Sierra Cosworth DOHC Engines – How to Power Tune Updated & Enlarged Edition (Hammill)
Ford V8 – How to Power Tune Small Block Engines (Hammill)
Harley-Davidson Evolution Engines – How to Build & Power Tune (Hammill)
Holley Carburetors – How to Build & Power Tune Revised & Updated Edition (Hammill)
Jaguar XK Engines – How to Power Tune Revised & Updated Color Edition (Hammill)
MG Midget & Austin-Healey Sprite – How to Power Tune Updated & Revised Edition (Stapleton)
MGB 4-Cylinder Engine – How to Power Tune (Burgess)
MGB V8 Power – How to Give Your, Third Color Edition (Williams)
MGB, MGC & MGB V8 – How to Improve (Williams)
Mini Engines – How to Power Tune on a Small Budget Color Edition (Hammill)
Motorcycle-engined Racing Car – How to Build (Pashley)
Motorsport – Getting Started (Collins)
Motorsports Datalogging (Templeman)
Nitrous Oxide High-Performance Manual (Langfield)
Rover V8 Engines – How to Power Tune (Hammill)
Sportscar/Kitcar Suspension & Brakes – How to Build & Modify Enlarged & Updated 2nd Edition (Hammill)
SU Carburettor High-Performance Manual (Hammill)
Supercar, How to Build (Thompson)
Suzuki 4x4 – How to Modify for Serious Off-Road Action (Richardson)
Tiger Avon Sportscar – How to Build Your Own Updated & Revised 2nd Edition (Dudley)
TR2, 3 & TR4 – How to Improve (Williams)
TR5, 250 & TR6 – How to Improve (Williams)
TR7 & TR8, How to Improve (Williams)
V8 Engine – How to Build a Short Block for High Performance (Hammill)
Volkswagen Beetle Suspension, Brakes & Chassis – How to Modify for High Performance (Hale)
Volkswagen Bus Suspension, Brakes & Chassis – How to Modify for High Performance (Hale)
Weber DCOE, & Dellorto DHLA Carburetors – How to Build & Power Tune 3rd Edition (Hammill)

Those were the days ... Series
Alpine Trials & Rallies 1910-1973 (Pfundner)
Austerity Motoring (Bobbitt)
Brighton National Speed Trials (Gardiner)
British Police Cars (Walker)
British Woodies (Peck)
Crystal Palace by (Collins)
Dune Buggy Phenomenon (Hale)
Dune Buggy Phenomenon Volume 2 (Hale)
MG's Abingdon Factory (Moylan)
Motor Racing at Brands Hatch in the Seventies (Parker)
Motor Racing at Goodwood in the Sixties (Gardiner)
Motor Racing at Oulton Park in the 1960s (McFadyen)
Motor Racing at Oulton Park in the 1970s (McFadyen)
Short Oval Racing in the 1980s (Neil)
Three Wheelers (Bobbitt)

Enthusiast's Restoration Manual Series
Citroën 2CV, How to Restore (Porter)
Classic Car Bodywork, How to Restore (Thaddeus)
Classic Car Electrics (Thaddeus)
Classic Cars, How to Paint (Thaddeus)
Reliant Regal, How to Restore (Payne)
Triumph TR2/3/3A, How to Restore (Williams)
Triumph TR4/4A, How to Restore (Williams)
Triumph TR5/250 & 6, How to Restore (Williams)
Triumph TR7/8, How to Restore (Williams)
Volkswagen Beetle, How to Restore (Tyler)
VW Bay Window Bus (Paxton)
Yamaha FS1-E, How to Restore (Watts)

Essential Buyer's Guide Series
Alfa GT (Booker)
Alfa Romeo Spider Giulia (Booker & Talbott)
BMW GS (Henshaw)
BSA Bantam (Henshaw)
BSA Twins (Henshaw)
Citroën 2CV (Paxton)
Citroën ID & DS (Heilig)
Fiat 500 & 600 (Bobbitt)
Jaguar E-type 3.8 & 4.2-litre (Crespin)
Jaguar E-type V12 5.3-litre (Crespin)
Jaguar/Daimler XJ6, XJ12 & Sovereign (Crespin)
Jaguar XJ-S (Crespin)
MGB & MGB GT (Williams)
Mercedes-Benz 280SL-560SL Roadsters (Bass)
Mercedes-Benz 'Pagoda' 230SL, 250SL & 280SL Roadsters & Coupés (Bass)
Morris Minor (Newell)
Porsche 928 (Hemmings)
Rolls-Royce Silver Shadow & Bentley T-Series (Bobbitt)
Subaru Impreza (Hobbs)
Triumph Bonneville (Henshaw)
Triumph TR6 (Williams)
VW Beetle (Cservenka & Copping)
VW Bus (Cservenka & Copping)

Auto-Graphics Series
Fiat-based Abarths (Sparrow)
Jaguar MkI & II Saloons (Sparrow)
Lambretta LI series scooters (Sparrow)

Rally Giants Series
Audi Quattro (Robson)
Big Healey – 100-Six & 3000 (Robson)
Ford Escort MkI (Robson)
Ford Escort RS1800 (Robson)
Lancia Stratos (Robson)
Peugeot 205 T16 (Robson)
Subaru Impreza (Robson)

General
$1^1/_2$-litre GP Racing 1961-1965 (Whitelock)
AC Two-litre Saloons & Buckland Sportscars (Archibald)
According to Carter (Skelton)
Alfa Romeo Giulia Coupé GT & GTA (Tipler)
Alfa Romeo Montreal - The Essential Companion (Taylor)
Alfa Tipo 33 (McDonough & Collins)
Anatomy of the Works Minis (Moylan)
Armstrong-Siddeley (Smith)
Autodrome (Collins & Ireland)
Automotive A-Z, Lane's Dictionary of Automotive Terms (Lane)
Automotive Mascots (Kay & Springate)
Bahamas Speed Weeks, The (O'Neil)
Bentley Continental, Corniche and Azure (Bennett)
Bentley MkVI, Rolls-Royce Silver Wraith, Dawn & Cloud/Bentley R & S-series (Nutland)
BMC Competitions Department Secrets (Turner, Chambers, Browning)
BMW 5-Series (Cranswick)
BMW Z-Cars (Taylor)
British 250cc Racing Motorcycles by Chris Pereira
British Cars, The Complete Catalogue of, 1895-1975 (Culshaw & Horrobin)
BRM – a mechanic's tale (Salmon)
BRM V16 (Ludvigsen)
BSA Bantam Bible (Henshaw)
Bugatti Type 40 (Price)
Bugatti 46/50 Updated Edition (Price & Arbey)
Bugatti T44 & T49 (Price & Arbey)
Bugatti 57 2nd Edition (Price)
Caravans, The Illustrated History 1919-1959 (Jenkinson)
Caravans, The Illustrated History from 1960 (Jenkinson)
Carrera Panamericana (Tipler)
Chrysler 300 – America's Most Powerful Car 2nd Edition (Ackerson)
Chrysler PT Cruiser (Ackerson)
Citroën DS (Bobbitt)
Cliff Alison - From the Fells to Ferrari (Gauld)
Cobra – The Real Thing! (Legate)
Cortina – Ford's Bestseller (Robson)
Coventry Climax Racing Engines (Hammill)
Daimler SP250 New Edition (Long)
Datsun Fairlady Roadster to 280ZX – The Z-car Story (Long)
Dino – The V6 Ferrari (Long)
Dodge Charger – Enduring Thunder (Ackerson)
Dodge Dynamite! (Grist)
Draw & Paint Cars – How to (Gardiner)
Drive on the Wild Side, A – 20 extreme driving adventures from around the world (Weaver)
Ducati 750 Bible, The (Falloon)
Ducati 860, 900 and Mille Bible, The (Falloon)
Dune Buggy, Building a – The Essential Manual (Shakespeare)
Dune Buggy Files (Hale)
Dune Buggy Handbook (Hale)
Edward Turner: the man behind the motorcycles (Clew)
Fiat & Abarth 124 Spider & Coupé (Tipler)
Fiat & Abarth 500 & 600 2nd edition (Bobbitt)
Fiats, Great Small (Ward)
Fine Art of the Motorcycle Engine, The (Peirce)
Ford F100/F150 Pickup 1948-1996 (Ackerson)
Ford F150 1997-2005 (Ackerson)
Ford GT – Then, and Now (Streather)
Ford GT40 (Legate)
Ford in Miniature (Olson)
Ford Model Y (Roberts)
Ford Thunderbird from 1954, The Book of the (Long)
Forza Minardi! (Vigar)
Funky Mopeds (Skelton)
Gentleman Jack (Gauld)
GM in Miniature (Olson)
GT – The World's Best GT Cars 1953-73 (Dawson)
Hillclimbing & Sprinting – The essential manual (Short & Wilkinson)
Honda NSX (Long)
Jaguar, The Rise of (Price)
Jaguar XJ-S (Long)
Jeep CJ (Ackerson)
Jeep Wrangler (Ackerson)
Karmann-Ghia Coupé & Convertible (Bobbitt)
Lambretta Bible, The (Davies)
Lancia 037 (Collins)
Lancia Delta HF Integrale (Blaettel & Wagner)
Land Rover, The Half-Ton Military (Cook)
Laverda Twins & Triples Bible 1968-1986 (Falloon)
Lea-Francis Story, The (Price)
Lexus Story, The (Long)
little book of smart, the (Jackson)
Lola – The Illustrated History (1957-1977) (Starkey)
Lola – All the Sports Racing & Single-Seater Racing Cars 1978-1997 (Starkey)
Lola T70 – The Racing History & Individual Chassis Record 3rd Edition (Starkey)
Lotus 49 (Oliver)
MarketingMobiles, The Wonderful Wacky World of (Hale)
Mazda MX-5/Miata 1.6 Enthusiast's Workshop Manual (Grainger & Shoemark)
Mazda MX-5/Miata 1.8 Enthusiast's Workshop Manual (Grainger & Shoemark)
Mazda MX-5 Miata: the book of the world's favorite sportscar (Long)
Mazda MX-5 Miata Roadster (Long)
MGA (Price Williams)
MGB & MGB GT – Expert Guide (Auto-Doc Series) (Williams)
MGB Electrical Systems (Astley)
Micro Caravans (Jenkinson)
Micro Trucks (Mort)
Microcars at large! (Quellin)
Mini Cooper – The Real Thing! (Tipler)
Mitsubishi Lancer Evo, the road car & WRC story (Long)
Montlhéry, the story of the Paris autodrome (Boddy)
Morgan Maverick (Lawrence)
Morris Minor, 60 years on the road (Newell)
Moto Guzzi Sport & Le Mans Bible (Falloon)
Motor Movies – The Posters! (Veysey)
Motor Racing – Reflections of a Lost Era (Carter)
Motorcycle Road & Racing Chassis Designs (Noakes)
Motorhomes, The Illustrated History (Jenkinson)
Motorsport in color, 1950s (Wainwright)
Nissan 300ZX & 350Z – The Z-Car Story (Long)
Pass the Theory and Practical Driving Tests (Gibson & Hoole)
Peking to Paris 2007 (Young)
Plastic Toy Cars of the 1950s & 1960s (Ralston)
Pontiac Firebird (Cranswick)
Porsche Boxster (Long)
Porsche 356 (2nd edition) (Long)
Porsche 911 Carrera – The Last of the Evolution (Corlett)
Porsche 911R, RS & RSR, 4th Edition (Starkey)
Porsche 911 – The Definitive History 1963-1971 (Long)
Porsche 911 – The Definitive History 1971-1977 (Long)
Porsche 911 – The Definitive History 1977-1987 (Long)
Porsche 911 – The Definitive History 1987-1997 (Long)
Porsche 911 – The Definitive History 1997-2004 (Long)
Porsche 911SC 'Super Carrera' – The Essential Companion (Streather)
Porsche 914 & 914-6: The Definitive History Of The Road & Competition Cars (Long)
Porsche 924 (Long)
Porsche 944 (Long)
Porsche 993 'King of Porsche' – The Essential Companion (Streather)
Porsche 996 'Supreme Porsche' – The Essential Companion (Streather)
Porsche Racing Cars – 1953 to 1975 (Long)
Porsche Racing Cars – 1976 on (Long)
Porsche – The Rally Story (Meredith)
Porsche: Three Generations of Genius (Meredith)
RAC Rally Action! (Gardiner)
Rallye Sport Fords: the inside story (Moreton)
Redman, Jim – 6 Times World Motorcycle Champion: The Autobiography (Redman)
Rolls-Royce Silver Shadow/Bentley T Series Corniche & Camargue Revised & Enlarged Edition (Bobbitt)
Rolls-Royce Silver Spirit, Silver Spur & Bentley Mulsanne 2nd Edition (Bobbitt)
RX-7 – Mazda's Rotary Engine Sportscar (updated & revised new edition) (Long)
Scooters & Microcars, The A-Z of popular (Dan)
Scooter Lifestyle (Grainger)
Singer Story: Cars, Commercial Vehicles, Bicycles & Motorcycles (Atkinson)
SM – Citroën's Maserati-engined Supercar (Long & Claverol)
Subaru Impreza: the road car and WRC story (Long)
Taxi! The Story of the 'London' Taxicab (Bobbitt)
Tinplate Toy Cars of the 1950s & 1960s (Ralston)
Toyota Celica & Supra, The book of Toyota's Sports Coupés (Long)
Toyota MR2 Coupés & Spyders (Long)
Triumph Motorcycles & the Meriden Factory (Hancox)
Triumph Speed Twin & Thunderbird Bible (Woolridge)
Triumph Tiger Cub Bible (Estall)
Triumph Trophy Bible (Woolridge)
Triumph TR6 (Kimberley)
Unraced (Collins)
Velocette Motorcycles – MSS to Thruxton Updated & Revised (Burris)
Virgil Exner – Visioneer: The official biography of Virgil M Exner designer extraordinaire (Grist)
Volkswagen Bus Book, The (Bobbitt)
Volkswagen Bus or Van to Camper, How to Convert (Porter)
Volkswagens of the World (Glen)
VW Beetle Cabriolet (Bobbitt)
VW Beetle – The Car of the 20th Century (Copping)
VW Bus – 40 years of Splitties, Bays & Wedges (Copping)
VW Bus Book, The (Bobbitt)
VW Golf: five generations of fun (Copping & Cservenka)
VW – The air-cooled era (Copping)
VW T5 Camper Conversion Manual (Porter)
VW Campers (Copping)
Works Minis, The Last (Purves & Brenchley)
Works Rally Mechanic (Moylan)

www.veloce.co.uk

First published in February 2008 by Veloce Publishing Limited, 33 Trinity Street, Dorchester DT1 1TT, England. Fax 01305 268864/e-mail info@veloce.co.uk/web www.veloce.co.uk or www.velocebooks.com.
ISBN: 978-1-84584-156-0/UPC: 6-36847-04156-4

Readers with ideas for automotive books, or books on other transport or related hobby subjects, are invited to write to the editorial director of Veloce Publishing at the above address.
British Library Cataloguing in Publication Data - A catalogue record for this book is available from the British Library. Typesetting, design and page make-up all by Veloce Publishing Ltd on Apple Mac.
Printed in India by Replika Press.

GM
IN MINIATURE

VELOCE PUBLISHING
THE PUBLISHER OF FINE AUTOMOTIVE BOOKS

CONTENTS

ACKNOWLEDGMENTS

THIS IS THE SECOND BOOK IN VELOCE PUBLISHING'S SERIES ABOUT MINIATURE cars and trucks. As its author, I have learned much from my first effort, *Ford in Miniature*. It is no small feat to create such a publication and I am indebted to many fine people without whom this book would simply be a dream:

First, I would like to thank Jerry Rettig, author of *American Wheels – A Reference*. Jerry's love for little scale model cars and trucks is quite simply contagious. I have drawn from his well of knowledge and photographs many times.

On the subject of photographs, I am once again grateful to David Larsen, Dirk Mathyssen, Alex Moskalev, Alan Novak, Bob Hooper, Dave Ronken, Christian Hardegger, Greg Gunn, and Mike Stephens for their superb images and background information. I would also like to thank new friends Steve Overy, Steve Williams, Deltrich Lohman, Brad Gorman, Will Martin, Andy Bradshaw, and Robert M Woolley (founder of *Model Car Journal*) for their superb photos.

In addition to their photographs, Ray Paskiewicz Jr, Margaret Stewart, Bruce Arnold, John Arnold, Jacqui Macnally, and John Roberts provided much information and colorful commentary that dramatically improved the quality of the finished work.

Others happily provided extensive information and time to improve the content and accuracy of the history of 1:43 scale models. I wish to acknowledge Chris Sweetman for his thoughtful history of die-cast models and Mike Coupe for sharing his knowledge about white metal models. I would be remiss if I did not express my gratitude to Rod Ward, Wayne Moyer, Gene Parrill, and Dick Browne who play such an important role in advancing the hobby and who have provided valuable information and advice.

This book would not exist without the patternmakers, builders, and other key people who breathe life into these little models. I have acknowledged many of these people throughout the book and in the Builders chapter.

Also, as a collector I have good relationships with many, many suppliers who keep me in models. I have provided their store details so that readers may visit them and add to their collection.

A TRIO OF MOTOR CITY USA 1950 MODELS, CLOCKWISE FROM BOTTOM: OLDSMOBILE 88 CONVERTIBLE, PONTIAC CHIEFTAIN SUPER DELUXE CATALINA, AND OLDSMOBILE 88 HOLIDAY. (AUTHOR COLLECTION)

THE AUTHOR, RANDALL OLSON, AND HIS HANDBUILT 1:43 SCALE 1952 CADILLAC EXECUTIVE SPEEDSTER BY ELEGANCE MODELS. (AUTHOR COLLECTION)

To fellow hobbyists on the Forum 43 board at www.diecast.org and all those of you who correspond with me, thank you once again for your friendship and passion for the hobby.

I am the author of this publication but it takes other gifted people to create a product that is worth reading and to bring it to the public. It is with gratitude that I recognize the folks at Veloce Publishing – my editor, Alec Grant who uses his creative talents to magically turn my photos and words into a readable, captivating book; and publisher, Rod Grainger, whose vision, wisdom and extreme dedication enabled this publication to find an audience that is not served by others.

Finally, I would like to thank Lucy and Lawrence Olson who brought me up in the world of mid-20th century cars, my sons, Alex and Mike, and my wife, Lindsay, who, even though she may not share my passion for it, supports my hobby and all that goes with it.

Randall Olson
British Columbia
Canada

Publisher's note –
A small number of the images in this book are of relatively poor quality because of the rarity of the models. However, these are important illustrations hence their inclusion.

ABOUT HANDBUILT MODELS 1

A very brief history

THERE ARE MODEL-BUILDING ENTHUSIASTS AND MODEL-COLLECTING enthusiasts. Enthusiast builders of automotive scale models used to have two choices if they wanted a model: to assemble a factory produced model kit from injection-molded plastic, or to scratch build one using whatever materials they could find.

Model kits from makers such as JoHan, AMT, Monogram, MPC, and Revell were popular from the 1950s onward and were most frequently issued in 1:24th scale with only a few 1:43 scale kits issued. Then, one day in the early 1970s, Mikansue introduced a model kit of a 1940 Dodge in 1:43 scale which was made of white metal. A few other producers followed suit.

Model-collecting enthusiasts could buy kits or factory built-up models known as 'promotionals'. Reasonably priced and quite detailed, the quality of the finished product was heavily dependent on the skill of the builder. Another source for collectors was die-cast toy models, most commonly 1:43 scale metal models which were fairly accurate and affordable but very common and tended to be confined to only a few dozen popular automobile subjects.

Gradually model kit producers such as Mikansue began to have their white metal and resin models built-up and sold as fully assembled models. Collectors were willing to pay the premium to have a professionally assembled and finished model known as a 'handbuilt' that was not toy-like but bore greater resemblance to the original vehicle. These handbuilts became popular with collectors during the 1980s. At the same time as the white metal and resin builders produced their replicas, mints such as Danbury

AN EARLY DIE-CAST 1939 OLDSMOBILE BY DINKY TOYS. (COURTESY ROBERT M WOOLLEY)

and Franklin began to sell well-detailed die-cast models at much higher prices than toy models. Collectors now had yet another source for their models.

The scale model car hobby continues to evolve. The mints have been almost completely overtaken by companies such as Minichamps which produce accurate and well-detailed die-cast models at a low selling price of $15-50. A few companies produce premium handbuilt models in the $100-400 price range, although the supply has diminished substantially since its early 1990s heyday.

Die-cast models by Chris Sweetman

The scale of 1:43 has quite a history and is derived from an unexpected source – model railways! It is generally accepted that the first model road vehicles in this scale were the cars in

the Modeled Miniatures range; these were introduced in 1933 to accompany Hornby 'O' gauge railways. Meccano Limited made both of these ranges. In 1934, Modeled Miniatures was renamed Dinky Toys.

The method used to produce the bodies was die-casting. The first road vehicles were die-cast from lead. However, this material was soon replaced by zinc alloy – also known as 'Zamak' – which provides a lighter casting that is more robust than lead.

Zamak was first developed during the 1920s by The New Jersey Zinc Company. The name is derived from Z – zinc, A – aluminum, MA – magnesium and K – kopper (German for copper). One of the first toy companies to use Zamak instead of lead was Tootsietoys for its model car range. It is possible that Tootsietoys used products from The New Jersey Zinc Company.

One of the problems of the zinc alloys used for some Dinky Toys ranges before WWII was that years later they developed inter-granular corrosion. Collectors know this as metal fatigue or sometimes as 'die-cast cancer' – toys develop cracks and can even crumble to dust! The reason for this problem is that impurities were accidentally added to the alloy mixture. It is now known that zinc alloys don't like the addition of lead, meaning that dies needed to be cleaned thoroughly before and after production. Remember the earlier Dinky Toys were cast in lead and if any of this was left on the die, it resulted in metal fatigue. However, workers in the 1930s would have had no idea that their product was going to be eagerly collected in the future and extremely high prices paid to obtain items. We should all be pleased to know that metal fatigue is uncommon in most post-WWII toy production, and has never been found in Matchbox models, Dinky Toys (British and French production) and Corgi Toys from 1945.

One of the most famous American model car ranges produced was the 39 series from Dinky Toys introduced in 1939. Despite appearances, the 39 series has nothing to do with the year it was introduced – a range of British scale models known as the 38 series was also released in 1939. The 39 series included an Oldsmobile (39b) and a Buick (39d). Production was halted in 1940 due to WWII. The series was re-introduced around 1946 and was made until 1952. In their day, they were the finest die-cast model cars available. Dinky Toys called its Buick a Buick Viceroy Sedan car. This particular car was available as a motorcar in the UK, and the name comes from the fact that these Buicks were Canadian built and given names that the British public could associate with. In the 1930s, cars from Canada did not have such an excessive import duty as those from the USA.

The complete Dinky Toys 39 series also consisted of: Packard Super 8 Touring Sedan (39a), Lincoln Zephyr Coupe (39c), Chrysler Royal Sedan (39e), and Studebaker State Commander (39f).

These models are not in 1:43 scale but 1:48. The reason for this is not that American Railroad 'O' Gauge is in this scale, but that die-casting blocks are one size to fit the die-casting machinery. This size could not accommodate the larger American model cars to 1:43 scale so a compromise was made.

Dinky Toys production methods may have been state-of-the-art in the 1930s but the same techniques were still being used in the 1960s. Die-casting was done by hand throughout this period. Financial problems facing Meccano led to its takeover by Lines Brothers (Tri-ang) in January 1964. However, it was Jack Odell who revolutionized die-cast manufacturing for Lesney Products (Matchbox). In 1956 he designed automatic die-casting machines from scratch and streamlined production to maximize productivity. Matchbox became the largest manufacturer of die-cast model cars reaching a high in the late 1960s and early 1970s. Unfortunately, for us collectors specializing in 1:43 scale, the vast majority of its production was in smaller scales.

The processes Matchbox used from initial selection of a model to mass production was a long affair. Photographs and technical drawings were first obtained from the full sized model. This was followed by the carving of a miniature replica from solid Perspex – a process that took several weeks to complete. When the replica was approved, draftsmen would then draw the parts required and, from these, skilled pattern makers hand-carved (from wood or resin) accurate patterns. These were made three to four times larger so that any error would show up immediately.

The pattern was then split in half and the reverse impression would be the basic shape from which the model would eventually be cast. All the measurements would be rechecked before a resin cast was made of each part. Using these, a quarter sized die was carved out of solid steel. A pantograph was then used to cut the delicate outline of the new mold in chrome-vanadium steel. After further checks the mold was filled with molten metal to see if it leaked. It was then hardened in an oven for two days at temperatures exceeding 1000°C. Finally, several models were run through to see if the mold was okay. If so, it was ready for the shop floor.

Because the main die-cast model car manufacturers were European, there were few scale models of North American cars produced for the period 1920-1954. The exceptions to this were the Marklin Buick, the Dinky Toys '53 Cadillac, the Dinky Toys France '52 Buick, the Prameta '46 Buick and Mercury Toys' Cadillac.

Even now there have not been many die-cast American GM models from this period cast in 1:43 scale. Again there are exceptions: Franklin Mint's Cars of the '50s contained some GM cars of this era; there are Solido's '50s Buick and '30s Cadillac as well as early 1950s Cadillac models from Vitesse and Ertl. More recently a few other die-cast models of GM vehicles such as Ixo's1930 Cadillac, Gearbox's 1941 Chevrolet pickup and Yatming/Road Champs' 1949 Cadillac have been produced.

However, it is largely left to the manufacturers of handbuilt resin and white metal models to provide replicas within the period set out in this book.

Handbuilt white metal models by Mike Coupe of Spa Croft Models

I am often asked, "What are white metal models, and why are they so expensive?" To answer this it is necessary to explain the production of white metal models. Spa Croft Models, and the other white metal model manufacturers, generally produce models that are not considered commercially viable by the die-cast manufacturers such as Corgi, as they often have a limited appeal. The metal used in the die-casting process is a hard metal, and can only be cast in steel dies. The tooling costs are, therefore, extremely high, and because of this, the manufacturer has to be

sure that his investment will be recouped. Subjects, therefore, have to have a wide appeal, and be capable of being produced in a variety of forms and liveries with little, or no alteration. On die-cast models, plastic is used to produce many of the smaller items such as radiator grilles, bumpers etc., and interiors, because this is also cheaper. Generally the only non-metal parts used in white metal models are rubber for the tires, and acetate for the windows. Everything else is metal that contributes to the weight of the model and its overall impression of quality.

Whilst the production of white metal models is still not cheap, because the metal used has a low melting point, rubber molds can be used to cast the models, by means of centrifugal casting, and it is this process that is much cheaper than die-casting, because tooling costs are much less. "Why is the end product so much more expensive?" I hear you ask. There are several reasons. Because of the limited appeal of many of the subjects of white metal models – for instance, they may only be known in the UK, and therefore have no interest worldwide – the recovery

A CONTEMPORARY HANDBUILT 1938 OLDSMOBILE F-SERIES BY DURHAM CLASSICS. (AUTHOR COLLECTION)

THE FIRST, PAINSTAKING STEP IN THE LIFE OF A HANDBUILT MODEL IS FOR THE SUBJECT VEHICLE TO BE MEASURED AND PHOTOGRAPHED FROM ALL ANGLES. MEASUREMENTS ARE THEN CONVERTED TO 1:43 SCALE. HAVING SPENT CONSIDERABLE TIME INTERNALIZING ALL ASPECTS OF THE VEHICLE, INCLUDING ITS PROPORTIONS AND CHARACTER, THE PATTERNMAKER IS READY TO PRODUCE A MASTER PATTERN. A VARIETY OF POSSIBLE TECHNIQUES AND MATERIALS ARE USED HERE, DEPENDING UPON THE PATTERNMAKER'S PREFERENCE. SOME CARVE THE MODEL OUT OF WOOD AND OTHERS SCULPT USING WAX.

WHATEVER THE SCULPTING MATERIAL USED, A MOLD OR IMPRESSION OF THE MODEL AND ITS PARTS (UP TO 100) IS CREATED, AND BRASS IS POURED INTO THE MOLD TO CREATE A MASTER PATTERN THAT CAN BE USED REPEATEDLY. THE BRASS MASTER PICTURED HERE IS FOR A '54 CHEVROLET HANDYMAN STATION WAGON BY BROOKLIN MODELS. (COURTESY JOHN ROBERTS)

MOLDS ARE THEN CREATED AROUND EACH PATTERN, ENSURING THAT THERE ARE NO AIR BUBBLES, WARPING, OR BUILD-UP OF EXCESS MATERIALS. WHITE METAL SUCH AS PEWTER, IS THE MOST COMMON MATERIAL POURED INTO THE MOLDS; RESIN IS ALSO USED. HERE, A TECHNICIAN POURS THE MOLTEN WHITE METAL INTO A MOLD. CENTRIFUGAL (SPINNING) MOLDING EQUIPMENT IS USED TO SPEED THE PROCESS AND IMPROVE THE QUALITY OF THE PRODUCT. (COURTESY DURHAM CLASSICS AUTOMOTIVE MINIATURES)

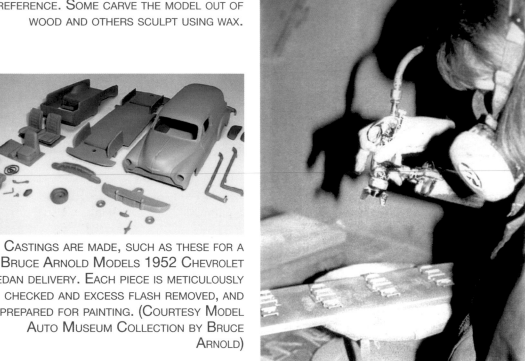

CASTINGS ARE MADE, SUCH AS THESE FOR A BRUCE ARNOLD MODELS 1952 CHEVROLET SEDAN DELIVERY. EACH PIECE IS METICULOUSLY CHECKED AND EXCESS FLASH REMOVED, AND PREPARED FOR PAINTING. (COURTESY MODEL AUTO MUSEUM COLLECTION BY BRUCE ARNOLD)

FINAL DETAILING OF PARTS SUCH AS POLISHING BRIGHTWORK IS PERFORMED BEFORE ASSEMBLY. MODELS ARE THEN HAND ASSEMBLED BY PEOPLE WITH EXCEPTIONALLY FINE MOTOR SKILLS. (COURTESY DURHAM CLASSICS AUTOMOTIVE MINIATURES)

GENUINE AUTOMOTIVE PAINT IS APPLIED, AND, IN THE CASE OF CHROME WHITE METAL PARTS SUCH AS BUMPERS, NICKEL PLATING IS OFTEN EMPLOYED. ON THE MORE EXPENSIVE MODELS, TINY, DELICATE PIECES SUCH AS SCRIPT AND WIPERS EMPLOY A PHOTO-ETCHING PROCESS WHERE ACID IS USED TO BURN AWAY SUPERFLUOUS MATERIAL TO CREATE PRECISE, MINUTE 1:43 SCALE, ACCURATE PIECES. (COURTESY DURHAM CLASSICS AUTOMOTIVE MINIATURES)

of tooling costs is spread over a smaller number of units, very often no more than 600 pieces. Each model is also handbuilt, and hand-finished, and in some cases, hand-polished. This is a very labour intensive part of the production of white metal models, and because production is wholly in the UK (or America and Europe), the white metal manufacturers cannot benefit from the much cheaper labour available elsewhere to our colleagues in the die-cast model industry.

"Why should I buy white metal models, then?" you may ask. Because you are getting a special model which, more often than not, no one else produces. For example, none of the models produced by Spa Croft Models are currently available from any other manufacturer, die-cast or white metal. White metal models are very often more accurate and have more detail than their die-cast counterparts, although the die-cast manufacturers are now recognising the demands of the discerning collector, and things are definitely improving; the finish of white metal models is of a greater quality because they are handbuilt; your collection will be closer to unique because there are fewer examples of each model around, and I suppose, to be a little light-hearted, you will not be filling your cabinets as quickly, because you will be buying less of the more expensive models, unless of course you are a lottery winner. Ultimately, the value of your collection may increase more because of the desirability of these little gems, but that's a bonus. Collecting is for the fun of it, and the intrinsic value of your collection.

Handbuilt resin models

As for resin models, builders who plan to make 100 or fewer models favor this material. Resin is a liquid that, somewhat like polystyrene, is poured into molds and allowed to harden. It is then removed, rough areas sanded and painted and assembled in much the same was as white metal models are. A resin mold is good for producing about 35 models, a white metal mold, 300 pieces. Hand building requires finishing and assembly of fifty to a hundred tiny parts to make one model.

Currently available handbuilt models of General Motors Company automobiles

Much like fine jewelers and instrument builders, such as Faberge and Stradivarius, very few people have the skill, tools, or inclination to produce these tiny works of art. There are perhaps a handful of expert patternmakers in the world. Add to this the nature of the materials and production techniques used, and it is apparent why the models are so rare. At the time this book went to press, there were only about a dozen builders of classic and modern period handmade North American car models in the world. Handbuilt models of General Motor Company cars were available at stockists or directly through the following builders:

Brooklin Models (UK). Located in Bath, England, Brooklin is the largest producer of handbuilt models. The builder issues ten or more models of American automobiles annually, sometimes with body style variations – usually from the 1930-69 time period. In 2006-07 Brooklin released several GM models ranging from a 1934 Buick to a 1954 Chevrolet Handyman station wagon. Brooklin's models are white metal, nicely proportioned, and well finished. They have become more detailed over the years as the builder has gradually added windshield wipers, door handles, and chromed parts for significant moldings and ornamentation. Clear headlight lenses are still omitted and windshield headers are sometimes painted – perhaps that is how the builder keeps these handbuilt models at a price near to $100.

Bruce Arnold Models (USA) has an affinity for General Motors products, especially late 1940s to early 1960s Cadillac motorcars. Bruce Arnold himself creates the patterns for its models. It has made a very detailed 1947 Series 75 that was sold under its own label as well as by Conquest Models, and a 1953 Cadillac in Eldorado and Sixty Special specifications. Models have tended to be limited to between 50-200 pieces with prices in the $300-400 range.

Conquest/Madison (USA). Conquest/Madison models are very well finished, carefully detailed, and accurately proportioned models at the high end of the scale around $225-250. Models are made for Conquest/Madison by Scale Model Technical Services (SMTS) of the UK. Between 1987 and 2000 Conquest/Madison was a Dutch concern operated under the name of Fa. Daimler House which issued more than 60 different models during that time. In 2005 it was purchased by its current American owner who immediately re-issued many General Motors replicas such as a 1948 Pontiac station wagon and 1952 Buick Super. In 2007 it began to release new models starting with a 1959 Pontiac convertible.

Durham Classics Automotive Miniatures (Canada) are still available at retail outlets and on eBay. It interrupted production in 2003 but has since resumed in a limited capacity. Durham Classics' models such as the 1934 LaSalle and 1941 Chevrolet are similar to Brooklin – very heavy with lustrous paint. They are not as abundant as most Brooklins.

Enchantment Land Coachbuilders (USA) is an artisan builder that continues to release a variety of resin scale models through direct purchase and through eBay auctions. Its production is very low and covers a broad spectrum of North American vehicles from the '20s to '60s; its eclectic range includes such models as the 1947 Buick Flxible ambulance.

Great American Dream Machines (USA) is dedicated to creating scale models of North American concept cars. Its line

1941 CHEVROLET SUBURBAN AND UTILITY PICKUP HANDBUILT WHITE METAL MODELS BY DURHAM CLASSICS WITH OMEN FIGURE OF MUSICIAN ACKER BILK. (AUTHOR COLLECTION)

includes most of the great Motorama display models such as the 1951 LeSabre and 1954 Wildcat II. Accurate in appearance and scale, these fine handbuilt white metal models sell in the $200-250 range in the builder's eBay store.

Milestone Miniatures (UK) distributes a line called Forty-Third Avenue (or "FTA") that includes a 1947 Cadillac. It tends to produce at the lower end of the price spectrum ($100–$125) and detailing reflects this. Milestone Miniatures produces models for other companies and has a broad range of British models, especially Jaguar. In 2006, the company issued a white metal 1936 Buick at $235 that is described in the Buick chapter.

Mini Marque (UK) issues 3-4 new, very detailed scale models per year. At $250-275, it has concentrated on Hudson and Packard but has produced models from Chevrolet and Cadillac-LaSalle under a previous owner and name (Mini Marque "43"). Mini Marque announced a new 1948 Cadillac Sixty Special in 2007.

Motor City USA (USA) is revered for its exquisitely built models of the Motor City Gold line in the medium ($125-$150), and its top of the line models in the premium ($275-$300) price ranges. Motor City USA's accuracy and build quality are incomparable. The company's last GM models were from 2005-06 and were a 1959 Oldsmobile 4dr hard-top and 1959 Cadillac

75. Since 2000, the builder has focused much of its efforts on 1:18 die-cast, hot rods and service cars (i.e. ambulances and hearses). The company brings out a new 1:43 scale model about once a year.

Victory Models (USA) is dedicated to the creation of scale models of North American cars and trucks from the World War II period. In collaboration with small builder CCC Models of France, Victory has produced some stunningly accurate Packard, Studebaker, Buick, LaSalle, and Cadillac models from 1938-42. Victory's handbuilt resin replicas are priced in the $159-239 range and seldom exceed 100 units of each model.

Western Models Limited (UK) was a renowned supplier of a broad range of models for other companies as well as its own range. Its North American automobiles include the 1941 Buick, 1941 Oldsmobile, and 1949 Cadillac of which it issued a new fastback in 2006. The company was in the business for thirty years and, up until the publication of this book, had issued a few new American models annually. Its founders retired and its doors closed. Western's products are slightly more detailed than Brooklin's and are produced in smaller numbers. They are moderately priced at around $150.

For all of the model builders I have listed, please check on the internet or at the stockists listed in the Suppliers chapter.

CHEVROLET 2

FROM ITS EARLY DAYS, CHEVROLET HAD A WELL-FOUNDED REPUTATION FOR producing some of the best quality cars for the dollar. If a person wanted reliable transportation, up-to-date features, a strong dealer network, and high resale value, it was all there in the 'bow tie brand'. For these reasons and others, Chevrolet consistently surpassed rival Ford in sales throughout the middle decades of the 20th century.

Because of its place in automotive history, popular culture, and peoples' lives, it is not surprising that many 1:43 scale models of Chevrolets have been made over the years.

Model-by-model — 1932-41

In the 1930s Chevrolet was producing attractively-styled and reliable transportation, overtaking Ford's number 1 position in the sales race.

As for Chevrolet scale models, Danbury Mint (USA) and Ashton Models (USA) produced a few white metal versions of

SOME FEATURED CHEVROLET MODELS

YEAR	MODEL	MANUFACTURER
1937	MASTER COUPE	BROOKLIN MODELS
1937	MASTER SEDAN	MADISON MODELS
1937	MASTER SEDAN	USA MODELS
1939	MASTER COUPE	USA MODELS
1941	SPECIAL DELUXE	DURHAM CLASSICS
1946	STYLEMASTER SEDAN	GOLDVARG COLLECTION
1947	STYLEMASTER SEDAN	CONQUEST MODELS
1947	STYLEMASTER SEDAN DELIVERY	BROOKLIN MODELS
1948	FLEETMASTER AND FLEETLINE	MOTOR CITY USA
1950	STYLELINE AND FLEETLINE	RECORD MODELS
1951	STYLELINE AND BEL AIR	USA MODELS
1953	BEL AIR	MOTOR CITY USA
1954	BEL AIR	USA MODELS
1954	BEL AIR AND 210 HANDYMAN	BROOKLIN MODELS

A TRIO OF 1947-48 CHEVROLET HANDBUILT SCALE MODELS, CLOCKWISE FROM TOP LEFT: '47 STYLELINE BY CONQUEST MODELS, '48 FLEETLINE AEROSEDAN AND '48 FLEETMASTER CONVERTIBLE INDY 500 PACE CAR, BOTH BY MOTOR CITY USA. (AUTHOR COLLECTION)

1930 CHEVROLET DELIVERY VAN DIE-CAST BY ERTL.
(COURTESY J RETTIG)

1932 CHEVROLET PHAETON TOP UP. DANBURY MINT NO 17.
(COURTESY J RETTIG)

1932 CHEVROLET ROADSTER TOP UP. ASHTON MODELS NO 4.
(COURTESY J RETTIG)

1932 CHEVROLET OPEN ROADSTER. HALLMARK. (COURTESY J RETTIG)

the 1932 Chevrolet in the 1970s that are available at auctions occasionally. These are simple models with few parts.

The first substantial scale model Chevrolet is Brooklin Models' 1937 coupe. Initially produced in Canada in 1986, and then England until 1991, it is a sturdy, handmade white metal model with an accurate shape, using polished white metal for major parts (radiator, bumpers, lights, etc). During its run, there were 13 variations of the Brooklin '37 Chevrolet including a police car in genuine San Francisco police livery made for the San Francisco Bay Brooklin Club and a 'Kool Kustom' version available in three bright custom colors by Dean Paolucci's DMP Studios.

Brooklin's coupe was followed by a slightly more detailed 1937 Master 4 door sedan built for Motor City USA by English builder SMTS. This accurately rendered white metal USA Models line replica was available for a little over $100 in a civilian version as well as a taxi, police car, and fire chief's car.

Fa. Daimler House used the same pattern for its Madison Models 1937 4 door sedan (see sidebar).

SMTS later produced an excellent 1939 5-window coupe in Tusk Ivory or Maroon, for the USA Line of Motor City USA. With moderate detailing such as chromed windshield wipers, script decals, and enamel headlight lenses, this model was a

AN EARLY CANADIAN BROOKLIN MODELS 1937 CHEVROLET COUPE IN HUMELL GREEN WITH GRAY WHEELS. BRK-4. (COURTESY D MATHYSSEN)

1937 CHEVROLET ISSUED IN 1991 FOR THE SAN FRANCISCO BAY BROOKLIN COLLECTORS CLUB. ONE OF 300. BRK-4. (COURTESY D MATHYSSEN)

1937 DELUXE SEDAN IN THE LIVERY OF THE LOS ANGELES POLICE DEPARTMENT. USA-27P. (COURTESY MOTOR CITY USA)

THE POPULAR 1937 CHEVROLET DELUXE SEDAN IN TAXI MODE. THIS HANDBUILT WHITE METAL MODEL WAS ISSUED BY MOTOR CITY USA. USA-27T. (COURTESY MOTOR CITY USA)

1937 DELUXE SEDAN IN GREEN WITH WHITEWALL TIRES. ALSO ISSUED IN GUN METAL GRAY AND MAROON. USA MODELS NO 27. (COURTESY MOTOR CITY USA)

IN 1989, BROOKLIN MODELS ISSUED 150 OF THESE NATTY RED 1937 CHEVROLET COUPES FOR J LEAKE3' 15TH ANNUAL AUCTION. BRK-4. (COURTESY D MATHYSSEN)

1937 DELUXE SEDAN FIRE CHIEF CAR, LOS ANGELES COUNTY. USA-27F. (COURTESY MOTOR CITY USA)

'37 CHEVROLET CONVERTIBLE IN RESIN. THIS IS A ONE-OF-A-KIND MODEL CONVERTED BY JERRY RETTIG FROM A MADISON MODELS SEDAN. (COURTESY J RETTIG)

bargain at around $125, especially because only 300 units were produced.

By 1941, Chevrolet cars had taken on the appearance that they would generally maintain throughout the decade, with enclosed fender-mounted headlights and a body that appeared designed as one piece common across the range. There is only one scale replica of the popular 1941 automobile and it is a good one, a 2 door coupe issued by Durham Classics in the early 1990s.

PROFILE – 1937 CHEVROLET MASTER SEDAN BY MADISON MODELS

IN 1992 HENK VAN ASTEN ISSUED HIS 7TH MADISON MODELS HANDBUILT WHITE METAL REPLICA. FOR HIS SUBJECT HE CHOSE THE SMTS-BUILT 1937 CHEVROLET MASTER 4 DOOR SEDAN. AVAILABLE IN THE AUTHENTIC COLORS OF BERYL GREEN (MID-GREEN) OR TORONTO BLUE (A LIGHTER SHADE THAN NAVY), IT SOLD FOR CLOSE TO $200 – WHICH WAS ALMOST TWICE THE PRICE OF THE USA MODELS OF THE TIME. FOR THIS PREMIUM, THE BUYER RECEIVED A SLIGHTLY MORE DETAILED MODEL WITH ENAMEL HEADLIGHTS, PHOTO-ETCHED WIPERS, AND SEPARATE CHROMED DOOR HANDLES. THE MODEL PICTURED HERE HAS EXCELLENT PROPORTIONS AND FINISHING. SMALL PARTS SUCH AS THE RADIATOR CAP ORNAMENT ARE CORRECTLY SIZED AND BRIGHT NICKEL-PLATED. THE SLIGHTLY BLACKWASHED GRILLE IS PARTICULARLY IMPRESSIVE WITH ITS CAREFUL VERTICAL SCORING THAT GIVES THE APPEARANCE OF THE DELICATE GRILLEWORK OF THE ORIGINAL.

THE INTERIOR IS DEVOID OF THE WINDOW WINDERS AND DOOR LEVERS THAT DISTINGUISHED LATER MADISON MODELS, BUT DOES HAVE SOME INTERIOR DETAIL WITH UPHOLSTERY BUTTONS AND PLEATS CAST INTO THE SEATS AND A MOLDED DASH THAT HAS THE MAJOR CONTOURS; INCLUDING THE VARIOUS CONTROL KNOBS OF THE ORIGINAL. THE INTERIOR APPEARANCE IS FINISHED OFF WITH A PERIOD-APPROPRIATE BLACK STEERING WHEEL AND LONG GEARSHIFT LEVER MOUNTED ON THE TRANSMISSION TUNNEL. (AUTHOR COLLECTION)

Patterned by Dick Armbruster, Durham's '41 Chevy is very similar to Brooklin Models' products from the same period. Sculpted from a single piece, Armbruster employed the laminated wood block method, carving the entire body including moldings, park lights, door handles, and shut lines directly into the original pattern. The few pieces that comprise the model are accurate to the original and fit together well. The little Durham replicas have a deep glossy paint finish, with early models sporting colors of gray or light blue.

As the 1990s progressed, Durham Classics offered a

CHEVROLET COUPE BY USA MODELS, HANDBUILT WHITE METAL. USA-40. (AUTHOR COLLECTION)

NEARING THE HEIGHT OF THE INDUSTRIAL DESIGN MOVEMENT'S INFLUENCE, THE 1939 CHEVROLET COUPE SHOWS INCREASED STREAMLINING AROUND THE GRILLE AREA IN CONTRAST WITH THE 1937 SEDAN. USA MODELS NO USA-40 AND MADISON MODELS NO MAD-7. (AUTHOR COLLECTION)

ALTHOUGH IT IS FROM MOTOR CITY USA's LESS EXPENSIVE USA MODELS LINE, THIS 1939 CHEVROLET COUPE IS HIGHLY-DETAILED AND LACKS ONLY MINOR SCRIPT-WORK, SOME WINDOW TRIM, AND INTERIOR PARTS FOUND IN THE MAKER'S HIGHEST PRICED MODELS. USA-40. (AUTHOR COLLECTION)

1941 CHEVROLET CONVERTIBLE BY DURHAM CLASSICS. DC-5D. (COURTESY COLLECTORS ANTIQUES)

1941 CHEVROLET COUPE BY DURHAM CLASSICS, HANDBUILT WHITE METAL. THIS PHOTOGRAPH SHOWS THE TYPICAL DURHAM CLASSICS MODEL OF THE TIME, CIRCA LATE 1980s, WITH DETAILS SUCH AS MOLDINGS CARVED INTO THE PATTERN AND ONLY MAJOR PARTS SUCH AS GRILLE AND HEADLIGHTS IN NICKEL-PLATED WHITE METAL. CASTINGS ARE VERY CLEAN AND THE PAINT IS THICK AND GLOSSY. DC-5. (COURTESY D LARSEN)

DURHAM CLASSICS RELEASED A TOP UP 1941 CHEVROLET IN SEVERAL COLORS. THIS EARLY VERSION HAS FENDER SKIRTS. DC-5D. (COURTESY COLLECTORS ANTIQUES)

1941 CHEVROLET CONVERTIBLE TOP DOWN IN DARK BLUE. DURHAM CLASSICS EVENTUALLY ADDED MORE CHROME TO ITS REPLICAS, SUCH AS A PROMINENT BELT LINE MOLDING. JERRY RETTIG HAS GIVEN THIS MODEL EXTRA FOIL DETAILING. DC-5D. (COURTESY J RETTIG)

1941 CHEVROLET UTILITY COUPE. DURHAM CLASSICS OFTEN SPUN OUT ITS PATTERNS BY ALTERING THE APPEARANCE OF THE MODELS WITH VARIATIONS IN COLORS, LIVERIES, AND BODY MODIFICATIONS. THE BUILDER'S 'UTE' WAS BASED ON ITS POPULAR COUPE. (AUTHOR COLLECTION)

1941 CHEVROLET ONTARIO PROVINCIAL POLICE (OPP) PATROL CAR 'NUMBER 50'. DURHAM CLASSICS ALSO CREATED A 'NUMBER 1' WITH A WHITE HOOD AND A MICHIGAN STATE POLICE VERSION WITH DISTINCTIVE MICHIGAN MAP SILHOUETTE DOOR LOGOS. DC-5. (AUTHOR COLLECTION)

1941 CHEVROLET UTILITY COUPE BY DURHAM CLASSICS. FROM THE REAR, IT IS APPARENT THAT EVEN THE FENDERS ARE PART OF THE ORIGINAL PATTERN, CARVED OUT OF A SINGLE PIECE OF MATERIAL BY PATTERNMAKER DICK ARMBRUSTER. THE DC-11 PICTURED HERE HAD A BLUE STEAMER TRUNK ADDED TO THE DRAWER-TYPE CARGO EXTENSION. (AUTHOR COLLECTION)

1941 CHEVROLET UTILITY COUPE IN SALVATION ARMY LIVERY. LIKE ITS COMPETITOR, BROOKLIN MODELS, DURHAM CLASSICS PURPOSELY TIED INTO SPECIAL EVENTS, CAUSES, AND HISTORICAL THEMES, CREATING SEVERAL COMMEMORATIVE MODELS. DC-11. (COURTESY D LARSEN)

1941 Chevrolet convertible in open and top up configurations, produced the coupe as a police and fire chief car, and introduced an interesting utility version of the coupe with a pickup-style box in place of a trunk. This latter version is historically accurate – Chevrolet saw a market for this type of vehicle almost two decades before introducing the El Camino. About a dozen different color combinations and model variations were made of the Durham Classics 1941 Chevrolet automobile. With 150-300 units of each issued, this company's replicas remain fairly common in the secondary market.

Model-by-model   1946-48

Post-WWII Chevrolet models picked up the 1942 styling with enclosed running boards and 'fade away' pontoon-like fenders to achieve a larger appearance. The public snapped them up as fast as it could. Scale modelers apparently liked these cars as well. Four builders chose the 1946-48 Chevrolet as the subject for 1:43 scale models.

Goldvarg Collection of Argentina was the first builder to create a handbuilt replica of the post-war Chevrolet in 1991-92. It chose the humble and ubiquitous (over 156,000 sold in

1946 STYLEMASTER SEDAN FROM THE GOLDVARG COLLECTION REPAINTED AND CHROMED BY JERRY RETTIG. GDV-2. (COURTESY J RETTIG)

A REAR VIEW OF THE SLIGHTLY BULBOUS 1946 STYLEMASTER SEDAN BY GOLDVARG. GDV-2. (COURTESY J RETTIG)

1947 STYLEMASTER SEDAN (LEFT) BY CONQUEST MODELS (CNQ-37) AND 1946 STYLEMASTER SEDAN FROM THE GOLDVARG COLLECTION (GDV-2). PHOTOGRAPHS OF THE ACTUAL VEHICLE SHOW THAT CONQUEST'S IS A MORE ACCURATE RENDERING OF THE SEDAN'S LONG HOOD, SHORT BACK PROFILE. HOWEVER, LINE-DRAWN ADVERTISEMENTS OF THE DAY TENDED TO EMPHASIZE THE CAR IN MOTION WITH A MORE FORWARD STANCE, AND WHAT APPEARS TO BE A MORE ROUNDED AND ELONGATED REAR, AS MODELED HERE BY GOLDVARG. (AUTHOR COLLECTION)

1947 STYLEMASTER SEDAN (LEFT) BY CONQUEST MODELS (CNQ-37) AND 1946 STYLEMASTER SEDAN FROM THE GOLDVARG COLLECTION (GDV-2). THE ARGENTINE BUILDER ADDED A SUN VISOR – COMMON TO THAT SUNNY COUNTRY. (AUTHOR COLLECTION)

GOLDVARG'S 1946 OHIO STATE POLICE CAR IS UNCOMMON.
(COURTESY J RETTIG)

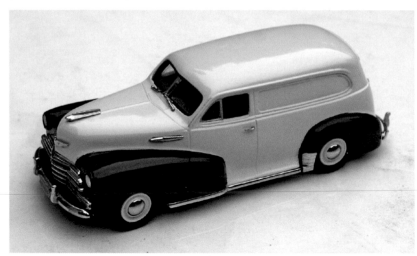

1947 CHEVROLET STYLELINE SEDAN DELIVERY BY BROOKLIN MODELS
BRK-136, INTRODUCED IN 2007 IN LIGHT GREEN WITH SIGNAGE FOR
A HARDWARE COMPANY. THE TWO-TONE MODEL PICTURED IS A ONE-OFF
CUSTOMIZATION PERFORMED BY JOHN WHITE. (COURTESY D LARSEN)

1947 CHEVROLET STYLEMASTER SEDAN IN OZONE BLUE. A PREMIUM
WHITE METAL HANDBUILT ISSUED IN 2007 BY CONQUEST MODELS.
CNQ-37. (AUTHOR COLLECTION)

1947 CHEVROLET STYLEMASTER SEDAN FROM CONQUEST MODELS.
CNQ-37 ALSO CAME IN SPORT BEIGE. (AUTHOR COLLECTION)

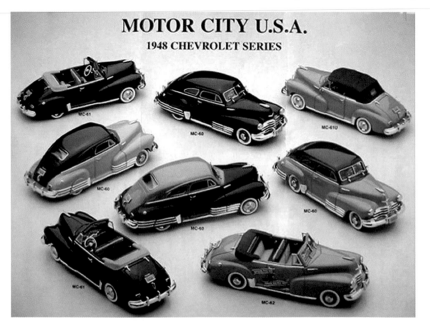

a short sales year) entry level 1946 Stylemaster 4 door sedan.
Goldvarg's substantial replica is made of white metal. Similar to
a Brooklin, it is generally accurate in detail with a chrome beltline
molding and sun visor, popular in bright Buenos Aires. Issued in
maroon and in a scarce black-and-white police car version, it has

IN THE LATE 1990S MOTOR CITY USA CREATED DELIGHTFUL 1:43
SCALE RESIN AND WHITE METAL REPLICAS OF THE 1948 FLEETLINE AERO
FASTBACK AND FLEETMASTER CONVERTIBLE. THE BUILDER TOUTED THESE
MODELS IN A FULL COLOR POSTER. (AUTHOR COLLECTION)

THE MOST COMMON 1948 CHEVROLET, WITH OVER 211,000 SOLD, WAS THE HIGH RANGE FLEETLINE AEROSEDAN. IN THAT YEAR'S SELLERS' MARKET PEOPLE WERE EAGER TO PAY A LITTLE MORE FOR A MORE DELUXE VEHICLE THAN THE MAKER'S STYLEMASTER. IN 2006, MOTOR CITY USA RE-ISSUED THE FLEETLINE AERO 2 DOOR FASTBACK SEDAN IN SILVER GREEN GRAY OVER LIVE OAK GREEN. AT A PRICE OF $275, THE MODEL WAS QUICKLY SNAPPED UP. (AUTHOR COLLECTION)

VERY FEW OF MOTOR CITY USA'S 1948 FLEETLINES WERE RELEASED IN THIS DISTINCTIVE GLOSSY BLACK FINISH. THE AUTHOR TRADED THIS HIGHLY COVETED MODEL FOR ANOTHER RARE MOTOR CITY USA MODEL FROM A PROMINENT COLLECTOR IN MICHIGAN. SUCH TRANSACTIONS BETWEEN COLLECTORS ARE FAIRLY COMMON BECAUSE SOME MODELS ARE SO SCARCE. MC-60. (AUTHOR COLLECTION)

PHOTO-ETCHED PARTS SUCH AS THE REAR WINDOW SURROUND, LOWER TAILLIGHT EMBELLISHERS, AND FLEETLINE SCRIPT ARE USED LIBERALLY IN THIS MUSEUM QUALITY PIECE. NOTE THE THIRD BUMPER OVERRIDER. MOTOR CITY USA MC-60. (AUTHOR COLLECTION)

good proportions from the cowl back but a curiously narrow front clip. Chevrolet collectors are not apt to mind this early and loving effort to model their favorite make.

Several years later, as it wound down its business, Fa. Daimler House issued a Conquest 1947 Stylemaster 4 door sedan in Oxford Maroon and Battleship Gray. Scarce at the time,

the author managed to acquire a version of this handbuilt white metal model for around $300. Although it is based on a somewhat plain subject, the proportions, detailing, assembly, and finishing of the model are worthy of its premium price. In 2007, this replica was re-issued in Ozone Blue and Sport Beige.

Brooklin Models debuted an entirely new body style for

PROFILE – 1948 CHEVROLET FLEETMASTER CONVERTIBLE BY MOTOR CITY USA

IN THE POST-WAR WORLD OF 1948, CHEVROLET SOLD 20,471 FLEETMASTER CONVERTIBLES FOR THE CALENDAR YEAR. CHEVROLET'S SECOND MOST EXPENSIVE MODEL (AFTER THE STATION WAGON) WAS SELECTED TO PACE THE INDIANAPOLIS 500 FOR 1948. RACE ORGANIZERS WERE PLEASED TO SEE THE MOST COLORFUL PROCLAMATION OF THE EVENT YET TO GRACE THE SIDES OF ITS PACE VEHICLE.

THE BUILDER CREATED SCALE MODELS OF THE 1948 FLEETMASTER CONVERTIBLE AS BOTH A TOP DOWN AND TOP UP MODEL (MC-61) AND AS A TOP DOWN PACE CAR IN DOVE GRAY (MC-63).

THESE 1:43 SCALE HANDBUILT MODELS ARE MADE, SURPRISINGLY, FROM RESIN WITH WHITE METAL BASES. IT IS THE FIRST TIME THAT THE CALIFORNIA BUILDER USED THIS MATERIAL FOR ITS REPLICA BODIES AND THE RESULT IS SUPERB.

MOTOR CITY USA'S LITTLE CHEVROLET HAS ACCURATE PROPORTIONS AND FLAWLESS FIT AND FINISH. THE LEVEL OF EXTERIOR DETAIL IS SO COMPLETE THAT A WELL-PHOTOGRAPHED MODEL COULD PASS FOR THE ACTUAL AUTOMOBILE. THIS IS ACHIEVED THROUGH THE USE OF BARE METAL FOIL FOR MOLDINGS AND PHOTO-ETCHING FOR SMALL DETAILS SUCH AS SCRIPT.

THE ACCURATE DETAILS CONTINUE IN THE MODEL'S INTERIOR. IN ADDITION TO THE UNCANNILY AUTHENTIC-LOOKING WOOD GRAINED DASHBOARD, INSTRUMENTS WITH DIALS, BANJO-TYPE STEERING WHEEL, DOOR HANDLES, AND WINDOW WINDERS, THE BUILDER EMPLOYED CLOTH-LIKE TEXTURED FLOCKING ON THE SEATING SURFACES TO SIMULATE MOHAIR. THE EFFECT IS REALISTIC. IN THE AUTHOR'S OPINION, MOTOR CITY USA'S 1948 CHEVROLET IS THE MOST REALISTICALLY DETAILED 1:43 SCALE MODEL OF A NORTH AMERICAN AUTOMOBILE THAT HAS BEEN PRODUCED.

(AUTHOR COLLECTION)

1:43 models in 2007 with its 1947 Styleline sedan delivery, no BRK-136. Outfitted in working garb with 'Main Hardware' on its quarter panels, this light green model is a delightful rendering of the service vehicle so popular with trades people and small businesses.

1948 was Chevrolet's last year for a body style that had served it well throughout the decade. Motor City USA chose the Fleetline 2 door fastback and top of the line Fleetmaster convertible as the basis for its replicas from the late 1990s. Motor City USA's Fleetline was originally released in a variety of colors such as Lake Como Blue (dark metallic) and Dove Gray, Marsh Brown (mid-brown) and Satin (light) Green, Oxford Maroon and Battleship Gray, and all black. In 2006, approximately twenty-five were re-issued in Live Oak Green and Silver Green. At $275 per copy, the collector is assured that they are getting authentic colors. 1948 was also one of the years that Chevrolet paced the Indianapolis 500. To recognize this, MCUSA created a convertible pace car (see sidebar).

In the late 1940s the genuine wood exteriors of a few luxury cars such as Chrysler's Town & Country captured buyers' interests. For a short while, even low-priced producer Chevrolet offered wood cladding in its Country Club trim package for $149.50. Between 1994 and 2001, Brooklin Models made a 1948 2 door Fleetline Aero fastback sedan replica in Dark Forest Green with the Country Club trim. The builder also provided a California Highway Patrol version to the Brooklin Collector club

A Powder Blue 1948 Fleetline Aerosedan towing a Wesley Slumbercoach. Brooklin Models created 165 sets of these in 1997 for the Wessex Models and Toy Collectors Club. BRK-50X and BRK-65X. (Courtesy D Mathyssen)

Brooklin Models issued this California Highway Patrol 1948 Fleetline Aerosedan model in 1997. The agency's archives show a Mercury patrol car for this year but no Chevrolet. BRK-50A. (Courtesy D Mathyssen)

A unique 1:43 scale model of a 1948 Chevrolet station wagon skilfully converted by Jerry Rettig from a white metal Brooklin Models sedan. This is believed to be the only one of its kind and resides in Jerry's extensive collection. (Courtesy J Rettig)

Today, many people are prepared to pay a substantial premium for 1940s wood-adorned motorcars. This was not the case in 1948 when Chevrolet offered optional wood grained treatment to its 2 door sedan as part of its $149.50 'Country Club' trim package. Not content with Brooklin Models' painted trim on its BRK-50 Aerosedan, Dave Ronken carefully cut, finished and fit genuine wood veneer to his re-painted and hand-foiled Brooklin. Few modelers have the skill or courage to undertake this type of modification to their expensive handbuilt models. In Dave's case the results were well worth the risk and effort. (Courtesy D Ronken)

and 165 units of a powder blue Fleetline pulling a tiny Wesley Slumbercoach.

Model-by-model   1949-52

A complete redesign of the world's number one selling automobile greeted buyers in 1949. Though its appearance was not as revolutionary as the slab-sided invention of rival Ford, the Chevrolet's overall design with its newly lowered hood and higher fenders achieved a more integrated overall appearance. The venerable Stovebolt 6 cylinder engine that had served the make so well since the 1930s remained under the hood of the new model.

The earliest handbuilt white metal 1950 Chevrolet was Mikansue's 4 door sedan. Available primarily in kit form during the 1970s, the majority of examples that surface in auctions were built by hobbyists with varying skill levels. Americana no 13. (Courtesy Robert M Woolley)

1951 CHEVROLET SHORT-WHEELBASE AMBULANCE BY ZAUGG MODELS. THE BUILDER HAD SOME FUN WITH THIS MODEL, EVEN CREATING 10 OR SO UNITS WITH WORKING FLASHING LIGHTS. THIS IS THE ONLY 1:43 SCALE MODEL MADE OF A 1949-52 CHEVROLET AMBULANCE. No 13B. (COURTESY J RETTIG)

1949 WAS THE YEAR FOR A NEW CHEVROLET BODY. NOT AS RADICAL A DESIGN AS COMPETITOR FORD, BUYERS LIKED WHAT THEY SAW AND PURCHASED MORE THAN 1 MILLION CHEVROLET UNITS, ENABLING THE DIVISION TO TAKE FIRST PLACE IN THE SALES RACE. HERE IS A SCALE MODEL THAT ALSO PROVED VERY POPULAR, FINDING TENS OF THOUSANDS OF BUYERS – SOLIDO MODELS' DIE-CAST 1950 CHEVROLET SEDAN ISSUED AROUND 1988 AT APPROXIMATELY $15. No 4508. (AUTHOR COLLECTION)

CHEVROLET'S HARD-TOP CONVERTIBLE COUPE DEBUTED IN 1950 IN THE BEL AIR LINE. SELLING OVER 70,000 MODELS THAT YEAR, IT GAINED IN POPULARITY THROUGH 1955. ZAUGG MODELS OF SWITZERLAND CHOSE THE 1951 BEL AIR HARD-TOP FOR ITS VERY FIRST SCALE MODEL IN THE 1970s. AS ONE CAN SEE, THE BUILDER HAS DONE A GOOD JOB OF CAPTURING THE AUTOMOBILE'S APPEARANCE BELOW THE GREENHOUSE. THIS REPLICA SCALES OUT AT CLOSE TO 1:45. No 1. (COURTESY J RETTIG)

STEEL-BODIED CHEVROLET STATION WAGONS WERE VERY POPULAR IN 1950, WITH 166,995 PURCHASED THAT YEAR. FRANCE'S PROVENCE MOULAGE PRODUCED THIS TRANSKIT WHICH USED PARTS FROM THE SOLIDO DIE-CAST MODEL. AVAILABLE AS BOTH A KIT AND BUILT-UP, IT IS NOT VERY COMMON TODAY AND TYPICALLY SELLS AT AROUND $100 ON THE AFTERMARKET. TK-27. (COURTESY J RETTIG)

How many 1951 Chevrolet funeral cars actually existed is open to conjecture. Here is a landau hearse complete with drapes from Zaugg Models. No 13C. (Courtesy D Larsen)

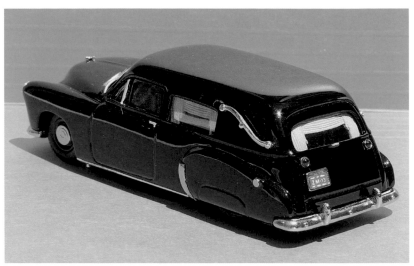

1951 Chevrolet short-wheelbase landau hearse by Zaugg Models. No 13C. (Courtesy D Larsen)

1951 Chevrolet Deluxe open convertible. Despite being a lower line USA Model this replica is well detailed, nicely finished, and has superb proportions. (USA-20). (Author collection)

1951 Chevrolet Deluxe open convertible. USA-20. (Author collection)

England's Mikansue, in its Americana series, introduced the first 1:43 scale white metal Chevrolet in 1970. Seldom seen these days, this Mike Richardson-patterned white metal model tends to surface on eBay every year or so in its original kit form or built-up by amateur modelers. Because Mike relied upon photographs and advertisements of the original, the scale model's proportions are somewhat impressionistic, and, in the author's opinion, the replica has a charming artisan-like quality rather like original art.

The first mass-produced scale model of a 1950 Chevrolet is Solido Model's low-priced die-cast 4 door sedan. This is an excellent rendition of Chevrolet's popular Styleline Deluxe model.

Though simply detailed, it is highly accurate. At the hands of a modeler who can dress it up with black paint behind the chromed polystyrene grille bars and some chrome foiled brightwork, it begins to hold its own next to handbuilts costing ten times as much. Solido's replica is easily obtainable as old stock at hobby shops and at on-line auctions.

Less common, and well worth its usual $100 price, is Provence Moulage Models' 1950 Chevrolet station wagon. This resin-bodied transkit that uses the Solido models' parts was sold as a built-up model. It has high-quality assembly and finishing. With its simulated wood-grain accents, it is a very attractive and accurate model.

FINISHED IN THISTLE GRAY WITH A BURGUNDY INTERIOR, THE DASHBOARD ON THIS MODEL IS ACCURATELY MOLDED, ALBEIT A LITTLE BRIGHT IN COLOR. 1951 CHEVROLET DELUXE OPEN CONVERTIBLE. USA-20. (AUTHOR COLLECTION)

If one visited a Chevrolet showroom in 1951, it was likely that the newest member of the Chevrolet family would be proudly displayed in the showroom center. The 2 door Bel Air hard-top coupe debuted the previous year, captivating the public, and becoming a staple body style of most automobile companies into the mid-1970s.

Motor City USA released a handbuilt replica of the '51 Bel Air 2 door hard-top

RECORD MODELS ISSUED A RESIN-BODIED 1952 CHEVROLET IN ALL BODY STYLES EXCEPT FOR STATION WAGON. 1952 CHEVROLET STYLELINE DELUXE 2 DOOR. NO 12. (COURTESY J RETTIG)

1951 BEL AIR BY MOTOR CITY USA. THIS MODEL HAS HAD SUBSTANTIAL WORK DONE, FOIL ADDED TO OUTLINE THE WINDOW OPENINGS AND WIPERS. ADDITIONAL TRANSPARENCIES TO REPRESENT SIDE WINDOWS HAVE BEEN INSERTED, AND FOIL ADDED TO DIVIDE THE DOOR AND REAR QUARTER SIDE GLASS. USA-4. (COURTESY A MOSKALEV)

A REAR VIEW SHOWING THE CHROME WORK ON THIS FATHOM GREEN OVER ASPEN GREEN 1951 BEL AIR. USA-4. (COURTESY A MOSKALEV)

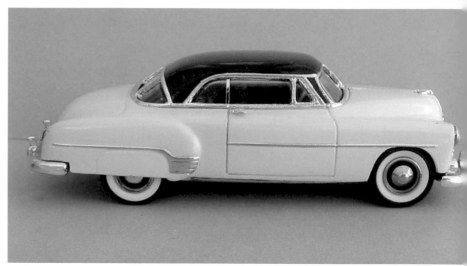

1952 BEL AIR. RECORD MODELS PRODUCED A KIT AND BUILT-UP VERSION OF THE CHEVROLET IN A VARIETY OF MONOCHROMATIC TONES. THIS MODEL HAS HAD THE ROOF PAINTED AND MUCH METAL FOIL ADDED TO MAKE IT CLOSELY RESEMBLE THE ORIGINAL SUBJECT. MODEL NO 8. (AUTHOR COLLECTION)

IN PROFILE, IT IS APPARENT THAT THE WHEELS OF THIS 1952 BEL AIR 2 DOOR HARD-TOP COUPE BY RECORD MODELS ARE TWO-PIECE, WITH A CENTER CHROMED HUB CAP SURROUNDED BY A PAINTED WHEEL, JUST LIKE THE ORIGINAL. NO 8. (AUTHOR COLLECTION).

THE MAJORITY OF RECORD MODELS' 1952 CHEVROLETS WERE FINISHED IN LIGHTER COLORS. HERE, A FASTBACK 2 DOOR SEDAN IS POSED BESIDE A 4 DOOR NOTCHBACK SEDAN. THE 4 DOOR SEDAN WAS CHEVROLET'S MOST POPULAR BODY STYLE WITH CLOSE TO 355,000 PURCHASED IN 1952. MODELS NO 9 AND 7. (AUTHOR COLLECTION)

1952 WOULD BE THE LAST YEAR FOR CHEVROLET'S FASTBACK DESIGN. RECORD MODELS NO 9. (COURTESY ROBERT M WOOLLEY)

DESPITE ITS SPORTY AND ATTRACTIVE APPEARANCE, SALES OF CHEVROLET'S 1952 CONVERTIBLE HAD DIMINISHED TO A THIRD OF WHAT THEY HAD BEEN IN 1950, DUE IN PART TO THE ADVENT OF THE OPEN AND AIRY HARD-TOP COUPE. RECORD MODELS NO 1002F. (COURTESY J RETTIG)

1952 CHEVROLET FASTBACK BY RECORD MODELS. NO 9. (COURTESY ROBERT M WOOLLEY)

A UNIQUE 1952 SEDAN DELIVERY THAT BRUCE ARNOLD MADE FOR 20TH CENTURY MODELS WHICH WAS NEVER RELEASED. (COURTESY MODEL MUSEUM COLLECTION, BRUCE ARNOLD MODELS)

CHEVROLET'S 1952 SEDAN DELIVERY CAME WITH ONLY A DRIVER'S SEAT AS STANDARD EQUIPMENT. THIS PROTOTYPE, PATTERNED AND DETAILED BY BRUCE ARNOLD, SHOWS THE PATTERNMAKER'S ATTENTION TO DETAIL. (COURTESY MODEL MUSEUM COLLECTION, BRUCE ARNOLD MODELS)

coupe as the 4th model in its low-line USA Models series. This white metal version has accurate proportions and is well finished with a moderate level of detailing such as chrome trim. To keep costs down, the builder used a one-piece top that includes the windshield portion. On early models this part is painted all one color. Later versions have the windshield picked out in chrome. Interior details are restricted to a formed dash and steering wheel with painted highlights. USA Models also created a convertible for the same year. It has a chromed white metal windshield frame.

For 1952, Zaugg Models of Switzerland's little convertible, 2 door hard-top coupe, and ambulance made their debut. The maker issued quite a few of these resin numbers with chrome trim and clear headlight lenses. While more realistic in overall appearance than the Americana version, the Zaugg has a pronounced narrowness to its roof and windshield header that is most apparent from a front view.

A more accurate version of the 1952 Chevrolet is Record Models/JPS' 1952 Styleline 4 door notchback sedan, 2 door hard-top, 2 door fastback sedan, convertible, business coupe, and pickup. These resin replicas were issued as kits or built-up from the factory. Fairly plentiful on the secondary market, the Record Models have details such as trim moldings cast into the body and lend themselves well to detailing with chrome foil. Built-up models from the factory are nicely painted with good fit and finish. Modeler Bruce Arnold notes: "the Record Model Chevrolets are 1/43 from the cowl forward ... 1/45 from there back."

Model-by-model   1953-54

History was made in 1953 with the introduction of General Motors' first sports car, the Corvette. Just like the actual vehicle, builders issued their versions in white. A very popular subject with scale model producers, no fewer than eight different replicas were made as handbuilts or die-cast models. Of these, Precision Miniatures and Western Models are the most intricate and costly handbuilts.

A makeover of the full-size Chevrolet line occurred for the 1953 and 1954 model years. The first 1:43 scale model of the Chevrolet is Marty Martino's 1953 Bel Air open convertible. In May of 2007 this resin handbuilt model was listed on eBay at a starting price of $74.95. It did not sell.

Other handbuilt scale models of the 1953 Chevrolets are limited to Motor City USA's 1953 Bel Air 2 door hard-top coupe, Bel

THE SPORTS CAR THAT WOULD EVENTUALLY EARN THE ADMIRATION OF MILLIONS STARTED OUT MODESTLY WITH 300 AUTOMOBILES VIRTUALLY HANDBUILT BY CHEVROLET IN 1953. THIS RESIN CAST PROVENCE MOULAGE SCALE MODEL CORVETTE WAS ISSUED IN SIMILARLY LOW NUMBERS. (COURTESY J RETTIG)

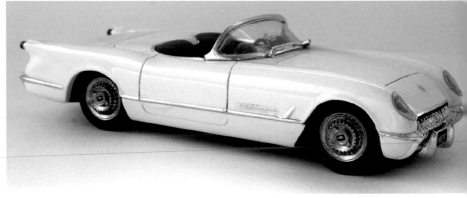

1953 CORVETTE IN WHITE METAL BY PRECISION MINIATURES. POSSIBLY THE NICEST EARLY '50S STOCK CORVETTE SCALE MODEL MADE. PMI-10. (AUTHOR COLLECTION)

MILESTONE USA ISSUED THIS RARE SCALE MODEL OF THE '53 CORVETTE. NO 1. (COURTESY ROBERT M WOOLLEY)

PRODUCTION OF THE CORVETTE ROSE TO 700 IN 1954 WITH SOME MODELS HAVING A NEWLY-AVAILABLE 8-CYLINDER ENGINE. A MUCH MODELED VEHICLE, THIS FRANKLIN MINT DIE-CAST METAL VERSION WAS VERY POPULAR AND IS FREQUENTLY ON OFFER AT AUCTIONS. (COURTESY J RETTIG)

1953 BEL AIR 2 DOOR HARD-TOP COUPE AND TOP DOWN CONVERTIBLE. THIS YEAR'S CHEVROLET HAD A MAJOR STYLING CHANGE WITH ONE-PIECE CURVED WINDSHIELD AND WRAPAROUND BACKLIGHT ON MOST MODELS, AS WELL AS HIGHER REAR FENDERS THAT INTEGRATED INTO THE BODY MORE THAN ITS PREDECESSOR'S HAD. MC-7 AND MC-8. (AUTHOR COLLECTION)

1953 BEL AIR TOP DOWN CONVERTIBLE CREATED BY MARTY MARTINO, AN EARLY MODELER OF NORTH AMERICAN CARS. MARTINO MODELS' NO 3 HANDBUILT RESIN CAST MODEL. (COURTESY J RETTIG)

AT THIS POINT (NUMBER EIGHT IN THE LINE) MOTOR CITY USA'S SCALE MODELS ARE HIGHLY-DETAILED, WELL-PROPORTIONED, AND FLAWLESSLY FINISHED. THE SUNGOLD MODEL PICTURED HERE HAS COLORED INSIGNIA AND QUITE A LOT OF INTERIOR DETAIL. MC-8. (AUTHOR COLLECTION)

Air open convertible, sedan delivery (finished in different liveries), and the intriguing Design Studio's National 'Ambulette'. The convertible and coupe (see sidebar) are particularly uncommon and, as white metal models, are without peer.

For 1954, Chevrolet gave a slight facelift to its line with park lights assuming an oval appearance and moving to the edges of the front to widen the car's aspect.

Two builders created replicas of the 1954 Chevrolet. The first handbuilt model is a white metal 4 door sedan released in dark metallic brown with beige roof or powder blue with white roof from Motor City USA's USA Models line. Externally, below the greenhouse, the builder packed much detail into this model including contrasting chrome trim outlined paint spears on the rear quarters. Building costs were kept down by the use of

patterned white metal headlights and monochrome one-piece roof insert that includes the windshield.

USA Models' competitor, Brooklin Models, created a superb 1954 Bel Air 2 door hard-top in 1997. This attractive Navajo Tan over Burnt Orange number has superb proportions and finishing. It is a much sought after piece that is apt to become more coveted because its pattern was used to create Brooklin's equally superb 1954 Chevrolet 210 Handyman station wagon which debuted in 2007.

The spectacular 1954 Nomad concept car was modeled brilliantly by Great American Dream Machines. Very nice versions of the Nomad and Corvair fastback show car were also created by Provence Moulage and Mini Marque '43. These models, especially the Mini Marque, are very rare.

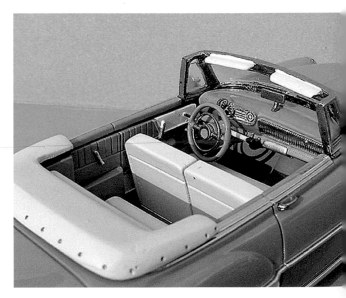

1953 BEL AIR OPEN CONVERTIBLE IN TARGET RED BY MOTOR CITY USA. CLOSE TO 30,000 CITIZENS BOUGHT NEW CHEVROLET CONVERTIBLES THAT MODEL YEAR, OF WHICH 5617 WERE MODEL 210S AND ABOUT 4 TIMES AS MANY WERE BEL AIRS. MC-8. (AUTHOR COLLECTION)

THE INTERIOR OF CHEVROLET'S MOST DELUXE 1953 MODEL IS WELL RENDERED BY MOTOR CITY USA. DECORATIVE CHROME – SUCH AS THAT ON THE INSTRUMENT PANEL FASCIA – WOULD BECOME EVEN MORE PREVALENT AS THE '50S WORE ON. MC-8. (AUTHOR COLLECTION)

THE SHORT-WHEELBASE AMBULANCE OR 'AMBULETTE' WAS PRODUCED DURING THE EARLY 1950S FOR LOW-PRICED STUDEBAKER AND CHEVROLET CHASSIS USING SEDAN DELIVERY AND STATION WAGON BODIES. THIS FINE HANDMADE WHITE METAL REPLICA OF A NATIONAL PRODUCT WAS PART OF MOTOR CITY USA'S DESIGN STUDIO LINE. IT HAS IMPRESSIVE FEATURES SUCH AS EMERGENCY LIGHT FAIRINGS, ROOF-MOUNTED 'GUMBALL MACHINE', SIGNAGE, PHOTO-ETCHED SCRIPT, AND EMBOSSED WHEEL COVERS. DS-9AMB. (AUTHOR COLLECTION)

NOTE THE INCREDIBLE REALISM OF THIS 1953 SEDAN DELIVERY MODEL DOWN TO THE WOOD LADDERS ON THE ROOF RACK. MOTOR CITY USA NO MC-9. (AUTHOR COLLECTION)

BEFORE THE DAYS OF MINI-VANS, SMALL BUSINESSES OFTEN HAD A SEDAN DELIVERY FOR LIGHT DUTY. THE 1953 CHEVROLET SEDAN DELIVERY WAS AVAILABLE TRIMMED AS A 150 WITH BLACK RUBBER REAR FENDER STONE GUARDS, OR HIGHER LINE 210 WITH CHROME GUARDS AND BODY MOLDINGS. MOTOR CITY USA ENVISIONED THIS 150 VERSION IN ITS FIRE AND RESCUE VEHICLE FLEET. MC 9. (AUTHOR COLLECTION)

THE ONLY 1:43 SCALE MODEL 1954 CHEVROLET 4 DOOR SEDAN IS USA MODELS' BEL AIR. NO 5 IN THE SERIES, IT HAS A MODERATE LEVEL OF DETAIL AND A RETAIL PRICE OF AROUND $100 WHEN RELEASED IN THE EARLY 1990S. CASHMERE BLUE AND POLO WHITE. (COURTESY ROBERT M WOOLLEY)

USA MODELS' 1954 CHEVROLET BEL AIR 4 DOOR SEDAN. THE BUILDER ADDED QUITE A BIT OF DETAIL TO THE LOWER BODY BUT USED A SIMPLE, UNADORNED, ONE-PIECE GREENHOUSE AND SINGLE VAC-FORM WINDOW INSERT TO KEEP COSTS DOWN. USA-5. (AUTHOR COLLECTION)

CHEVROLET BEL AIR 4 DOOR SEDAN BY USA MODELS IN SADDLE BROWN AND SHORELINE BEIGE. USA-5. (AUTHOR COLLECTION)

PROFILE – 1953 CHEVROLET BEL AIR 2 DOOR SPORT COUPE BY MOTOR CITY USA

TODAY, WE TEND TO REFER TO THE BODY STYLE OF THIS BEL AIR AS A 2 DOOR HARD-TOP COUPE. IN 1953, CHEVROLET CALLED IT A "2 DOOR SPORT COUPE". EVEN THOUGH IT ACCOUNTED FOR ONLY 7 PER CENT OF THE DIVISION'S TOTAL SALES THAT YEAR, THE SPORTY 2 DOOR HAD 99,047 BUYERS, WHICH JUST ABOUT DOUBLED THE TOTAL NUMBER OF KAISER AND HUDSON AUTOMOBILES PRODUCED THAT YEAR. IN 1953, GENERAL MOTORS' COLOR PALETTE WAS BECOMING LARGER WITH A GREATER RANGE OF AVAILABLE COLORS AND COMBINATIONS. THIS '53 BEL AIR BY MOTOR CITY USA (MC-7) IS FINISHED IN AN AUTHENTIC AND TASTEFUL WOODLAND GREEN OVER CAMPUS CREAM.

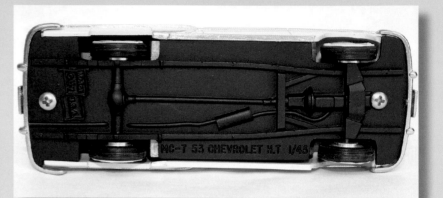

PRODUCED IN THE EARLY 1990S, THE MCUSA REPLICA LACKS CHROME FOIL AND PHOTO-ETCHING, BUT STILL HAS EFFECTIVE DETAILING THAT ENABLES IT TO RESEMBLE THE ACTUAL AUTOMOBILE. PROPORTIONS ARE EXCELLENT AND, WHEN WELL PHOTOGRAPHED, IT LOOKS LIKE THE REAL CAR. PARTICULARLY IMPRESSIVE IS THE INTERIOR WITH ITS NICELY DETAILED DASHBOARD AND INSTRUMENT PANEL, AND A PRINTED SEAT FABRIC THAT CLOSELY RESEMBLES THE TOP OF THE LINE MODEL'S UPHOLSTERY. ALTHOUGH IT LACKS A FEW SEPARATE CHROME GOODIES SUCH AS WINDOW WINDERS AND DOOR RELEASES, THESE DETAILS ARE CAST INTO THE INTERIOR TUB AND PICKED OUT EFFECTIVELY IN SILVER. THIS IS A BEAUTIFUL HANDBUILT SCALE MODEL. (AUTHOR COLLECTION)

EARLY 1950S STEEL BODIED STATION WAGONS WERE POPULAR WITH THE MANY YOUNG FAMILIES THAT GREW UP AFTER WWII. CHEVROLET MADE MORE THAN 56,000 WAGONS IN 1954, AND THIS CHEVROLET 210 HANDYMAN WAS THE MOST POPULAR MODEL. JOHN ROBERTS HAS PAINTED AND DETAILED THIS CORAL BRK-132, RELEASED ORIGINALLY IN SHORELINE BEIGE IN MARCH 2007. (AUTHOR COLLECTION)

THE TOP OF THE LINE 1954 CHEVROLET MODELS WERE THE BEL AIR HARD-TOP COUPE AND CONVERTIBLE. BROOKLIN MODELS ISSUED THIS EXCELLENT WHITE METAL REPLICA IN AUTHENTIC PUEBLO TAN AND SHORELINE BEIGE. BRK-68. (COURTESY D MATHYSSEN)

USA MODELS' BEL-AIR AND BROOKLIN MODELS' 1954 HANDYMAN. (AUTHOR COLLECTION)

AN INTRIGUING SHOW CAR THAT MADE THE GM MOTORAMA FOR THE 1954 MODEL YEAR WAS THIS 'NOMAD' CORVETTE VARIANT. SEVERAL BUILDERS, INCLUDING PRECISION MINIATURES, MINI MARQUE '43' AND GREAT AMERICAN DREAM MACHINES, HAVE PRODUCED THIS MODEL. THIS EXAMPLE IS FROM PROVENCE MOULAGE. NO 274. (COURTESY J RETTIG)

1954 CHEVROLET NOMAD DREAM CAR. PROVENCE MOULAGE. NO 274. (COURTESY J RETTIG)

PONTIAC 3

THE QUINTESSENTIAL 'MID-PRICED' CAR, THE PONTIAC WAS INTRODUCED in 1926. By the Second World War, it had carved out a rather deep niche for itself as the fifth most popular automobile. Positioning itself as the maker of deluxe-type vehicles at a price just slightly above the low-priced three of Ford, Plymouth, and Chevrolet, Pontiac took few chances and produced a solid, albeit unspectacular, product until the 1960s when it began to differentiate itself from its competitors with 'wide-track Pontiacs', and sporty continental-flavoured Grand Prix models.

There is a plethora of scale model handbuilt and die-cast Chevrolet and Cadillac models from the 1920s to 1954, but relatively few different Pontiac models for this same time period.

SOME FEATURED PONTIAC MODELS

YEAR	MODEL	MANUFACTURER
1948	TORPEDO AND STREAMLINER	CONQUEST MODELS
1950	CHIEFTAIN	RECORD MODELS
1950	CHIEFTAIN	MOTOR CITY USA
1953	CHIEFTAIN SEDAN DELIVERY	BROOKLIN MODELS
1954	STAR CHIEF	CONQUEST MODELS

Model-by-model   1940-48

There is only one model of a pre-WWII Pontiac, which was issued in tiny numbers. Day Dreamer's (USA) 1940 Torpedo is a scarce pewter replica in a reputed 1:45 scale. It is crude by today's modeling standards.

On the other hand, Conquest Models' 1:43 scale handbuilt

1950 CHIEFTAIN SUPER DELUXE CATALINA BY MOTOR CITY USA. MC-47. (AUTHOR COLLECTION)

white metal replica of the early post-war Pontiac melds artistry, materials and technology to produce a masterpiece. Pontiac produced the original automobile in 1948. At this point, the

Following the war, Pontiac used two body and chassis types. Here is the A-bodied 1948 Torpedo convertible which shared its body with the Chevrolet and Oldsmobile S66, and the 1948 Streamliner wagon which used the same B body as the Oldsmobile S76 and Buick Special. Conquest Models CNQ-14 and CNQ-27. (Courtesy A Moskalev)

Pontiac's 1948 Streamliner station wagon was built in the traditional fashion using wood in its structure and a canvas roof. It was the division's most expensive model and lowest seller. Conquest Models CNQ-27. (Courtesy A Moskalev)

1948 Torpedo 8 Deluxe open convertible in Frances Ivory. Built by SMTS for the Conquest Line of Fa. Daimler House in 1993, this scale model has a high level of interior and exterior detail. CNQ-14. (Courtesy A Moskalev)

Conquest Models' 1948 Streamliner replica is an elaborate model that mimics its subject closely by having a six-piece body. Handbuilt in 1996, it was priced at $225-250. CNQ-27. (Courtesy A Moskalev)

The 1948 Torpedo 8 Deluxe convertible weighed in at 3530lb, which was about 200lb more than a Ford. This Conquest Model CNQ-14 also came in Genessee (not Tennessee) Green Metallic. A high-end model that was made in small numbers of less than 500 total. CNQ-14. (Courtesy A Moskalev)

1948 TORPEDO 8 DELUXE TOP UP CONVERTIBLE. CONQUEST MODELS CNQ-14. (AUTHOR COLLECTION)

Madison Avenue advertising people were attempting to 'out name' the competition to attract sales of their clients' merchandise. The moniker of Pontiac's entry in the mid-size class was grandiose: Pontiac Torpedo Eight Deluxe.

That year the slang word 'torpedo' had many connotations, including a sleekly-designed automobile, usually a fastback or convertible. Pontiac used this word to refer to its shorter wheelbase models. Of course, eight cylinders – even Pontiac's inline flathead eight configuration – were better than six, and 'deluxe' indicated something that was above the norm. Therefore, by the convention of the day, a Torpedo Eight Deluxe must have been a pretty special car. And looking back these many years, it was. Though sales figures by body style are not available from 1948, only 35,000 of Pontiac's 250,000 vehicles were Torpedo Eights. These were spread across all body styles, including the business coupe, sport coupe, sedan coupe, 2 door sedan, 4 door sedan, and convertible, which was the most costly model in the line. The 1948 open Pontiac weighed in at 3600lb and had a length of 204.5in, which made it about 250lb and 7in longer than a comparable Chevrolet convertible.

The first handbuilt model 1948 Pontiac was produced for Henk van Asten by SMTS in 1993. Marked as Conquest Models No 14, it was an open convertible in Genessee Green Metallic or Frances Ivory. Conquest also released a top up version in buff over Blue Lake Metallic or Parma Wine Metallic.

BY 1952 PONTIAC'S ONCE POPULAR FASTBACK BODY HAD PRETTY WELL RUN ITS COURSE. THIS IS THE RECORD MODELS OF FRANCE RENDITION OF THE 1950 CHIEFTAIN 2 DOOR SEDAN. MODEL NO 82. (COURTESY J RETTIG)

Model-by-model 1949-52

The 1949 model year featured all new styling for the majority of General Motors' offerings. For that year, Pontiac unveiled automobiles that began to integrate fenders more into the overall body to appear lighter and lower. Also, though it was longer by 5-6in, the Pontiac bore a strong resemblance to the Chevrolet due to the sharing of many key body components.

There are several scale models of the 1950 Pontiac thanks

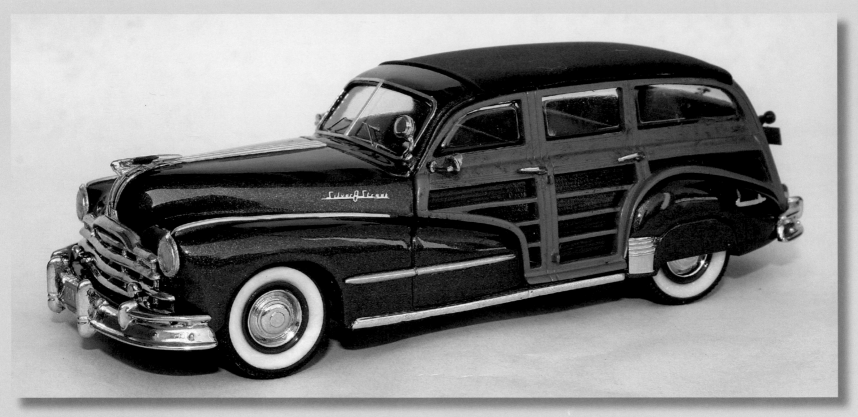

PROFILE – 1948 PONTIAC STREAMLINER EIGHT DELUXE STATION WAGON BY CONQUEST MODELS
FOLLOWING ITS 1948 PONTIAC CONVERTIBLE, CONQUEST DEBUTED AN EVEN MORE COMPLEX MODEL IN 1996. THIS TIME THE MAKER CHOSE THE FLAGSHIP OF THE PONTIAC FLEET, THE MAGNIFICENT 1948 PONTIAC STREAMLINER EIGHT DELUXE STATION WAGON. ASSIGNED MODEL NUMBER CNQ-27, THIS REPLICA OF THE WOOD-BODIED WAGON IS A TOUR DE FORCE THAT STANDS AS A TESTAMENT TO THE BUILDER'S SKILL. FIRST IMPRESSIONS ARE THAT THIS WAS A CURVACEOUS AUTOMOBILE WITH BOLD ACCENTS TO SET IT APART FROM CHEVROLET AND OTHER LOW-PRICED MOTORCARS. THE GRILLE IS MASSIVE AND COMPLICATED, MAKING A STATEMENT WITH ITS WIDE HORIZONTAL BARS AND SECONDARY VERTICAL ACCENTS ADDED FOR THE 1948 MODEL YEAR. CONQUEST'S PONTIAC IS A WELL-PROPORTIONED REPLICA. I HAD THOUGHT THAT THE PATTERNMAKER HAD MADE

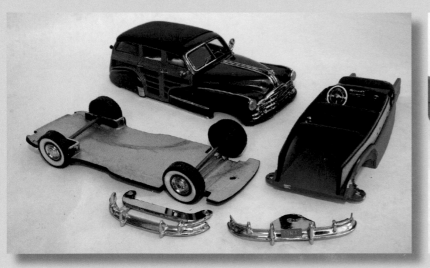

THE FRONT CLIP TOO LARGE BUT, UPON CLOSER INSPECTION OF PHOTOGRAPHS OF THE ACTUAL CAR, HAVE CHANGED MY MIND. ALL STYLING COMPONENTS THAT HAVE BEEN CREATED BY THE PATTERNMAKER AND BUILDER ARE SPOT ON. THE CONQUEST MODEL HAS EXCELLENT FINISHING WITH AUTHENTIC AUTOMOTIVE PAINT. THE LEVEL OF DETAIL ON THE MODEL IS PEERLESS. THE BUILDER HAS MADE LIBERAL USE OF CHROME FOIL TO CAPTURE THE MANY MOLDINGS, INCLUDING THE THREE BOLD PONTIAC TRADEMARK 'SILVER STREAKS' THAT RUN THE LENGTH OF THE CENTER HOOD. THE DISTINCTIVE, STYLIZED PONTIAC CHIEF MASCOT IS CAREFULLY CRAFTED AND TO SCALE. THE 'SILVER 8 STREAK' SCRIPT IS PHOTO-ETCHED METAL AND IN THE PROPER PLACE ON EACH SIDE OF THE HOOD IN FRONT OF THE COWL. INTERIOR DETAILS ARE THOROUGH AND INCLUDE FULL GAUGES, STEERING WHEEL CHROME TRIM, GEARSHIFT, AND CHROME WINDOW DOOR HANDLES. WITH A SIX-PIECE BODY AND A TOTAL OF 83 PARTS, ALL HAND-FITTED AND ASSEMBLED, THIS IS AN OUTSTANDING MODEL. THE TREATMENT OF THE WOOD DETAIL IS PERFORMED WITH GREAT EXPERTISE. THE PATTERNMAKER AND BUILDER HAVE CAPTURED THE TEXTURE, COLORING, AND LOOK OF THE REAL WOOD VERY ACCURATELY. IT CONTRASTS EFFECTIVELY WITH THE PARMA WINE METALLIC AND VOLUNTEER GREEN METALLIC COLORS THAT WERE AVAILABLE ON THE 1996 SCALE MODEL. ORIGINALLY AVAILABLE AT AROUND $235, STOCKISTS RAN OUT OF CONQUEST MODELS PONTIACS AROUND 2002. FORTUNATELY FOR ENTHUSIASTS, THREE-DOZEN OF THE STATION WAGONS WERE REISSUED IN 2006 IN RIO RED OR FRANCES IVORY. CONQUEST MODELS' ORIGINATOR, HENK VAN ASTEN, IS TO BE COMMENDED FOR BREATHING LIFE INTO THIS MODEL; ALSO DAVE KIRKEL FOR PERPETUATING IT A DECADE LATER. (AUTHOR COLLECTION)

to Record Models of France and Motor City USA. In the 1980s, Record issued an impressive range of 1:43 scale resin 1950 Pontiac models in kit and built-up form. Four body styles were available at around $40: 2 door hard-top coupe, open convertible, 4 door fastback sedan, and 2 door fastback sedan. When purchased as a factory built model, these replicas look fairly plain with relatively few parts. However, the castings are very detailed with moldings, emblems, and other features in high relief. In the hands of a skilled modeler who is in possession of some chrome foil, these scale models can be brought up to a high level of accuracy.

Bruce Arnold comments: "Record's Pontiacs apparently

use the shorter Canadian wheelbase. Provence Moulage's GM offering, the 50 Chevy Woody wagon, was different because it was based on the correct Solido die-cast."

Motor City USA's 1950 Pontiac was released in the late 1990s as an open convertible with a small number of top up models made available and as a 2 door hard-top coupe (see sidebar).

PONTIAC WAS A MASTER OF THE 'NAME GAME', FREQUENTLY ADDING ADJECTIVES TO ITS MODEL NAMES TO CONVINCE BUYERS TO UPGRADE THEIR PURCHASE. TOP OF THE LINE FOR 1950 WAS THE CHIEFTAIN SUPER DELUXE CATALINA. HERE IS AN EXPERTLY BUILT MODEL WITH AN ABUNDANCE OF CHROME FOIL FROM RECORD MODELS. NO 79. (COURTESY J RETTIG)

1950 CHIEFTAIN FASTBACK SEDAN BY RECORD MODELS. NO 82. (COURTESY ROBERT M WOOLLEY)

1950 PONTIAC CHIEFTAIN OPEN CONVERTIBLE. RECORD MODELS NO 80. (COURTESY J RETTIG)

1950 PONTIAC CHIEFTAIN 4 DOOR SEDAN. PONTIAC'S MOST POPULAR MODEL HELPED THE DIVISION SELL MORE THAN 446,000 UNITS THAT YEAR. RECORD MODELS NO 81. (COURTESY J RETTIG)

AFTER RECORD MODELS PRODUCED ITS RANGE OF FINELY SCULPTED RESIN MODELS, MOTOR CITY USA INTRODUCED A SUPERB WHITE METAL BUILT-UP. PICTURED IS ITS VERSION OF THE 1950 CHIEFTAIN SUPER DELUXE CATALINA. THIS GRAY REPLICA IS A COLOR TEST WITH ONLY VERY FEW ISSUED. MC-47. (AUTHOR COLLECTION)

1950 CHIEFTAIN SUPER DELUXE CATALINA BY MOTOR CITY USA. ENCLOSED REAR FENDER WELLS WERE COMMON ON THE PONTIAC. MC-47. (AUTHOR COLLECTION)

PROFILE – 1950 CHIEFTAIN SUPER DELUXE CATALINA BY MOTOR CITY USA

THE CALIFORNIA STUDIOS OF MOTOR CITY USA HAVE DONE A FABULOUS JOB OF CAPTURING THE EXACT PROPORTIONS AND DETAILS OF THE 1950 PONTIAC CONVERTIBLE (MC-46).

FROM THE CRIMSON-DOTTED FULL WHEEL COVERS, CHROMED REAR FENDER STONE SHIELDS AND FULL-WIDTH DOOR SIDE MOLDINGS (CAST IN POLISHED WHITE METAL NOT BRIGHT METAL FOIL), TO THE MULTIPLE SILVER STREAKS AND AMBER 'CHIEF' MASCOT, THIS IS ONE PRECISION PIECE. OF NOTE ARE CHROME DOOR HANDLES, BACK-UP LIGHTS, LICENSE PLATE LIGHTS, INDIVIDUAL HAND-PAINTED CONVERTIBLE BOOT FASTENER HEADS, AND EMBOSSED REAR DECK LID HANDLE. HEADLIGHTS HAVE CLEAR LENSES AND PARK/TURN INDICATORS ARE WHITE.

THE SILVER STREAK INSIGNIA ON THE FRONT FENDER HAS A PHOTO-ETCHED '8' BETWEEN THE TWO WORDS TO PROCLAIM THAT THE CAR HAS THE L-HEAD STRAIGHT 8 CYLINDER MOTOR. THIS POWER PLANT PUT OUT 113HP VERSUS THE STANDARD 93HP SIX-CYLINDER ENGINE. THIS WAS STILL 22HP LESS THAN OLDSMOBILE'S 303CI V8, AND WOULD HAVE PRODUCED LEISURELY ACCELERATION COMPARED TO THE OLDS. THE 1950 PONTIAC CONVERTIBLE'S INTERIOR IS QUITE AUSTERE, PARTICULARLY FOR A DELUXE MODEL. HOWEVER, LEATHER UPHOLSTERY WAS THE NORM FOR RAGTOP MODELS. THE INTERIOR IS ACCURATE, THE DASHBOARD AUTHENTIC DOWN TO THE RADIO GRILLE, DOOR HANDLE AND WINDOW-WINDER KNOBS. THE QUALITY OF PAINT IS FLAWLESS AS WELL. MY VERSION HAS A LUSTROUS METALLIC BLUE WITH OXBLOOD INTERIOR. ONCE AGAIN, MOTOR CITY USA WAS AT THE TOP OF ITS GAME ON THIS ONE. (AUTHOR COLLECTION)

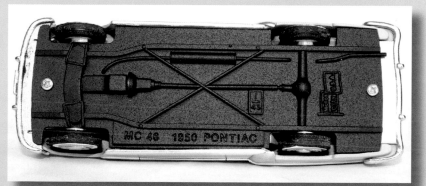

1950 HARD-TOP AND OPEN CONVERTIBLE. THESE EXAMPLES ARE HANDBUILT WHITE METAL 1:43 SCALE MODELS FROM CALIFORNIA'S MOTOR CITY USA. MC-47 AND 46. (AUTHOR COLLECTION)

RIGHT: THE 1952 PONTIAC CHIEFTAIN STATION WAGON WITH WOOD GRAIN WAS ONCE AGAIN THE DIVISION'S MOST EXPENSIVE MODEL AT $2699 FOR THE 8-CYLINDER VERSION, COMPARED TO $2444 FOR THE MOST DELUXE CONVERTIBLE AND $1724 FOR THE LOWEST PRICED PONTIAC SEDAN. THE MODEL PICTURED HERE IS A VERY RARE BRUCE ARNOLD MODELS REPLICA THAT HAS EXQUISITE PROPORTIONS AND DETAILING; BOTTOM-RIGHT: 1952 CHIEFTAIN STATION WAGON IN THE EXCLUSIVE STATION WAGON COLOR OF IMPERIAL MAROON THAT CONTRASTS NICELY WITH THE LIGHT COLORED WOOD GRAIN. BRUCE ARNOLD MODELS. (COURTESY B ARNOLD)

ANOTHER '52 CHIEFTAIN STATION WAGON FROM PROLIFIC BUILDER JERRY RETTIG WHO CLEVERLY CONVERTED THIS ONE-OF-A-KIND MODEL FROM A JPS/RECORD SEDAN. (COURTESY J RETTIG)

Model-by-model 1953-54

Redesigned for 1953, Pontiacs looked longer as the rear fender flowed more into the body and a precursor to fins appeared with a raised portion at the back to house the taillight assembly.

Brooklin Models produced a 1953 sedan delivery that is described in the chapter on light trucks. Craftsman, John Roberts converted several Brooklin sedan delivery models into station wagons. By applying new paint, often in two and three tone combinations, scraping the paint strategically to bare shiny metal, cutting open a tailgate and adding luggage or golf clubs, and a figure or two, John has created models that sell for prices many times the original. In 2006 a John Roberts-converted BRK-31 garnered over $1300 on eBay.

ABC Models and Conquest Models have modeled the 1954 Pontiac Star Chief as a high-end replica.

Carlo Brianza who also is responsible for the Playtoy 1953 Buick Skylark and 1948 Chrysler Town & Country created ABC Models' version. The Brianza Star Chief Custom Catalina is an open convertible in Coral Red with buff interior. Available at

over $200, this resin model was issued in small quantities (low hundreds) and has a fineness of detail, mirror-like paintwork, and feeling of delicacy that characterizes the work of the best French and Italian patternmakers and builders. Brianza's rendering of the model is also a little impressionistic, particularly the squared-off windshield and rather upright folded top that resembled European tops of the time. This reminds collectors that these are handmade replicas with patterns sculpted by an artist rather than a machine.

Conquest Models' 1954 Pontiac Star Chief Custom Catalina appeared in 1991 as an open convertible and in 1994 as a 2 door hard-top. Considering that this model is less than 5 inches in length, the patternmaker and builder (SMTS) have managed to pack much detail into the finished product. All five silver streaks are present on the hood, interspersed by the amber face of the chief on the chromed hood mascot; on the original this feature lit-up but on this replica we have to use our imagination. Conquest's is a highly-detailed model complete down to the widow winders, door handles, and armrests of the original. It even has a five piece front seat.

Build quality, as with other Conquest Models of this time, is excellent and the paint finish is both good and authentic. Colors for the convertible in 1991 were Shannon Green (light blue-green) and Arlington Maroon. In 1997 Picador Red was introduced. The 2 door hard-top came in white over Maize Yellow, and white over red. In 2005-06, the new Conquest Models brought out 18 more of the 2 door hard-top in Coral Red over Biloxi Beige, and 6 in black. In these small numbers, and at the price of $225-235, they sold quickly.

PICTURED IS A RELATIVELY PLAIN CHIEFTAIN SPECIAL CONVERTED FROM BROOKLIN MODELS' BRK-31 BY JERRY RETTIG. THE LINDEN GREEN JERRY HAS CHOSEN WAS A PONTIAC COLOR FOR THAT YEAR. (COURTESY J RETTIG)

TO DATE, NO BUILDER HAS MASS-PRODUCED PONTIAC'S ALL STEEL 1953 STATION WAGON. HOWEVER, JOHN ROBERTS AND JERRY RETTIG ISSUED A HANDFUL OF CUSTOM VERSIONS BASED ON BROOKLIN'S SEDAN DELIVERY. THIS IS JOHN ROBERTS' VERSION THAT GARNERED A WINNING BID OF $1300 IN A 2006 EBAY AUCTION. (COURTESY W MARTIN)

PONTIAC MADE A MILD STYLING CHANGE TO ITS 1954 MODELS, MOST NOTICEABLY THE OVAL GRILLE TREATMENT, TO DISTINGUISH THEM FROM THE 1953 PRODUCTS. 1954 STAR CHIEF CUSTOM CATALINA HARD-TOP WHITE METAL SCALE MODEL MADE BY CONQUEST MODELS IN 1994 AND REISSUED IN 2006. (AUTHOR COLLECTION)

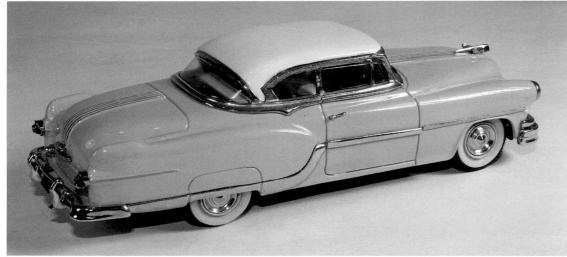

DESPITE SHARING MANY STRUCTURAL COMPONENTS WITH THE CHEVROLET, THE REAR EXTENSION MADE THE SENIOR PONTIAC LOOK MUCH LONGER. 1954 STAR CHIEF CUSTOM CATALINA. CONQUEST MODELS CNQ-17. (AUTHOR COLLECTION)

To justify its position in the mid-priced market segment, Pontiac packed on the chrome and weight. Compared to the post-war version, the 1954 convertible gained the weight of two small passengers – it now weighed 3776lb. Conquest Models no CNQ-8. (Author collection)

The extraordinary detail in this Conquest Models' 1954 Pontiac Star Chief replica is typical of the models issued by Fa. Daimler House in 1991. The seating alone comprises five different pieces, all of which had to be patterned, cast, finished, painted, and assembled. CNQ-8. (Author collection)

Produced in Arlington Maroon, Piccador Red, or this model's Shannon Green, Conquest's 1954 Pontiac convertible was only available as a top down model. CNQ-8. (Author collection)

Italy's master patternmaker, Carlo Brianza, created a 1954 Pontiac open convertible in his ABC line. Handcrafted in resin. ABC-22. (Courtesy J Arnold)

Two Bonneville Specials were created for GM's popular Motorama in 1954 in green and reddish bronze. Both exist today. Pictured is a handmade white metal version of the dream car by Highway Travellers. It is the 6th and last model produced by Illustra for Paul Patterson's company. (Courtesy J Rettig)

OLDSMOBILE

"SOME MEN ARE BAPTISTS, OTHERS CATHOLICS. MY FATHER WAS AN Oldsmobile man."

This line is from Jean Shepherd's classic, *A Christmas Story*. The brand that Ransom E Olds founded in 1907 was a significant part of North American culture. From the popular song, *In My Merry Oldsmobile* to the mass production of 'clutchless' driving, this icon symbolized what was good about the American way of life. It was a sad day when, on April 28, 2004, the last Oldsmobile pulled off the line in the Lansing, Michigan plant, 107 years after the first.

ONE OF THE EARLIEST SCALE MODEL OLDSMOBILES IS THIS 1934 SEDAN FROM MINIATURE VEHICLE CASTING. REMINISCENT OF THE POPULAR AUBURN RUBBER AND TOOTSIETOY MODELS OF THE TIME, IT HAS SURPRISINGLY GOOD PROPORTIONS AND DETAILS IN RELIEF. WHEN PAINTED, FOILED AND WITH A WINDSHIELD ADDED, IT IS A PRETTY NICE MODEL. LEAD CAST IN 1:41 SCALE. MVC-18. (COURTESY J RETTIG)

SOME FEATURED OLDSMOBILE MODELS

YEAR	MODEL	MANUFACTURER
1938	F SERIES TRUNKBACK SEDAN	DURHAM CLASSICS
1941	DYNAMIC CRUISER 4 DOOR SEDAN	WESTERN MODELS
1941	SERIES 66	ELC
1942	SERIES 66 CONVERTIBLE	NEWBANK
1947	76 DYNAMIC CRUISER CLUB COUPE	CONQUEST MODELS
1947	SERIES 66 4 DOOR SEDAN	MADISON MODELS
1948	SERIES 98 CONVERTIBLE	BROOKLIN MODELS
1949	SERIES 98 HOLIDAY	BROOKLIN MODELS
1949	SERIES 88 CLUB COUPE	BROOKLIN MODELS
1949	SERIES 88 CONVERTIBLE	TRON
1950	SERIES 88 CLUB COUPE	TRON
1950	SERIES 98 FASTBACK	MADISON
1950	SERIES 88	MOTOR CITY USA
1953	FIESTA	BROOKLIN MODELS
1954	SERIES 98	CONQUEST MODELS

Despite its early origin and popularity, the Oldsmobile has not been modeled often in 1:43 scale. Perhaps this is because, aside from the 1953 Fiesta, the maker turned out few of the dream cars or limited edition models so favored by collectors.

Model-by-model   1938-47

Dinky Toys (1:48th scale) made the 1938 Super 6 one of its range of late-'30s American automobiles, as did the Auburn Rubber Company, but it was not until the late 1990s that a builder saw fit to make an adult collectible Oldsmobile from the decade of the Depression. This model was Durham Classics' very good 1938 F Series 6 cylinder 4 door trunkback sedan (see sidebar).

1937 OLDSMOBILE SUPER 6 BY BUCCANEER MODELS. THIS IS A COPY OF THE COMMON DINKY TOY DIE-CAST CAR ISSUED IN THE 1940s AS ONE OF SIX PRE-WAR AMERICAN SEDANS. THIS MODEL IS SIGNIFICANT BECAUSE IT IS AN EXAMPLE OF DINKY TOYS' EARLY SUCCESSFUL EFFORT TO DEPICT WITH ACCURACY THE SHAPE AND DETAILS OF ITS SUBJECT VEHICLE. (COURTESY J RETTIG)

MUCH LIKE BROOKLIN MODELS, DURHAM CLASSICS RELEASED SEVERAL TRIM AND COLOR VARIATIONS OF ITS 1938 OLDSMOBILE TO AMORTIZE ITS INVESTMENT IN THE ORIGINAL PATTERN AND MOLDS. HERE IS A DARK MAROON VERSION WITH CHROME SIDE TRIM, FENDER SKIRTS, AND WHITEWALL TIRES. DC-27. (COURTESY D LARSEN)

THE ONLY PLACE YOU ARE LIKELY TO SEE A 1:43 SCALE VERSION OF OLDSMOBILE'S 1938 CONVERTIBLE COUPE IS IN JERRY RETTIG'S VAST MODEL COLLECTION. HERE, THE BUILDER HAS CONVERTED DURHAM CLASSICS' SEDAN INTO A VERY SPORTY OPEN 6-CYLINDER CONVERTIBLE WITH CONTRASTING RED WHEELS. (COURTESY J RETTIG)

1941 DYNAMIC CRUISER 4 DOOR SEDAN BY WESTERN MODELS IN METALLIC MAROON. WMS-84. (COURTESY J RETTIG)

PROFILE – 1938 OLDSMOBILE F SERIES 4 DOOR SEDAN BY DURHAM CLASSICS AUTOMOTIVE MINIATURES

OLDSMOBILE'S 1938 F SERIES DIFFERED FROM THE L SERIES IN A FEW SIGNIFICANT WAYS, SUCH AS HAVING A 230CI SIX-CYLINDER ENGINE VERSUS THE L'S 257CI STRAIGHT EIGHT. VISIBLE DIFFERENCES INCLUDE A SHORTER 117IN WHEELBASE FOR THE F COMPARED TO THE L'S LARGER 124IN AND FEWER LARGER BARS USED IN THE F SERIES' GRILLE.

ISSUED BY THE CANADIAN MODEL MAKER AROUND THE TURN OF THE MILLENNIUM, DURHAM CLASSICS' REPLICA WAS MADE USING METHODS INTRODUCED DECADES EARLIER. IT IS CONSTRUCTED OF HEAVY WHITE METAL, USES A FEW NICKEL-PLATED PIECES TO SET OFF MAJOR BRIGHTWORK, AND IS DEVOID OF INTRICATE DETAILING. FOR EXAMPLE, DOOR AND TRUNK HANDLES ARE MOLDED INTO THE MAIN BODY. OTHER OBSERVATIONS OF NOTE ARE THAT THE PAINT IS GLOSSY AND WHEELS ROLL FREELY, IN THE DURHAM CLASSICS TRADITION.

INTERIOR DETAILING OF THIS LITTLE OLDS IS MINIMAL, WITH PARTS CONFINED TO PLEATED SEATS AND DASHBOARD IN A DARKER TONE THAN THE FLOOR AND INSIDE DOOR PANELS, THREE-SPOKE STEERING WHEEL, AND GEARSHIFT LEVER. THE PATTERNMAKER HAS ALSO REPRESENTED OLDSMOBILE'S INNOVATIVE 'SAFETY DASH' WITH ALL CONTROLS AND INSTRUMENTS CLUSTERED BEHIND THE STEERING WHEEL.

DURHAM CLASSICS ISSUED 1250 PIECES OF THIS MODEL DURING 2000-03 IN A VARIETY OF COLORS AND LIVERIES, INCLUDING A US ARMY STAFF CAR, NEW YORK GENERAL CAB COMPANY TAXI IN YELLOW, DETROIT SAFETY POLICE CAR WITH MASSIVE ROOF-MOUNTED LOUDSPEAKER, A RATHER PLAIN-LOOKING, BRIGHTWORK-FREE, CREAM-COLORED SEDAN, DARK BLUE WITH CHROME MOLDINGS, AND MAROON WITH DETAILED DASH, FENDER SKIRTS AND ADDED BODY BRIGHTWORK. CURIOUSLY, THE LATTER THREE CIVILIAN MODELS ALL RETAILED AT AROUND $135, REGARDLESS OF THE DEGREE OF ADDED BRIGHTWORK AND FENDER SKIRTS. (AUTHOR COLLECTION)

PROFILE – 1941 OLDSMOBILE DYNAMIC CRUISER 4 DOOR SEDAN BY WESTERN MODELS

IN THE AUTHOR'S OPINION, WESTERN MODELS' 1941 DYNAMIC CRUISER IS ONE OF THIS VENERABLE COMPANY'S BEST REPLICAS. CRAFTED IN WHITE METAL FROM AN EXCELLENT PATTERN, IT IS VERY ACCURATELY PROPORTIONED TO THE ORIGINAL AUTOMOBILE. WHEREAS THE SHORTER-BODIED GM MODELS WERE SLIGHTLY BUSTLE-BACKED, THE SENIOR SERIES OF 1941 OLDSMOBILE MODELS WERE LONG AUTOMOBILES WITH SMOOTH, ROUNDED LINES THAT FLOW PLEASINGLY ON A MORE HORIZONTAL PLANE FROM THE FRONT TO THE REAR OF THE AUTOMOBILE. HORIZONTAL CHROME MOLDINGS ADD BRIGHTNESS AND A TOUCH OF STREAMLINING TO THE OVERALL APPEARANCE.

THE FRONT OF THE 1941 OLDSMOBILE IS QUITE BUSY, AND WESTERN HAS DONE AN EXCELLENT JOB OF CAPTURING ITS MIXTURE OF BOLD HORIZONTAL AND FINER VERTICAL GRILLEWORK. AS WITH ITS OTHER MODELS, WESTERN HAS USED CLEAR HEADLIGHT LENSES TO ADD TO THE REALISM. THE REAR TREATMENT IS REALISTICALLY CAPTURED WITH RED REFLECTIVE TAILLIGHTS AND LARGE TRUNK ORNAMENT. OLDSMOBILE LETTERING IS DONE WITH DECALS, AND CONNECTICUT LICENSE PLATES ARE A NICE TOUCH (THOUGH APPLIED CROOKEDLY TO MY MODEL).

AS A MID-PRICED HANDBUILT MODEL, THE BUILDER HAS REDUCED EXPENSE

BY HAVING A SIMPLE INTERIOR WITH MOLDED DASHBOARD AND THE STEERING WHEEL, GEARSHIFT, AND COLUMN COMBINED IN ONE PIECE. SEATS ARE SMOOTH AND PAINTED IN ONE COLOR. AS FOR EXTERIOR COLORS, WESTERN MADE GRAY, MAROON, AND ORANGE AVAILABLE, THE LATTER AN UNUSUAL CHOICE BUT ONE THAT OLDSMOBILE OFFERED FOR 1941. (AUTHOR COLLECTION)

In 2003, Newbank Models (UK) introduced the only 1:43 scale model of a 1942 Oldsmobile. All Oldsmobiles that year were named 'B-44' by the divisions' advertising brain trust, to commemorate the forty-forth year of the marque's automobile production. The last models produced by Oldsmobile before the war, Newbank's '42 Series 66 convertible, coincidentally was the last model this company issued before halting production.

Made by SMTS, Newbank's '42 Olds handmade white metal replica was issued in one color, Ambassador Red Poly (maroon) with a buckskin interior. Some models had a removable tan convertible top. Production figures are estimated at around 200 pieces.

The scale model has high-quality reflective lenses. The grille appears a little disconcerting to some because, despite being nicely cast and showing obvious skill and care by the patternmaker, it lacks 'three dimensionality'. It appears to be all of one piece and would have benefited from a blackwash treatment or perhaps photo-etched grillework.

The Newbank replica Oldsmobile is well-proportioned and solidly constructed. Like the original automobile, it is somewhat

A METALLIC GREEN, ONE-OF-A-KIND 1941 OLDSMOBILE IN A CLUB COUPE CONFIGURATION FROM JERRY RETTIG, WHO USED WESTERN MODELS' 4 DOOR SEDAN AS THE BASIS FOR THIS CONVERSION. (COURTESY J RETTIG)

austere in appearance with little brightwork, non-patterned upholstery, hubcaps mounted on body-colored wheels, and black wall tires. It does, however, have pleated door panels, window winders, door handles and a fully-detailed instrument panel. Despite its accurate detailing, some collectors were not enthused about this replica. Like the actual automobile, it is a little plain for the price. In 2007, Conquest Models issued 15 units of the same model in blue with whitewall tires.

Model-by-model   1947-49

After World War II, Oldsmobile introduced slightly restyled models based upon the 1942 edition. For Conquest/Madison, SMTS created white metal models of an exceptionally realistic 1947 Oldsmobile Series 76 Dynamic Cruiser Club Coupe (see sidebar) and in 1998, an equally impressive Madison Models 1947 Series 66 4 door sedan.

Madison Models' 1947 Series 66 4 door sedan is an accurate rendering of Oldsmobile's upright profiled family sedan. It is as detailed as a typical later edition Conquest Model and has the solid build quality and finishing as the fastback (see sidebar). Fa. Daimler House (Conquest/Madison) issued a few hundred of these sedan replicas in 1998. They came in Caspian Blue Metallic over Nightshade Blue Metallic or Saxon Gray Metallic over Chateau Gray Metallic.

THE LAST PRE-WAR OLDSMOBILE BUILT WAS A 1942 B-44 SERIES 66 CONVERTIBLE, FAITHFULLY RENDERED HERE BY CONQUEST MODELS. NO 39. (AUTHOR COLLECTION)

1940-48 OLDSMOBILE STATION WAGONS CONTINUED TO BE CONSTRUCTED OF TRADITIONAL WOOD FRAMES, WOOD VENEERS, AND CANVAS MATERIALS. THIS 1:43 SCALE HANDBUILT RESIN REPLICA OF A 1941 MODEL IS A CONVERSION OF WESTERN MODELS' OLDSMOBILE SEDAN AND JERRY'S OWN 1941 BUICK PATTERN. (COURTESY J RETTIG)

1941 OPEN OLDSMOBILE CONVERTIBLE COUPE CONVERSION IN BLACK BY JERRY RETTIG. (COURTESY J RETTIG)

PERHAPS THE MOST RARE 1941 OLDSMOBILE AVAILABLE TODAY, THE REPLICA CONVERTIBLE SEDAN HERE IN A BUTTERCUP YELLOW WITH REALISTIC-LOOKING OXBLOOD 'LEATHER' INTERIOR IS EVEN RARER THAN THE ACTUAL MOTORCAR. IT IS ANOTHER ONE-OFF CONVERSION OF A WESTERN MODELS SEDAN BY JERRY RETTIG. (COURTESY J RETTIG)

1942 B-44 SERIES 66 CONVERTIBLE NEXT TO ITS POST-WAR SUCCESSOR, SERIES 76 FASTBACK SEDAN. GONE WERE THE DISPARATE GRILLE AND FRONT FASCIA PARTS IN FAVOR OF A LARGE 'FROWNING' OR 'FISH MOUTH' TREATMENT THAT MADE THE OLDSMOBILE DISTINCTIVE. BUILT ON THE MID-SIZED B BODY, THE OLDS SEEMED MORE MASSIVE AND LUXURIOUS THAN ITS PREDECESSOR. NEWBANK NO 2 AND CONQUEST MODELS CNQ-23. (AUTHOR COLLECTION)

1947 OLDSMOBILE S66 SEDAN. MADISON MODELS ISSUED THIS HANDBUILT WHITE METAL MODEL IN 1998 IN THE COLORS CASPIAN BLUE METALLIC/NIGHTSHADE METALLIC AND TWO-TONE GRAY. MAD-12. (AUTHOR COLLECTION)

1947 OLDSMOBILE SERIES 66 SEDAN BY MADISON MODELS. OLDSMOBILE'S LOWEST PRICED MODEL SHARED GENERAL MOTORS' SMALLEST 'A BODY' WITH CHEVROLET AND PONTIAC'S TORPEDO. NOT AS SLEEK AS THE 70 OR 98 SERIES, THE S66 STILL OFFERED PLENTY OF COMFORT, THE AVAILABILITY OF AN AUTOMATIC TRANSMISSION, AND THE UPWARDLY MOBILE STATUS OF THE OLDSMOBILE NAME. MAD-12. (AUTHOR COLLECTION)

PROFILE – 1947 OLDSMOBILE SERIES 76 DYNAMIC CRUISER CLUB COUPE BY CONQUEST MODELS

ORIGINALLY PRODUCED IN 1995, CONQUEST MODELS' 1947 DYNAMIC CRUISER CLUB COUPE IS A FLAWLESSLY PROPORTIONED, WHITE METAL, HANDMADE SCALE MODEL THAT EFFECTIVELY CAPTURES THE STREAMLINED 'FASTBACK' LINES OF THE ORIGINAL.

BUILT BY SMTS, CONQUEST'S OLDSMOBILE IS A PREMIUM PIECE THAT SPARES NO DETAIL. THE BUILDER HAS USED PHOTO-ETCHING FOR TINY DETAILS SUCH AS EMBLEMS, AND CHROME FOIL FOR MOLDINGS. THE MULTI-PIECE WHEELS ARE A WORK OF ART, WITH A RED OUTER RING, CHROME TRIM RING, RED INNER RING, AND POLISHED 'MOON' CENTER CAP — EACH WHEEL HAS FOUR PARTS. INTERIOR DETAILS SUCH AS WINDOW WINDERS, DOOR PULLS, GEARSHIFTS AND INSTRUMENTATION (DECALS) ARE ALL PRESENT.

../..

CON 23
1947 OLDSMOBILE SERIES
76 DYNAMIC CRUISER

2 Door Club Sedan
Black 1 of 6

Handcrafted in the United
Kingdom

PAINTWORK AND ASSEMBLY IS FIRST RATE. WHEN IT WAS ORIGINALLY ISSUED, THE MODEL CAME IN A COUPLE OF LUSTROUS (AND TIME-CONSUMING TO PRODUCE) METALLIC TWO-TONE PAINT COLOR COMBINATIONS: HAVANA BEIGE (A TOBACCO-LIKE COLOR) ON LIGHT PAWNEE BEIGE, AND MID-SEAFOAM GREEN ON LIGHT IVY GREEN. IN 2006 THESE MODELS WERE RELEASED AGAIN WITH EIGHTEEN IN THE BEIGE COMBINATION AND SIX PIECES IN ALL-BLACK. THE MODEL PICTURED HERE CAME IN A NUMBERED BOX AND HAS A HAND-NUMBERED BASE. (AUTHOR COLLECTION)

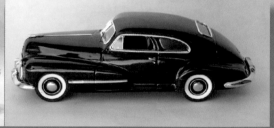

Oldsmobile's first all-new post-war model was its Series 98. Following a GM practice of first debuting special features such as the later panoramic windshields and hard-top body styles on senior models, the '48 employed new styling with a lowered hood line that converged toward a higher fender line. Oldsmobile called its new model 'Futuramic'.

The only 1:43 1948 scale model Olds is Brooklin Models' 98 convertible made for the Brooklin Collectors Club in 2001. Produced in a limited run of 250 units with a white metal Omen figure of American celebrity pianist Hoagy Carmichael, this little car was finished in a rich mid-blue with light blue interior. It is typical of later Brooklin products, in that it is well-proportioned with accurate styling, major details cast into the body or picked out with chrome parts, durable paint, and a solid feel to it. It has a fully chromed one-piece windshield frame. The interior, once again, is simple but has accurately-shaped seats, steering wheel, and dashboard. Originally issued to club members in the mid-$100 range, today, this model would command two to three times that amount on the open market.

An interesting coincidence is that Dirk Mathyssen, who provided many of the photographs of Brooklin models for this book, sold his Hoagy model (see photo) in November 2006 to none other than Hoagy Bix Carmichael, son of the great performer who was very pleased to acquire this rare memento of his father.

1948 OLDSMOBILE 98 CONVERTIBLE WITH OMEN FIGURE OF FAMOUS PIANIST HOAGY CARMICHAEL. 1 OF 250 MODELS PRODUCED IN 2001 FOR THE BROOKLIN COLLECTORS CLUB, THE MODEL PICTURED HERE WAS LATER PURCHASED ON eBAY IN 2006 BY CARMICHAEL'S SON, HOAGY BIX CARMICHAEL. (COURTESY D MATHYSSEN)

THE FIRST ENTIRELY NEW POST-WAR OLDSMOBILE WAS THE 98, AND THE FIRST NEW BODY STYLE WAS THE 1949 HOLIDAY 'HARD-TOP CONVERTIBLE COUPE'. BROOKLIN MODELS NO 73. (COURTESY D MATHYSSEN)

A ONE-OF-A-KIND 1949 OLDSMOBILE 98 SEDANET CREATED BY JOHN ROBERTS. SHOWING WHAT A GREAT CUSTOMISER CAN DO, JOHN TOOK BROOKLIN'S 1949 BUICK SEDANET AND SOMEHOW MARRIED IT TO THE SAME COMPANY'S 1949 OLDSMOBILE 98 HOLIDAY TO PRODUCE THIS UNIQUE SCALE MODEL. (COURTESY D LARSEN)

JOHN ROBERTS USED GREAT SKILL TO CREATE THE REAR OF THIS UNIQUE 1949 OLDSMOBILE 98 SEDANET. (COURTESY D LARSEN)

1949 OLDSMOBILE 88 CLUB COUPE. A VERY GOOD VERSION WAS MADE BY BROOKLIN MODELS IN 2005. THIS IS THE STANDARD MODEL IN SERGE BLUE METALLIC WITH TURQUOISE INTERIOR. BRK-114.
(COURTESY D MATHYSSEN)

A POWERFUL AUTOMOBILE, THE OLDSMOBILE 88 WAS A FITTING PURSUIT VEHICLE FOR THE CALIFORNIA HIGHWAY PATROL. BROOKLIN RELEASED THIS AS THE 11TH MODEL IN ITS INTERNATIONAL POLICE VEHICLE SERIES.
(COURTESY D MATHYSSEN)

Oldsmobile's revolutionary 1949 'hard-top convertible coupe' was modeled by Brooklin in 1998. Brought out in a Tawnee Buff with dark metallic brown, it enjoyed a short production run of 16 months; this was during a time that GM wanted scale model manufacturers to pay royalties to the large company for the use of its images. Brooklin's model is, of course, based on the Series 98 and is a credible albeit simply detailed replica.

In 2005 Brooklin issued its 114th model, a mid-blue 1949 Oldsmobile 88 Club Coupe with light blue wheels and whitewall tires. An accurately proportioned scale model, it has separate chromed windshield wipers, hood mascot, hood emblem, and door handles, rocker panel molding and hefty chrome stone shield on each rear fender. It is a very nicely made model that Brooklin also introduced as a California Highway Patrol cruiser in its International Police Vehicle line. In black with the 'CHiPS' emblem prominently displayed on each of the vehicle's white doors, the model appears to be historically authentic. The Highway Patrol usually purchased one type of car each year for its fleet, usually a heavier high-powered automobile that would hug the road. It used Oldsmobile 88s in 1954 and Buicks in 1955.

In 1949, an Oldsmobile Rocket 88 convertible paced the Indianapolis 500 Race. Two builders issued scale models to commemorate this event. The first was a 1980s Chris Boyer patterned offering from Paolo Rampini's Tron Models (Italy). Provence Moulage, now Provence Miniatures, cast all Tron models. Available as a built-up model and in kit form, the little resin convertible is a credible small sized copy of the original. In fact it is quite tiny at around 1:45 scale. The maker achieved a high level of realism with this replica with careful casting of detail directly into the body and interior and plated white metal parts for large pieces such as bumpers and the distinctive pace car's rocket ship on the front fenders.

Bruce Arnold points out, "There were two Tron Olds convertibles, a '49 and a '50. The '49 was a pace car and had cast-in vent windowpanes. The other used the hard-top photo-etched pieces that were wrong for a convertible. It looks like the '49 Olds pace car convertible, with its correct, different rocker panel trim, was purpose built, but the '50 Olds was an afterthought conversion of their 2 door sedan. Like the castings Provence Moulage made for Record, the Tron Olds were a scale all of there own."

Two decades later, Motor City USA created a 1949 Indy Pace Car primarily as an open convertible with a few top up models made.

Model-by-model 1950-54

For 1950, the 98 was modeled by Conquest/Madison in open convertible and 2 door club coupe versions. Appearing in 1994 as a Madison Model, this slightly stubby replica of the 1950 club coupe came in Crest Blue, Alder Green Metallic, and a limited edition of 50 units in Garnet Maroon Metallic. By this point in its production, the patternmaker and the builder SMTS were hitting their stride and issuing for Fa. Daimler House many nicely-detailed and well-constructed scale models.

Madison Models' 1950 Futuramic 98 convertible was introduced in 1996. Available only as an open model, it had the

OLDSMOBILE'S FUTURAMIC 98 WAS ALTERED NOTABLY IN THE REAR SECTION FOR 1950. THE CONVERTIBLE WAS A POPULAR BODY STYLE ACCOUNTING FOR 6.6 PER CENT OF ALL CONVERTIBLES PRODUCED IN AMERICA DURING THE CALENDAR YEAR. ISSUED BY MADISON MODELS IN 1996, THIS CANTO CREAM VERSION IS SCARCE TODAY, AS ARE THE OTHER MODELS OF THE SAME TYPE IN CHARIOT RED AND FLINT GRAY METALLIC. MAD-17. (AUTHOR COLLECTION)

FA. DAIMLER HOUSE ISSUED ONLY 50 OF THESE GARNET MAROON METALLIC CLUB SEDAN BEAUTIES IN 1994. MADISON MODELS MAD-9. (AUTHOR COLLECTION)

THIS 1950 98 AND ITS 88 SIBLING WOULD BE THE LAST OF THE FASTBACKS PRODUCED BY OLDSMOBILE UNTIL THE 1965 REVIVAL OF THE BODY STYLE. MADISON MODELS MAD-9. (COURTESY ROBERT M WOOLLEY)

A FEW HUNDRED CREST BLUE 1950 S98 FASTBACKS WERE MADE FOR MADISON MODELS, WHICH ALSO SOLD AN ALDER GREEN METALLIC VERSION. A SUBSTANTIAL WHITE METAL MODEL, IT SELDOM BECOMES AVAILABLE ON THE AFTERMARKET. (COURTESY ROBERT M WOOLLEY)

OLDSMOBILE'S 'MUSCLE CAR', THE 88 2 DOOR SEDAN, HAD THE NEW V-8 IN THE LIGHTER 76 BODY PRODUCING A DYNAMIC (PUN INTENDED) PERFORMER. TRON MODELS MADE A BUILT-UP AND KIT MODEL OF THE POPULAR AUTOMOBILE IN RESIN. THE CREATIVE JERRY RETTIG HAS CAREFULLY APPLIED EXTENSIVE CHROME FOIL AND PAINT TO THIS REPLICA. NOTE THE OCEAN BLUE HOOD EMBLEM. TRON NO 8. (COURTESY J RETTIG)

same high-quality of the other Fa. Daimler House products of the time. The convertible version of Madison Models' Series 98 came in three colors of Chariot Red, Canto Cream, and Flint Gray Metallic, all with a red interior.

Also for the 1950 model year, Tron created a Super 88 convertible and Club Coupe as a kit and factory built-up. (For a judgement about this model, see comments about 1949 pace car above.)

The stylish 'hard-top convertible coupe' body style was bestowed upon the Super 88 line in 1950. The first replica

TRON MODELS' 1950 SERIES 88 2 DOOR SEDAN IN METALLIC GRAY AS CRAFTED BY CONSUMMATE MODELER, BRUCE ARNOLD. (COURTESY D LARSEN)

THE REAR OF TRON'S 1950 S88 HAS BEEN CORRECTED BY BRUCE ARNOLD TO REFLECT ITS PROPER INSIGNIA AND ORNAMENTATION. TRON'S OLDSMOBILE MODELS WERE WELL CRAFTED WITH CRISPLY SCULPTED LINES AND DETAILS. ITS OLDSMOBILE WAS CLOSE TO 1:45 SCALE. (COURTESY D LARSEN)

PACING THE 1949 INDIANAPOLIS 500 WAS THE JOB OF OLDSMOBILE'S NEW 'ROCKET' ENGINE IN THE SERIES 88 CONVERTIBLE. TRON MODELS OF ITALY ISSUED THIS RESIN HANDBUILT MODEL WITH ITS DISTINCTIVE CHROMED ROCKET SHIP TRIM PIECE. (COURTESY J RETTIG)

A SKILFULLY CREATED, UNIQUE 1950 OLDSMOBILE STATION WAGON VERSION WITH HAND-PAINTED WOOD GRAIN BY THE INCOMPARABLE JERRY RETTIG. (COURTESY J RETTIG)

1950 SUPER 88 CONVERTIBLE BY TRON MODELS. NO 36. (COURTESY ROBERT M WOOLLEY)

FEWER THAN 6 PER CENT OF OLDSMOBILE DIVISION'S 1950 MODELS WERE SERIES 76 AND 88 CONVERTIBLES AND HOLIDAY COUPES. THIS MADE THEM QUITE EXCLUSIVE THEN AND COVETED TODAY. MOTOR CITY USA HANDCRAFTED THESE EXAMPLES IN THE MID-1990S AND AGAIN IN 2004. MC-69 AND MC-70. (AUTHOR COLLECTION)

1950 S88 DELUXE HOLIDAY COUPE IN WHITE METAL BY MOTOR CITY USA. THIS CLOSE-UP DISTORTS THE MODEL'S TRUE APPEARANCE SOMEWHAT, SHOWING THE CHALLENGE OF PHOTOGRAPHING MINIATURES. NOTE THE MANY PIECES THAT COMPRISE THE FRONT END OF THE MODEL. EVEN PERFECTIONIST MOTOR CITY USA CHOSE A DECAL TO REPRESENT THE OLDSMOBILE SCRIPT. SOME BUILDERS, SUCH AS TRON AND BROOKLIN, WOULD ATTEMPT TO CARVE THE SCRIPT IN THE MASTER PATTERN AND PICK IT OUT IN SILVER PAINT DURING FINISHING. THIS DELICATE WORK REQUIRES SUBLIME PATIENCE AND SKILL. MC-70. (AUTHOR COLLECTION)

THIS VIEW SHOWS THE PHENOMENAL PROPORTIONAL ACCURACY OF MOTOR CITY USA'S 1950 OLDSMOBILE 88 HOLIDAY COUPE: IT IS AS THOUGH THE MAKER HAD SOMEHOW SHRUNK A REAL AUTOMOBILE. 1 IN 12 OF ALL HARD-TOPS PRODUCED IN AMERICA IN 1950 WERE FROM OLDSMOBILE DIVISION. MC-70. (AUTHOR COLLECTION)

MOTOR CITY USA'S 1950 OLDSMOBILE S88 CONVERTIBLE FULLY DETAILED INTERIOR. MC-69. (AUTHOR COLLECTION)

OLDSMOBILE'S 1950 S88 CONVERTIBLE IN CHARIOT RED WITH BUFF LEATHER INTERIOR. RENDERED IN WHITE METAL BY MOTOR CITY USA. MC-69. (AUTHOR COLLECTION)

BY THE MID-1990S, MOTOR CITY USA'S LEVEL OF DETAIL AND FINISHING WAS PEERLESS. IT IS HARD TO BELIEVE THAT THIS AUTHENTIC REPLICA 1950 S88 CONVERTIBLE IS ONLY 5IN LONG. MC-69. (AUTHOR COLLECTION)

THE 1953 FIESTA WAS LIMITED TO 458 UNITS. BROOKLIN MODELS RELEASED THIS WHITE AND BLUE OPEN CONVERTIBLE MODEL IN THE EARLY 1990S. BRK-39. (COURTESY D LARSEN)

THIS EXAMPLE OF A BROOKLIN MODELS 1953 FIESTA HAS BEEN WELL DETAILED. BRK-39. (COURTESY D LARSEN)

hard-top is Motor City USA's 1950 Super 88. It was released in the late 1990s in white metal and again around 2002, in white metal and resin. It came as a 2 door hard-top coupe and convertible in open or closed versions. It is a tribute to the builder's talents that all but a few experts were unable to discern which materials were used in the two different production runs.

Buyers could choose from numerous colors for MCUSA's 1950 Oldsmobile. The hard-top came in a lustrous dark blue with cream top, cream over maroon, and black over cream with black interiors. Convertibles were black, Chariot Red, and blue with buff interiors.

The Motor City USA replica Super 88's are from the builder's top of the line series. Therefore they are as detailed as a static model can be, with polished chrome bumpers, taillight housings and grille, chromed script, colored emblems in all the right places, photo-etched vent window frames, abundant skilfully applied chrome foil, authentic full wheel covers with body colored wheels, and a fully detailed interior with correct gauges including separate dash-mounted clock, authentic dashboard shape and trim, and

door handles. The price today for one of these terrific replicas is around $275 at your stockist and likely more at auction.

As with Buick, no die-cast or handbuilt 1:43 scale replicas have been made for Oldsmobile's 1951 and 1952 model years. For 1953, Brooklin Models did issue a very nice white metal replica of the Fiesta with continental kit and 'propeller' wheel covers that became popular with car customisers. Oldsmobile's special model for 1953 featured the same cut down windshield, and unique trim and styling touches that Cadillac and Buick reserved for their Eldorado and Skylark, respectively. Producing just 458 units for 1953, the Fiesta was a rare car in its day. Brooklin's accurate rendition was released as a standard white and blue open model in the early 1990s. In 1993, 1000 models were issued as a red and white top up special. These models are nicely proportioned, moderately detailed, and solidly built. The special versions usually sell at $125 and up, with the standard version hovering around its initial $85 price.

1954 Oldsmobile replicas were issued by one company – Fa. Daimler House which introduced the Oldsmobile Starfire 98 open convertible as its first Conquest Model in 1987. Available initially in a mid-metallic blue or Willow Green Metallic, the little convertible was made by SMTS.

Conquest's CNQ-1 has good proportions and a high level of detail. Colors are authentic and assembly quality is good. Unlike models introduced by the company half-a-dozen years later, the hood emblem has no pigmentation, a pity,

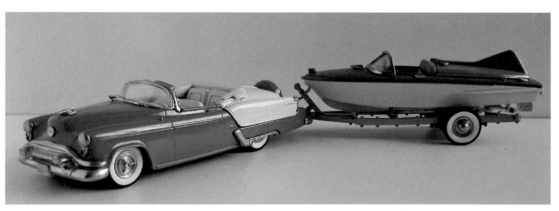

A 'FACTORY SPECIAL' SPEEDBOAT AND 1953 FIESTA FROM BROOKLIN MODELS FOR THE BROOKLIN COLLECTORS CLUB. ONE OF 300 SETS. BRK-39X AND BRK-71X. (COURTESY D MATHYSSEN)

THE 1954 SENIOR GM MODELS GAINED A NEW 'PANORAMIC' WINDSHIELD THAT HAD APPEARED ON THE FIESTA THE YEAR BEFORE. THIS FEATURE REMAINED WITH OLDSMOBILE UNTIL THE END OF THE 1962 MODEL YEAR. THOUGH IT REDUCED PILLAR STRENGTH AND CONTRIBUTED TO MANY A BANGED KNEE, IT INCREASED GLASS AREA AND GAVE A LIGHT, AIRY APPEARANCE. CONQUEST MODELS' FIRST REPLICA WAS THIS FLARE RED AND POLAR WHITE 98 CONVERTIBLE. CNQ-1. (AUTHOR COLLECTION)

A STELLAR EFFORT WHEN INTRODUCED IN 1987, CONQUEST MODELS' 1954 98 OPEN CONVERTIBLE HAD A HIGHLY-DETAILED INTERIOR IN GENUINE COLORS. CNQ-1. (AUTHOR COLLECTION)

A REAR VIEW OF CONQUEST'S OLDSMOBILE 98 ILLUSTRATES THE HIGH LEVEL OF DETAILING WITH TOUCHES SUCH AS THE AUTHENTIC 98 SCRIPT AND THE UNDER-BUMPER CHROMED TAIL PIPE. ON THE RIGHT IS CONQUEST MODELS' 1954 98 HOLIDAY CNQ-5 WHICH DEBUTED IN 1990. (AUTHOR COLLECTION)

THE 1954 98'S SEAT PATTERN AND MATERIALS DIFFERED ACCORDING TO BODY STYLE. ORIGINATOR OF FA. DAIMLER HOUSE, HENK VAN ASTEN ENSURED THAT THE INTERIOR OF THE HARD-TOP AND CONVERTIBLES WERE AUTHENTICALLY FINISHED. THIS 1954 98 HOLIDAY IS FINISHED IN WILLOW GREEN METALLIC AND POLAR WHITE. CNQ-5. (AUTHOR COLLECTION)

as the Oldsmobile globe of this time period was quite distinctive. Also, SMTS which adopted amazingly fine photo-etched script for its 1952 Buick Super, used decals to depict the block capital 'O-L-D-S-M-O-B-I-L-E' on the leading edge of the hood. The interior of the Conquest '54 98 is captured accurately and the dual pods of the instrument panel and glove compartment door are nicely picked out in chrome. As with other Conquest/Madison scale models, the chassis/base is plain black with no detailing, just the model name, number, and maker.

In 1988, the convertible was released in two-toned color combinations of Capri Blue/Polar White and Flair Red/Polar White. Particularly when seen in conjunction with the two-tone interior, these combinations added more visual interest to the model and helped to justify its retail price of over $200. Two years later, Conquest's 1954 98 Holiday 2 door hard-top made its appearance. Not just a scale model of a convertible with a hard-top added, Fa. Daimler House's Henk van Asten ensured that SMTS made an authentic interior for the closed car. A comparison between the convertible and hard-top shows the convertible's two-toned bucket seat style of upholstery pattern and the hard-top's more horizontal pattern that runs halfway up the seat. Both models are nicely done.

BUICK 5

THIS ESTEEMED MAKE FROM FLINT, MICHIGAN PREDATED THE FORMATION OF General Motors. In fact, Buick was, for a short period of time (1908), the largest producer of motorcars in North America and has been a key part of General Motors' success throughout much of the company's life. An early innovator with its efficient overhead valve engine, Buick automobiles were noted for their power, reliability, and prestige.

As for scale models of Buick cars, ever since Dinky Toy's simple rendition of the 1939 Viceroy sedan and Prameta's 1947 clockwork Super sedan, Buick has been a subject for many modelers, at least for the immediate pre-WWII period and for the years following.

SOME FEATURED BUICK MODELS

YEAR	MODEL	MANUFACTURER
1934	96-S COUPE	BROOKLIN MODELS
1935	96-S COUPE	BROOKLIN MODELS
1936	MCLAUGHLIN-BUICK FORMAL SEDAN	MILESTONE MINIATURES
1938	Y-JOB CONCEPT CAR	GREAT AMERICAN DREAM MACHINES
1938	SPECIAL	VICTORY MODELS
1939	MCLAUGHLIN-BUICK ROYAL TOUR CAR	MAE SCALE MODELS
1940	SUPER	VICTORY MODELS
1941	CENTURY	WESTERN MODELS
1947	ROADMASTER	DESIGN STUDIO

Model-by-model   1934-37

The earliest model year for a Buick replica, aside from a toy-like Matchbox 1911 model, is Brooklin Models' 1934 96-S coupe (see sidebar, p64).

In the summer of 2007 Brooklin Models astounded collectors with the announcement of its new Buick Collection, pledging: "Over the ensuing years this range will grow to eventually represent all the standard styles and series produced by Buick during these six years. This will mean some 130 variants in total."

Shortly after this announcement, Brooklin quickly introduced two variants, a sand colored 1934 96S coupe with sidemounts and blackwall tires BRK-BC 02, and a maroon 1935 96-S coupe BRK-BC01.

YEAR	MODEL	MANUFACTURER
1947	FLXIBLE	ELC
1948	ROADMASTER	MOTOR CITY USA, BROOKLIN MODELS
1949	ROADMASTER	MOTOR CITY USA, BROOKLIN MODELS
1950	SUPER AND ROADMASTER	PROVENCE MOULAGE
1952	SUPER	CONQUEST MODELS
1953	SKYLARK	BROOKLIN MODELS, PLAYTOY
1954	SKYLARK	MARTINO MODELS
1954	CENTURY/SKYLARK	MOTOR CITY USA

In 2006, Milestone Miniatures introduced an original model of its highly anticipated 1936 Buick limousine. The model is based on the McLaughlin-Buick limousine used by King Edward VIII during the dramatic period when he decided to marry the American divorcée, Wallace Simpson and abdicate the throne. Because of this, some wag dubbed it "the most romantic car in the world". The model is a Series 90 long-wheelbase sedan with blind rear quarters, right-hand drive, royal crest, and blue spotlight. Introduced at a price of $230, only 100 were issued, making it a rare replica.

ONE OF A KIND: 1936 McLAUGHLIN-BUICK SERIES 90 RENDERED AS A 4 DOOR SEDAN BY JERRY RETTIG. (COURTESY J RETTIG)

1936 McLAUGHLIN-BUICK SERIES 90 LIMOUSINE USED BY KING EDWARD VIII. MILESTONE MINIATURES ISSUED 100 OF THESE HANDBUILT WHITE METAL REPLICAS IN 2006. (COURTESY DOMINION MODELS)

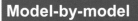

Model-by-model   1938-39

Emerging from the financially ruinous Depression where one year the division sold a little over a measly 40,000 units, Buick introduced the lower-priced Special in 1936. Like Packard's 120, it broadened the line's market and increased sales.

The 1938 Buick Special models from Victory Models were issued in 1999 in 4 door trunkback sedan, business coupe, and convertible in both open and top up configurations. These were the first replicas brought out under the 'La Familia' title, which was founder Ray Paskiewicz Jr's concept of a lower-priced line ($125-135) of family-oriented vehicles. The 1938 Buick models were a joint venture between Ray

and builder Georges Pont of CCC Models. They were available in Europe through a handful of stockists and from the USA only through Ray Paskiewicz Jr's Lilliput Motor Car Company.

The La Familia Buick models have a resin body and base. Thus, they are quite light at around 4oz. The models

VICTORY MODELS' LA FAMILIA LINE FROM THE LATE 1990s DEBUTED WITH THIS 1938 BUICK SPECIAL SEDAN IN TITIAN MAROON. HANDCRAFTED FOR VICTORY IN RESIN BY CCC OF FRANCE. VL-1. (AUTHOR COLLECTION)

PROFILE – 1934 BUICK 96-S COUPE BY BROOKLIN MODELS

BASED IN THE PICTURESQUE, HISTORIC CITY OF BATH, ENGLAND, BROOKLIN MODELS HAS STEADILY BECOME THE MOST PROLIFIC BUILDER OF HANDBUILT SCALE MODEL CARS AND TRUCKS. RELEASED IN APRIL OF 2007, ITS 1934 BUICK S-96 COUPE IS TYPICAL OF THE COMPANY'S ATTENTION TO FINE QUALITY AND VALUE.

THE '34 BUICK IS A FAITHFUL RENDITION OF THE ORIGINAL AUTOMOBILE. A MASSIVE VEHICLE WITH A 136IN WHEELBASE, AND POWERED BY A 344CI STRAIGHT EIGHT, THE 96-S WEIGHED 4546LB AND SEATED ONLY TWO PEOPLE IN ITS PASSENGER COMPARTMENT. EQUIPPED WITH A RUMBLE SEAT FOR TWO MORE PASSENGERS, IT WAS AN EXPENSIVE AND SOMEWHAT IMPRACTICAL AUTOMOBILE AT $1875 WHICH COMPETED WITH PACKARD AS AN 'IMAGE CAR'. 137 WERE SOLD. AS A 1:43 SCALE HANDBUILT REPLICA, BROOKLIN MODELS' ROYALE BLUE BUICK IS QUITE THE MODEL FOR AROUND $100. STARTING WITH THE WHITE METAL BODY, THE REPLICA HAS PERFECT PROPORTIONS THAT CAPTURE THE APPEARANCE OF THE ORIGINAL AND LOOK RIGHT FROM ANY ANGLE. MAJOR CHROME PARTS ARE SHINY AND FREE OF ROUGHNESS. LESSER EXTERIOR DETAILS, SUCH AS CHROME DOOR HANDLES AND THE HOOD MASCOT, ARE PRESENT AND SCALE ACCURATE. THE RUNNING BOARDS AND ROOF INSERT ARE FINISHED IN AN AUTHENTIC RUBBERY-LOOKING MATERIAL. THE GRILLEWORK IS TERRIFICALLY UNIFORM AND INTRICATE. TYPICAL OF BROOKLIN MODELS, WINDOW FRAMES ARE PAINTED AND HEADLIGHT LENSES ARE CAST IN WHITE METAL.

TO SAVE EXPENSE, THE INTERIOR IS SIMPLY RENDERED WITH ONE-PIECE MOLDED SEAT, ONE-PIECE DASH WITH MINOR SCULPTING, STEERING WHEEL AND COLUMN, AND CHROME FLOOR SHIFTER.

PAINT IS GLOSSY AND EVENLY APPLIED AND THE MODEL IS FREE OF GLUE RESIDUE AND SCRATCHES. ALL IN ALL, IT IS ANOTHER SUPERIOR EFFORT BY BROOKLIN TO MODEL A SCARCE AUTOMOBILE. (AUTHOR COLLECTION)

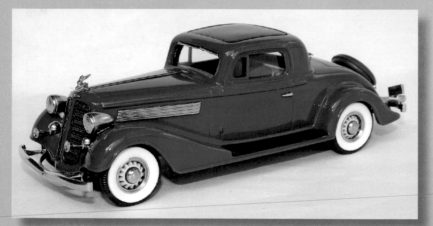 

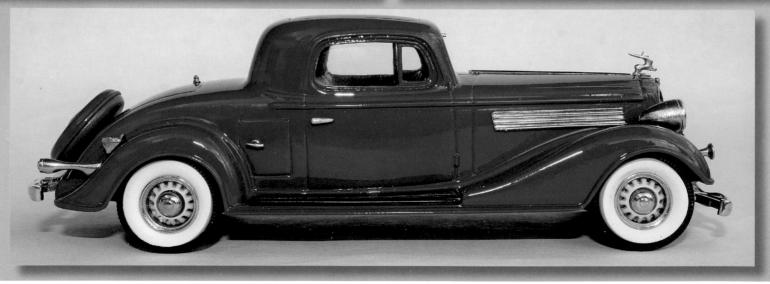

1938 BUICK SPECIAL BUSINESS COUPE IN VAN DYCK BROWN.
LA FAMILIA VL-2. (COURTESY VICTORY MODELS)

1938 BUICK SPECIAL BUSINESS COUPE IN CAROT BEIGE BY LA FAMILIA
OF VICTORY MODELS. VL-2. (COURTESY J RETTIG)

are well-proportioned and have a moderate level of exterior detailing and simple interiors comprising 4-5 parts. La Familia's 1938 replica is a fine model of a late 1930s family car. Ray's penchant for historical accuracy is reflected in the models' variety of authentic colors including Boticelli Blue, Titian Maroon, Carot Beige, Raphael Green, Homer Gray, and Van Dyck Brown.

Switzerland's Rextoys Models once issued a brochure of its die-cast products depicting the foregoing Buick models as well as a top up phaeton version and a streamlined sedan. None of these were built. Could it be that the patterns originally intended for Rextoys became available to CCC/Victory? I asked Ray Paszkiewicz Jr if Victory's 1938 Buick was made from a master pattern intended for Rextoys. His response was that Victory Models' masters are made from scratch in France, using Ray's documentation, photos and drawings. He went on to say, "We usually have more detail than some of the other manufacturers, there is no one to copy. If anything, we would be copied."

The run of 1938 Buick replicas from Victory and CCC was

LEFT, TOP TO BOTTOM: OPEN AND CLOSED 1938 BUICK CONVERTIBLES. LA FAMILIA VL-5. (COURTESY VICTORY MODELS)

BY 1938, STANDALONE HEADLIGHTS WITH FAIRINGS, RUNNING BOARDS, AND SIDE MOUNTS HAD JUST ABOUT RUN THEIR COURSE. THIS ELABORATE EXAMPLE OF A FULLY OUTFITTED 1938 SPECIAL TOP UP CONVERTIBLE IN VAN DYCK BROWN IS FROM VICTORY MODELS. WITH A TOTAL OF 100 OPEN AND CLOSED MODELS MADE, THIS LA FAMILIA VL-5 IS IN ONLY A FEW COLLECTIONS. (COURTESY J RETTIG)

Buick Division's first show car was Harley Earl's design team's 1938 Y-Job. Great American Dream Machine (GADM) issued a rendition of this dream car as the third model built by Phil Alderman and later, Paul Burt's company. GADM's version captures the look of the original accurately. With its slightly bulbous fenders, low slung profile, cut-down windshield, emphatic chrome striping, and unique taillight fairings – precursors to the fabulous fins of the '50s, this was an amazing dream car and makes for an equally pleasing replica.

very limited. Victory Models estimates that 150-175 sedans and 100-125 coupes were built. Convertibles were not so plentiful, with perhaps only 100 units being made.

For the 1939 model year, Mini Auto Emporium Scale Models created an impressive McLaughlin-Buick Royal Tour Car (see sidebar, p68).

GROUNDBREAKING IN SO MANY WAYS, BUICK'S Y-JOB CONCEPT CAR WAS PRODUCED BY GREAT AMERICAN DREAM MACHINES IN 1:43 SCALE AS A WHITE METAL REPLICA. GADM-3. (COURTESY J RETTIG)

A RARE 1939 ROADMASTER CONVERTIBLE COUPE FROM ENCHANTMENT LAND COACHBUILDERS THAT IS ENTIRELY HANDMADE. (COURTESY J RETTIG)

BUICK HAD THE HONOR OF PACING THE 1939 INDIANAPOLIS 500 RACE. THE DIVISION SELECTED ITS TOP OF THE LINE ROADMASTER CONVERTIBLE SEDAN FOR THE JOB. JERRY RETTIG OF ENCHANTMENT LAND COACHBUILDERS CRAFTED THIS HISTORICAL VEHICLE, COMPLETE WITH REAR TONNEAU COVER AND AUTHENTIC DOOR SIGNAGE. ELC-B10. (COURTESY J RETTIG)

BUICK
Built for Royalty

RARE ROYAL OFFERING

1939 MCLAUGHLIN BUICK LIMITED
Convertible Limousine (ROYAL TOUR CAR)

This is one of only two built for the visit of King George VI and Queen Elizabeth, the Queen Mother, to North America in 1939. It has since been used by visiting Royalty, including the Duke of Kent, Prince Charles, Lady Diana, Queen Elizabeth and the Duke of Edinburgh, and Prince Edward on a recent visit. The other one is in Canada's National Museum.

The car is Royal Maroon in color with matching interior, wood trim and regal appointments. It has a wheel base of 155 inches, is over 20 feet in length, weighs nearly 3 tons and is powered by a 320 cu. in. Buick straight 8 engine. It is one of the most photographed automobiles in the world.

PROFILE – 1939 McLAUGHLIN-BUICK ROYAL TOUR CAR BY MINI AUTO EMPORIUM SCALE MODELS (MAE)

IN THE 1990s, MINI AUTO EMPORIUM (MAE) OF CANADA RELEASED A REPLICA OF THE 1939 McLAUGHLIN-BUICK ROYAL TOUR CAR. BY THIS TIME McLAUGHLIN WAS THE SOLE REMAINING CANADIAN AUTOMAKER. HOWEVER, LIKE THE AUSTRALIAN HOLDEN, IT WAS TO ALL INTENTS ANOTHER BUICK, IF A FINE ONE AT THAT. THE ADVENT OF A CROSS-COUNTRY TOUR BY THE REIGNING MONARCH, KING GEORGE VI AND HIS WIFE, ELIZABETH, PROVIDED McLAUGHLIN WITH ONE LAST HURRAH, TO CREATE A SPECIAL CANADIAN VEHICLE.

A PAIR OF ROYAL TOUR CARS WAS BUILT. BASED UPON THE McLAUGHLIN-BUICK SERIES 90 SEVEN-PASSENGER SEDAN, THEY WERE REINFORCED AND STRETCHED AN ADDITIONAL 18IN TO ACCOMMODATE DUAL-FACING REAR SEATS, AND MADE INTO CONVERTIBLES. A MICROPHONE-SPEAKER SYSTEM ALLOWED THE CHAUFFEUR AND PASSENGERS TO COMMUNICATE. MAE's 1:43 HANDBUILT SCALE MODEL IS OVER 5½IN LONG AND WEIGHS JUST UNDER 1LB. MASTERED BY MIKE J MACNALLY, IT IS A NICELY DETAILED MODEL THAT HAS DUAL SIDE MOUNTS, BLACK RUNNING BOARDS, AND NUMEROUS CHROME TRIM PIECES, INCLUDING TRUNK LATCH AND FOG LIGHTS. ITS INTERIOR IS WELL TURNED OUT WITH A STEERING WHEEL THAT HAS A CHROMED HORN RING, GEARSHIFT LEVER, CHROMED DASH PIECES,

ARMRESTS, WINDOW WINDERS, DOOR HANDLES, AND TWO-PIECE CHROME AND PERSPEX WINDOW BETWEEN PASSENGER AND DRIVER COMPARTMENTS. THE MODEL WAS SUPPLIED WITH A ROYAL STANDARD FOR WINDSHIELD MOUNTING, PLUS OTHER FLAGS BUT, SADLY, THESE ARE OFTEN MISSING FROM THE FEW MODELS THAT ARE RESOLD.

JACQUI MACNALLY COMMENTS: "THE MCLAUGHLIN-BUICK WAS A VERY SPECIAL LIMITED EDITION VEHICLE. WE OBTAINED PERMISSION FROM THE MUSEUM IN OTTAWA TO GO THERE AND ACTUALLY TAKE MEASUREMENTS OF THE REAL CAR. IT WAS GREAT TO BE ABLE TO GET BEHIND THE ROPES AND TAKE ALL THE DIMENSIONS THAT WE NEEDED IN ORDER TO MAKE A MODEL THAT WAS AS ACCURATE AS POSSIBLE. THE BRITISH FLAG WAS HAND-PAINTED BY MIKE USING A HIGH-POWERED MAGNIFYING GLASS, AND WAS AS CLOSE TO SCALE AS WE COULD MAKE IT."

THE OPEN CONVERTIBLE IS MAE MODEL NO 107. A TOP UP MODEL WAS LISTED AS NO 116 BUT IS SCARCE. THE ACTUAL NUMBER OF PIECES OF THE TWO MODELS THAT THE BUILDER ISSUED IS UNKNOWN BUT IS LIKELY FEWER THAN 500. (AUTHOR COLLECTION)

The only 1:43 scale model of a 1940 Buick is Victory Models' terrific Super Series 50 4 door sedan and convertible (see sidebar, p71).

1941 was the zenith of Art Deco and industrial design. With its flowing lines and artfully placed fender skirt filigrees, the author considers the stylish 1941 Series 66 fastback sedan aka 'Sedanet' as Buick's high water mark for the period. Pioneer scale model maker, Mike Stephens and his Western Models chose the '41 S66 Sedanet as the subject for its first Buick. Western's fastback was followed shortly by both an open and top up convertible, station wagon with simulated wood panels, and more recently a 4 door sedan. Western also produced a realistic 1941 Buick 2 door Sedanet as a California Highway Patrol vehicle.

At around $150, Western's 1941 Buick came in a range of colors, including two-tone treatments for a slight premium over the basic cost. Models are solid and made from white metal. They have accurate proportions, excellent paintwork, and high-quality assembly. Early models had less exterior detail than later versions that were built with photo-etched wipers; individual chrome door handles and colored emblems. Interiors are simple and have few parts. Grilles are chromed and headlights have enamel lenses to give a translucent appearance. An indication of the quality of the Western Buick Sedanet is that Motor City USA

BY 1940 THE GREAT MAJORITY OF CONVERTIBLE MODELS SOLD BY BUICK WERE OF THE 2 DOOR VARIETY, SUCH AS THIS SERIES 50 SUPER IN SEQUOIA CREAM. THIS RESIN HANDBUILT IS NO VL-10 FROM VICTORY MODELS. (COURTESY RAY PASZKIEWICZ JR)

1940 BUICK SUPER SERIES 50 SEDAN IN ROYAL MAROON. 1 OF 50 MODELS HANDCRAFTED IN THIS COLOR IN RESIN FOR VICTORY MODELS. NO VL-3. (COURTESY D LARSEN)

IN 1941 BUICK MOTORCARS UNDERWENT A DESIGN CHANGE THAT MADE THEM APPEAR MORE MASSIVE AND AERODYNAMIC. DECORATIVE ELEMENTS SUCH AS THE CHROMED FENDER SKIRT EMBELLISHERS SEEN ON THIS CENTURY FASTBACK SEDAN EMPHASIZED THE SENSE OF MOTION SOUGHT BY HARLEY EARL'S STYLISTS. WESTERN MODELS CRAFTED THIS WHITE METAL MODEL WMS-67. (AUTHOR COLLECTION)

1941 BUICK CENTURY CONVERTIBLE COUPE WITH TOP UP. A HEAVY WHITE METAL MODEL THAT DOES A GOOD JOB OF CAPTURING THE APPEARANCE OF THE ORIGINAL MOTORCAR. WESTERN MODELS WMS-78. (COURTESY D LARSEN)

PROFILE – 1940 BUICK SUPER BY VICTORY MODELS

RELEASED IN 2002, AS A COLLABORATIVE EFFORT WITH CCC MODELS, THE SUPER WAS A FLAWLESS PRODUCT FROM VICTORY'S LA FAMILIA LINE OF MODELS.

WITH MAJOR STRUCTURAL COMPONENTS SUCH AS THE BODY AND BASE CAST IN RESIN, THE LITTLE SUPER HAS PERFECT PROPORTIONS AND GOOD DETAIL. ISSUED AT $139, IT HAS NUMEROUS FEATURES OF THE MOST EXPENSIVE MODELS INCLUDING EMBOSSED HUBCAPS, BODY-COLORED WHEELS WITH OUTSIDE TRIM RINGS, CHROME-TRIMMED, GLASS-LIKE REFLECTIVE HEADLIGHT LENSES, AND REAL RUBBER TIRES. INTERIORS ARE SIMPLE BUT HAVE A STEERING WHEEL WITH CHROME HUB AND HORN RING, COLUMN-MOUNTED GEARSHIFT, AND INSTRUMENT DECALS.

COLORS FOR THE 1940 VICTORY LA FAMILIA BUICK SUPER 50 SEDAN (V-L 3) ARE ENGLISH GREEN OR ROYAL MAROON. THE 1940 VICTORY LA FAMILIA BUICK SUPER 50 CONVERTIBLE (V-L 10) COLORS ARE BANDOLIER BLUE OR SEQUOIA CREAM. IN 2007 VICTORY ANNOUNCED PLANS TO REISSUE THESE MODELS IN ITS VICTORY LINE WITH WHITE METAL BASES, MORE EXTERIOR DETAILING, AND A REMOVABLE TOP AND BOOT COVER FOR THE CONVERTIBLE. APPROXIMATELY 100 SEDANS AND 75 CONVERTIBLES WERE PRODUCED AS LA FAMILIA PIECES. (AUTHOR COLLECTION)

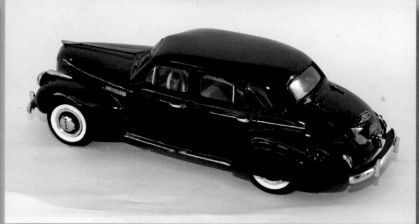

acquired 200 of Western's units to issue under its Design Studios label. In 2006, one of these models was purchased on eBay for more than $300.

Shortly after Western's 1941 Buick Sedanet was introduced, Jerry Rettig and his Enchantment Land Coachbuilders produced several variations of the '41 model, including a club coupe, station wagon, landaulet hearse, and a 4 door touring sedan. These resin models make use of chrome foil and were produced in very small quantities (fewer than 25 pieces for each body style). As an artisan, ELC can sometimes customize models or create models in colors that the customer wants.

THE CLUB COUPE CONTINUED TO BE A POPULAR BODY STYLE WITH CUSTOMERS BECAUSE IT PROVIDED A LARGE TRUNK, COZY COMFORT FOR REAR PASSENGERS, AND A LIGHTER APPEARANCE THAN SEDAN VERSIONS. THE 1941 CENTURY PICTURED HERE IS ONE OF ABOUT 25 MADE IN RESIN BY ENCHANTMENT LAND COACHBUILDERS. ELC-B11. (COURTESY J RETTIG)

FOR 1941 BUICK DIVISION'S MOST COSTLY REGULAR PRODUCTION MODEL WAS ITS STATION WAGON. WITH EXTENSIVE STRUCTURAL WOOD COMPONENTS REQUIRING SPECIALIZED PATTERNS TO CUT THE WOOD AND JIGS TO SHAPE MATERIALS, THESE WERE COMPLEX CARS TO BUILD. THEY ARE ALSO A FAVORITE OF SCALE MODELERS. THIS RESIN MODEL IS NUMBER B-12 FROM ENCHANTMENT LAND COACHBUILDERS. (COURTESY J RETTIG)

WESTERN MODELS RELEASED A NICELY FINISHED WHITE METAL 1941 BUICK STATION WAGON REPLICA WMS-96 IN THE EARLY 2000s. (COURTESY J RETTIG)

1941 BUICK SEDAN WITH EXTENSIVE DETAIL USING METAL FOIL. HANDMADE IN RESIN BY ENCHANTMENT LAND COACHBUILDERS. (COURTESY J RETTIG)

Model-by-model   1946-48

There were minimal styling changes to Buicks between 1946 and 1948. Motor City USA was the first builder to release a 1947 Buick, as open or top up convertibles under the Design Studio label. The high-end model is very accurate and carefully detailed. All major interior and exterior features are present, including chromed window winders, door handles, and instrument panel chrome and gauges. Headlights mimic glass and have a slight textured pattern as well as reflectors inside. This effect is very well done.

Careful inspection of the Design Studio model will reveal the state of the model maker's art during its mid-1980s origin.

Buick's 1941 convertible sedan is a rare automobile today. It is even rarer as a 1:43 scale model with only a handful or two of these resin models issued by Enchantment Land Coachbuilders. (Courtesy J Rettig)

A long-wheelbase 1947 Buick by Enchantment Land Coachbuilders no B-7. Enchantment Land Coachbuilders also made a red fire service version. (Courtesy J Rettig)

Jerry Rettig's goal was to create a replica of every body style produced for Buick in 1941. Here is a rare art-carved hearse and limousine model of the top of the line Buick. Enchantment Land Coachbuilders. (Courtesy J Rettig)

The Flxible Company of Ohio produced buses and Buick hearse and ambulance models such as the 1947 limousine-style and landau hearses here. Enchantment Land Coachbuilders created these nicely finished rich metallic green and glossy black handbuilt resin models. B-6 and B-5. (Courtesy J Rettig)

OLYMPIC FIGURE SKATER, BECKY SCOTT, SITS IN A BROOKLIN MODELS 1948 ROADMASTER FOR CTCS. BRK-45. (COURTESY D MATHYSSEN)

1948 BUICK ROADMASTER OPEN CONVERTIBLE IN HONOLULU BLUE METALLIC. BROOKLIN MODELS BRK-45. THIS WAS THE STANDARD MODEL ISSUED 1993 TO 1995. (COURTESY D MATHYSSEN)

SINGER-ACTOR BING CROSBY WAS AN AVID GOLFER. BROOKLIN MODELS ISSUED 200 SETS OF 1948 ROADMASTER STATION WAGONS WITH THESE OMEN FIGURES FOR THE SAN FRANCISCO BAY BROOKLIN CLUB IN 2004. BRK-95X. (COURTESY D MATHYSSEN)

The only photo-etched materials are the windshield wipers. Bare metal foil did not exist so chromed moldings are made by scraping through the paint to reveal the shiny surface of the white metal. Decals are used for script and emblems are painted by hand. This is a nicely made model that required much time and skill.

Motor City USA's next Buick was again a Design Studio, this time a 1948 Sedanet. Similar in appearance to the 1947 convertible, it has a few differences from the model that was issued earlier. Whereas there were some gaps between the grille and the body of the convertible, the Sedanet's grille fits better, perhaps from the more uniform temperatures and cooling rates of the white metal. The headlight lenses are white metal. Paradoxically, wipers are white metal rather than photo-etched, and chrome

BUICK'S 1948 ROADMASTER CONVERTIBLE WAS A HEAVY 'ROAD HUGGING' AUTOMOBILE AT 4315LB. DESPITE A $2837 LIST PRICE THAT WAS DOUBLE THAT OF MOST CHEVROLETS, MORE THAN 11,000 BUYERS LAID THEIR MONEY DOWN TO PURCHASE ONE. DESIGN STUDIOS DS-2. (AUTHOR COLLECTION)

1948 BUICK FASTBACK SEDAN. USA MODELS USA-39.
(COURTESY COLLECTORS ANTIQUES)

1948 BUICK ROADMASTER SEDANET IN ROYAL MAROON. USA MODELS
USA-39. (AUTHOR COLLECTION)

THE SEDANET CONTINUED TO SELL WELL FOR BUICK IN 1948, ALTHOUGH AS ONE MOVED UP THE RANGE IT BECAME MUCH LESS POPULAR THAN THE 4 DOOR SEDAN. ALTHOUGH PART OF THE LESSER USA MODELS LINE FROM MOTOR CITY USA, THE 1:43 WHITE METAL HANDBUILT IN THIS PHOTO HAS BEEN CAREFULLY AND LABORIOUSLY DETAILED. USA MODELS USA-39. (AUTHOR COLLECTION)

foil is used extensively to pick out exterior detail. Moreover, the Sedanet is ½in longer than the convertible. Once again, I am reminded that handbuilt models have their eccentricities and this is what makes them interesting and collectible.

Motor City USA also issued the 1948 Buick as a less-detailed USA Models version with less chroming and fewer detailed parts. Whereas the Design Studio version sold in the low $200 range, the USA Models was available at around $100.

Similar in detail to the USA Models version is Brooklin's 1948 Buick Roadmaster convertible, released in 1994. Available initially in a blue metallic, this accurate and substantial white metal scale model enjoyed a two-year run in which eight color variations were offered.

Brooklin reprised the 1948 Buick as a station wagon in 2002. An attractive model, with its glossy dark paint contrasting nicely with simulated wood panels, it was difficult to make. John Roberts – who is noted for his superior building and customization of white metal models – remarked that the Buick build process was, "a nightmare" (see sidebar).

Once again, Enchantment Land Coachbuilders offered

a few service car variations on the 1946-48 Buick, notably a 1947 Flxible Landaulet hearse, Flxible Limousine hearse, and ambulance. Crafted in resin, these are fascinating replicas of a somewhat obscure specialist subject. Each model reveals its handbuilt nature. Chrome foil is used and Jerry has hand-painted the colorful hood emblems. These models aren't in everyone's collection.

Model-by-model 1949-53

Buick Division's all new post-war product has been modeled in 1:43 scale by major and minor builders.

Brooklin Models produced a 1949 Roadmaster sedanet in the late 1980s. It is a somewhat plain model with fewer parts

JOHN ROBERTS DESCRIBES THE DIFFICULTIES IN HAND BUILDING BROOKLIN'S 1948 BUICK ROADMASTER STATION WAGON: "THE BASIC SHELL HAD THE SIDES, BACK, AND ROOF SECTION FITTED. GREAT CARE HAD TO BE TAKEN TO ENSURE THAT EVERYTHING LINED UP. IF THE SIDES OR BACK WERE NOT EXACT, THE ROOF DIDN'T FIT. IF ANY PIECE WASN'T RIGHT THE VAC FORM (WINDOWS) WOULDN'T FIT, AND IF THIS WAS WRONG IT FOULED THE SEATS AND CREASED. EACH STAGE HAD TO BE ALLOWED TO DRY, MEANING THE MODEL WAS ON THE BENCHES FOR LONGER THAN USUAL. "A LOT WERE MADE SO IT'S NOT RARE. THIS WAS A GOOD MODEL – TAKE IT OFF YOUR SHELF AND LOOK AT IT. THE MAROON BITS ARE ALL ONE CASTING. THE ROOF IS ATTACHED TO THE REST BY TWO THIN A POSTS AND TWO THIN C POSTS. WHEN THE BODIES WERE FIRST CAST THEY WERE BREAKING UP COMING OUT OF THE MOLDS. SIDEBARS HAD TO BE CAST IN AND THEN, WHEN THE SHELLS WERE CLEANED UP, THEY HAD TO BE REMOVED. "MOST WOODIES WERE DESIGNED WITH THREE 'WOOD' SECTIONS – TWO SIDES AND A BACK. WHEN CASTING WHITE METAL, TEMPERATURE IS CRITICAL. MINUTE VARIATIONS CAUSE VARIATIONS IN THE SIZE OF CASTING. IN A ONE- OR TWO-PIECE BODY THIS CAN BE OVERCOME. A WOODY WILL HAVE FOUR, OR EVEN FIVE (THE ROOF) SECTIONS. IF THE TEMPERATURE WAS SLIGHTLY DIFFERENT SOME PIECES MAY NOT FIT PROPERLY, CAUSING EXTRA FETTLING OR MELTING DOWN AND RECASTING ... ALL TIME-CONSUMING. ADD TO THIS THE SPRAYING OF THE 'WOOD' SECTIONS WHICH MUST ALL MATCH OVER A TWO-STAGE PROCESS, AND THE EXTRA EFFORT NEEDED BECOMES APPARENT. IT IS UNLIKELY THAT BROOKLIN WILL RE-ISSUE THE BUICK STATION WAGON, AS THERE MUST HAVE BEEN NO PROFIT IN IT."

BROOKLIN MODELS 1948 BUICK STATION WAGON. BRK-95. (AUTHOR COLLECTION)

2299 IONIA BODIED 1948 BUICK STATION WAGONS WERE MADE FOR 1948. BROOKLIN MODELS CRAFTED THIS MODEL NO. 95 IN 2002-2004. REPAINTED AND DETAILED BY JOHN ROBERTS. (AUTHOR COLLECTION)

than Brooklin's handbuilt models of today. Understandably, much attention was given to the distinctive grillework of the '49 and this is credibly done, albeit the chrome on some models would benefit from polishing. Some early castings were missing a hood ornament but this was rectified in later editions. Nine different variations in colors and details occurred during the lifecycle of this replica.

Far rarer, with just 250 pieces released, is the 1949 Roadmaster convertible issued in 1997 for the Brooklin Collectors Club of the UK. A slightly more detailed rework of the sedanet, it is a white metal replica of the car used in the critically acclaimed

1949 BUICK ROADMASTER FASTBACK SEDAN. AN EARLY BROOKLIN MODELS WHITE METAL REPLICA MADE IN 1991. BRK-10. (COURTESY COLLECTORS ANTIQUES)

AN EXTENSIVELY DETAILED BROOKLIN MODELS 1949 BUICK. BRK-10. (COURTESY D LARSEN)

1949 BUICK WOOD-BODIED STATION WAGON. JERRY RETTIG, WHO HAS THE AMAZING VISION AND SKILL TO CREATE VIRTUALLY ANY MODEL HE WANTS, PERFORMED THIS ONE-OFF CONVERSION OF A BROOKLIN SEDANET. (COURTESY J RETTIG)

1949 BUICK ROADMASTER CONVERTIBLE WITH OMEN FIGURES OF TOM CRUISE AND DUSTIN HOFFMAN AS THEY APPEARED IN THE 1988 MOVIE, RAIN MAN. THIS MODEL IS 1 OF 250 ISSUED FOR THE BROOKLIN COLLECTORS CLUB IN 1997. BRK-10X. (COURTESY D MATHYSSEN)

1988 movie *Rain Man*. The replica has the same cream exterior with red interior as the movie car and seats two Omen figures of Dustin Hoffman and Tom Cruise.

ELC also offered Code 3 versions of the Brooklin 1949 Buick as an open convertible and, before any other builder issued one, a 2 door hard-top.

The tiny concern of Prototypo issued 9 or 10 copies of a resin model kit patterned after a 1949 Riviera pickup truck. This obscure and very simple model builds up nicely in the hands of a skilled modeler.

Following the release of the Brooklin and ELC editions, Motor City USA produced a series of 1949 Roadmaster replicas

FOUR 1:43 SCALE HANDBUILT REPLICAS OF 1949 BUICK ROADMASTER PASSENGER CARS BY MOTOR CITY USA. FROM LEFT TO RIGHT: SEDANET AM-8, RIVIERA MC-26, OPEN CONVERTIBLE MC-27, AND STATION WAGON MC-76. (AUTHOR COLLECTION)

THE 1949 ROADMASTER CONVERTIBLE BY MOTOR CITY USA HAS A HIGH LEVEL OF DETAIL AND AUTHENTIC COLORS SUCH AS THIS SEQUOIA CREAM, WHICH REMAINED A COMMON BUICK COLOR FOR SEVERAL YEARS. MC-27. (AUTHOR COLLECTION)

IN THE 1949 ROADMASTER CONVERTIBLE THE SEAT, WINDOWS, AND TOP WERE ALL OPERATED BY ELECTRIC SWITCHES. THE FUTURE HAD ARRIVED. LEATHER UPHOLSTERY WAS STANDARD AS WELL. MOTOR CITY USA MODEL MC-27. (AUTHOR COLLECTION)

between 1998 and 2003 priced at $275. Included in the producer's full Motor City USA line-up is a convertible, 2 door hard-top coupe, and wood-bodied station wagon. Later, under the 'Sunset Coach' banner, the company issued an ambulance, limousine hearse and landau hearse. These models sold out quickly and are currently unavailable.

All of Motor City USA's 1949 Buick replicas are nicely proportioned, and have perfectly accurate detailing and colors. The open convertible came in a beautiful Sequoia Cream with contrasting oxblood interior and convertible boot. Six pieces each were also produced in dark gray, medium blue metallic,

green, and black, some with top up. The interior is highly-detailed and comes complete with all of the chromed hardware for power windows and vents as well as door release latches.

The popular 1950s Buick with its front fender 'Ventiports' has been a favorite of modelers since Dinky Toys issued its 1952 Roadmaster in the mid 1950s. Solido produced the next modern mass-produced die-cast Buick in 1985. Its 1950 Buick Super convertible, in open and top up configurations, was part of Solido's l'Age d'Or series honoring the 'Golden Age' of North American automobiles. This slightly chubby toy originally retailed for $10-12 and has given birth to a remarkable number of handbuilt models.

AN INFLUENTIAL NEW 1949 BODY STYLE INTRODUCED MID-YEAR WAS THE RIVIERA 2 DOOR COUPE. 4314 BUYERS ENJOYED THE AIRY FEELING OF THIS MODEL WITHOUT SUFFERING THE INCONVENIENCE OF A SOFT-TOP. MOTOR CITY USA NO MC-26. (AUTHOR COLLECTION)

THIS PHOTOGRAPH OF MOTOR CITY USA'S ROADMASTER STATION WAGON SHOWS THE REPLICA'S HIGH LEVEL OF FINISHING, INCLUDING THE REALISTIC LOOKING WOOD CLADDING. THE ISSUE PRICE OF THIS MC-76 WAS $275. (AUTHOR COLLECTION)

Jurgens (USA) made a station wagon with real wood mounted on a cut down Solido convertible. It was available at a few stockists until recently for $90. Finally, for a people carrier of a different type, Jones Models (USA) handcrafted a '50 Buick landaulet hearse and limousine type hearse using the Solido pattern.

For 1951, no 1:43 scale models of Buick street vehicles were made. However,

No fewer than nine variations on the little Solido '50 Buick have been issued by four companies, the most common Solido-based handbuilts being the 1950 Buick resin transkits and built-up models from Provence Moulage of France. These models came as a sedanet, 2 door Riviera, station wagon with simulated wood panelling, and a Roadmaster 4 door sedan. Still available occasionally at auctions, these little resin models are very nice, especially if one overlooks their slightly over-wide appearance. The built-up models from the factory have nice detailing with silver paint picking out moldings and emblems and richly colored paint. The transkits tend to have more subdued colors, often pastel-like.

For some reason the 1950 Buick Super station wagon has been popular with other builders. Miniature One Models once offered a professionally built-up Provence Moulage wagon and

1949 BUICK LANDAU HEARSE BY FLXIBLE. MOTOR CITY USA INTRODUCED ITS VERSION OF THIS MODEL IN 2003 AS PART OF ITS SUNSET COACH LINE. IT WAS MADE IN SMALL NUMBERS AND QUICKLY SNAPPED UP BY DISCERNING COLLECTORS. MC-87K. (COURTESY MOTOR CITY USA)

A WINDOWED, LIMOUSINE-STYLE 1949 BUICK FUNERAL CAR BY MOTOR CITY USA. (COURTESY MOTOR CITY USA)

1949 BUICK FLXIBLE AMBULANCE IN WHITE. MOTOR CITY USA. (COURTESY MOTOR CITY USA)

AN UNUSUAL SUBJECT FOR A SCALE MODEL IS THIS 1949 ROADMASTER-BASED PICKUP. ISSUED BY THE OBSCURE PROTOTYPO BRAND, IT IS ONE OF ONLY 10 KNOWN TO EXIST. A SIMPLE RESIN MODEL WITH FEW PARTS, THIS EXAMPLE HAS BEEN SKILFULLY PAINTED AND ASSEMBLED BY RESPECTED BUILDER, GREG GUNN. (COURTESY G GUNN)

FIRE DEPARTMENTS OFTEN USED THEIR OWN AMBULANCES TO RESPOND TO EMERGENCY CALLS. THIS 1949 BUICK VERSION IS BY MOTOR CITY USA. (COURTESY MOTOR CITY USA)

BUICK'S 1950 SPECIAL WAS GREAT VALUE AT $1856, ROUGHLY THE PRICE OF A STUDEBAKER COMMANDER. THIS SCALE MODEL OF THE SEDANET IS BY PROVENCE MOULAGE. PM-TK21. (AUTHOR COLLECTION)

Great American Dream Machines modeled Buick's second concept car, the LeSabre. Made by SMTS, this is a well-crafted model.

As the Korean Conflict accelerated, American automobile manufacturers lowered the quality of the chromium that adorned bumpers and grilles. As a result, vehicles from this era suffered from thinning and flaking of chrome parts. No such phenomenon is apparent on the fine 1952 Buick Super 2 door hard-top coupe produced by Conquest Models in 1995. This white metal model is a well-proportioned and finely detailed scale model that rivalled those produced by Motor City USA; it sold for around $225.

A year later, Conquest issued an open 1952 Super convertible in the same price range. On it, the builder made maximum use of photo-etching with 'Super' script on the rear fenders, delicate

DIECAST IN THE TENS OF THOUSANDS BY SOLIDO OF FRANCE IN THE EARLY 1980S, THESE 1950 BUICK SUPER CONVERTIBLES HAVE RECEIVED MINOR DETAILING BY WELL-KNOWN MODELER JERRY RETTIG. SOLIDO NOS 4511 AND 4512. (COURTESY J RETTIG)

1950 BUICK SUPER 2 DOOR HARD-TOP COUPE. PROFESSIONALLY BUILT FROM A PROVENCE MOULAGE TRANSKIT. PM-TK23. (AUTHOR COLLECTION)

1950 ROADMASTER 4 DOOR SEDAN BY PROVENCE MOULAGE. BUILT-UP PROFESSIONALLY, THIS REPLICA HAS TWO-TONE PAINT AND MANY DETAILS. PM-TK28. (AUTHOR COLLECTION)

1950 BUICK SUPER 2 DOOR HARD-TOP COUPE. THIS PROFESSIONALLY BUILT RESIN TRANSKIT HAS EXTENSIVE DETAILING, INCLUDING CHROMED FOIL ROOF MOLDINGS. THOUGH THE MAKER LISTS IT AS A 'ROADMASTER', THE MODEL HAS ONLY 3 VENTIPORTS AND THE SHORTER WHEELBASE OF A SUPER. PROVENCE MOULAGE NO TK23. (AUTHOR COLLECTION)

MORE THAN 51,000 CUSTOMERS LAID THEIR MONEY DOWN FOR A NEW 1950 ROADMASTER 4 DOOR SEDAN. AN AUDACIOUS DESIGN, ITS HEAVILY-CHROMED, 'TOOTHY' GRILLE AND BUMPER SCULPTURING INSPIRED MOVIE DIRECTOR, TIM BURTON, TO HAVE SEVERAL SINISTER '50 BUICK SEDANS PLY THE STREETS AND ALLEYWAYS OF GOTHAM IN BATMAN RETURNS. PROVENCE MOULAGE TK28. (AUTHOR COLLECTION)

chrome tail fins, ventiports, and reflective glass-like headlight lenses. One of the last models issued by Fa. Daimler House was a Conquest 1952 Buick Roadmaster woody station wagon. This 1999 release sold out quickly. A few years later I saw one selling for more than $400 in a European shop.

Fortunately, American Dave 'Buz' Kirkel, admired for his devotion to the hobby, resurrected Conquest Models and, in 2005, began reissuing some of the original models. That year he brought out a dozen '52 Super convertibles in Sequoia Cream and six in all-black. In 2006 and 2007, he released roughly four dozen '52 Roadmaster station wagons in a variety of colors. There is a strong demand for these rare and beautifully crafted replicas.

There are no other 1:43 scale models of the 1952 Buick of note except for some simple Nostalgic Miniatures white metal models and a few Dinky-based replicas by Equipe Gallois that are obviously toy-like.

The big news from Buick for 1953 was the introduction of its dream car for the American highway, the Skylark. At a price significantly exceeding the Cadillac Series 62 convertible, Buick's prestigious entry into what later became known as the 'personal luxury' segment sold a respectable 1690 vehicles. It is safe to say that there are many times that number of scale model Skylark copies in peoples' display cases, closets, and toy boxes. At last

TOP OF THE BUICK LINE FOR 1950 WAS THE ROADMASTER STATION WAGON. A TRANSITION PERIOD FOR BUICK, STRUCTURAL WOOD WAS STILL USED BY THE AUTOMAKER IN ITS WAGONS. THUS, THIS WAS AN EXPENSIVE AUTOMOBILE TO MANUFACTURE. THE SCALE MODEL HERE ALSO HAS REAL WOOD. IT IS BUILT BY JURGENS AND USES PARTS FROM THE SOLIDO BUICK DIE-CAST MODELS PICTURED EARLIER. JURGENS NO 50B. (AUTHOR COLLECTION)

AN UNUSUAL MODEL, JURGENS CONTINUED TO SELL THIS 1:43 WOOD, METAL AND RESIN 1:43 SCALE ROADMASTER STATION WAGON UNTIL THE EARLY 2000s FOR AROUND $90. JURGENS NO 50B. (AUTHOR COLLECTION)

LEFT: HARLEY EARL'S 1951 LE SABRE SHOW CAR PREVIEWED SEVERAL FEATURES THAT WOULD BE SEEN ON PRODUCTION BUICKS OF THE LATE 1950s. GREAT AMERICAN DREAM MACHINES HAS MADE IT ITS BUSINESS TO PROVIDE LOVELY SCALE MODELS OF MANY AMERICAN CONCEPT CARS FROM THE 1950s. PICTURED IS NUMBER ONE IN ITS SERIES OF BEAUTIFUL WHITE METAL REPLICAS. GADM-1. (COURTESY J RETTIG)

RIGHT: A PAIR OF HANDBUILT WHITE METAL 1952 BUICK MODELS FROM CONQUEST MADISON MODELS. BEHIND THE MADISON SUPER OPEN CONVERTIBLE (MAD-16) IS A CONQUEST ROADMASTER STATION WAGON (CNQ-35). (AUTHOR COLLECTION)

MADISON'S 1952 SUPER CONVERTIBLE WAS ISSUED IN 1996 IN SEQUOIA CREAM AND SURF BLUE. A DECADE LATER ANOTHER 18 WERE REISSUED AT $225 EACH. THIS IS ONE OF THE LATTER RUN. NOTE THE REALISTIC INTERIOR, INCLUDING THE CHROMED CENTER RADIO AND HEATER CONTROL PANEL. MAD-16. (AUTHOR COLLECTION)

LEFT: 1952 BUICK ROADMASTERS IN GLENN GREEN AND APACHE RED. A PALTRY 359 ROADMASTER STATION WAGONS WERE MADE IN THE KOREAN CONFLICT-SHORTENED PRODUCTION YEAR. LESS THAN HALF THAT NUMBER WERE ISSUED BY CONQUEST MODELS. CNQ-35. (AUTHOR COLLECTION)

JUST LIKE THE REAL AUTOMOBILE, THE BODY OF CONQUEST'S WHITE METAL SCALE MODEL VERSION OF THE ROADMASTER STATION WAGON IS CONSTRUCTED OF SEVERAL PARTS. FLAWLESSLY DETAILED TO RESEMBLE THE ORIGINAL WOODWORK AND CAREFULLY ASSEMBLED, IT IS A SUPERLATIVE HANDMADE REPLICA OF THE TOP BUICK FOR 1952. CNQ-35. (AUTHOR COLLECTION)

1952 BUICK SUPER RIVIERA IN SKY GRAY OVER VICTORIA MAROON. HANDCRAFTED IN WHITE METAL BY SMTS FOR CONQUEST IN 1905 AND REISSUED IN SMALL NUMBERS IN 2006. CNQ-26. (AUTHOR COLLECTION)

RIGHT: 1953 SKYLARK. THE FIRST 1:43 HANDBUILT REPLICA OF THIS MODEL WAS INTRODUCED BY NOSTALGIC MINIATURES IN OPEN (NO 273) AND CLOSED (NO 290) CONFIGURATIONS. (AUTHOR COLLECTION)

1953 SKYLARK BY NOSTALGIC MINIATURES. NO 273. (AUTHOR COLLECTION)

RIGHT: AN ATTRACTIVE SILVER WITH DARK BLUE TOP, 20 OF THESE MODELS WERE PRODUCED BY BROOKLIN MODELS AND RAFFLED FOR A CHARITY DRAW. BRK-20X. (COURTESY D MATHYSSEN)

RIGHT: NOT TO BE OUTDONE, BRITAIN'S JOHN ROBERTS CUSTOMIZED BROOKLIN'S 1953 SKYLARK TO CREATE THIS FINE SCALE MODEL. BRK-20. (COURTESY D LARSEN)

POPULAR WITH BUILDERS, THE SKYLARK OF 1953 WAS MODELED BY BROOKLIN MODELS. THIS TOP UP VERSION IS THE STANDARD ISSUE. BRK-20. (COURTESY COLLECTORS ANTIQUES)

LEFT: DMP STUDIOS CUSTOMIZED 50 BROOKLIN 1953 SKYLARK MODELS TO YIELD THIS GLOSSY RED NUMBER. IN ADDITION TO RE-SPRAYING THE EXTERIOR, HAND PAINTING THE TWO-TONED INTERIOR, AND POLISHING THE CHROME, CRAFTSMAN DEAN PAOLUCCI ADDED EXPENSIVE BBR PHOTO-ETCHED WIRE WHEELS. BRK-20. (COURTESY D MATHYSSEN)

LEFT: 1953 SKYLARK OPEN CONVERTIBLE BY BROOKLIN MODELS CUSTOMIZED BY JOHN ROBERTS. THIS REPLICA USES THE ORIGINAL WHEELS PRODUCED BY BROOKLIN FOR THE MODEL. BRK-20. (COURTESY D LARSEN)

count, 8 different companies had produced Skylark models in 1:43 scale either handbuilt in white metal or die-cast.

In chronological order: Nostalgic Miniatures' (USA) version is an early effort to bridge the gap between toy and collectible replica. Like most scale models from this maker, the replica

BUICK'S 1953 SKYLARK BY FRANKLIN MINT. NO 50-2. (COURTESY J RETTIG)

PRODUCED IN THE 1980S, THIS DIE-CAST FRANKLIN MINT SKYLARK HAS OPENING DOORS. NO 50-2. (COURTESY COLLECTORS ANTIQUES)

MATCHBOX/DINKY RELEASED A VERY NICELY PROPORTIONED AND FINISHED DIE-CAST STATIC MODEL IN THE EARLY 1990S. DY04. (COURTESY J RETTIG)

has many of the characteristics of the original upon which it is patterned but is still somewhat impressionistic. Part of this is due to the small number of parts used and some slightly awkward proportions.

A more realistic looking white metal model is Brooklin Model's '53 Skylark. Released in 1985 as a top up model in light metallic green with white top, it has a solid, high-quality feel to it. Unlike Brooklin's 21st century efforts, this model has little detailing.

The most formidable handbuilt 1953 Skylark 1:43 scale model is Belgian maker, Playtoy's no 3. This Carlo Brianza-patterned replica has accurate proportions and exceptional details. From its expensive photo-etched wire wheels to chrome outlining the rolled up windows, this is a museum quality piece. There is little wonder that, when it debuted during the mid-1980s, it commanded a price roughly three times that of the Brooklin edition. Occasionally this model comes up for sale where it appears to hover around its original issue price. Perhaps the failure of this model to appreciate in value is due in part to some collectors' scepticism about resin models or a reaction to the plethora of Skylark replicas available.

Hallmark's (USA) annual 1:43 scale tree ornament, Welly's (China) 1:40th scale model, Franklin Mint's (USA) Cars of the Fifties and slightly confusing permutations of Dinky/Matchbox/Dinky comprise the die-cast producers of the '53 Skylark in 1:43. Of these, the Franklin Mint and Dinky/Matchbox models are quite good, particularly for their typical selling price of $20-30. With accurate proportions and realistic detail, they look perfectly appropriate in any '50s model or Buick collection. In early 2007, Brooklin brought out a replica of the one-off 1953 Buick hard-top, reputedly for Harley Earl's wife.

1954 saw the first wrap-around 'panoramic' windshield on the senior GM motorcars. This feature and the distinctive vertical

THE MOST INTRICATE AND RARE (THIS IS NO 96 OF 100 UNITS MADE) 1:43 SCALE MODEL 1953 BUICK SKYLARK IS FROM CARLO BRIANZA'S PLAYTOY MODELS. CAST IN RESIN AND COMPRISING MORE THAN 70 PARTS, MANY PHOTO-ETCHED, MODEL NO P3 WAS ISSUED IN 1984. (AUTHOR COLLECTION)

1954 BUICK CENTURY 2 DOOR HARD-TOP. A BEAUTIFUL WHITE METAL REPLICA WITH SUPERB PROPORTIONS, ISSUED BY MOTOR CITY USA UNDER ITS DESIGN STUDIO LABEL. DS-17. (AUTHOR COLLECTION)

THE 1954 BUICK HAD THE TRADEMARK VERTICAL BARS OF ITS EARLY '50S PREDECESSORS, AS WELL AS THE NEW PANORAMIC WINDSHIELD THAT, THOUGH ATTRACTIVE, SUBSTANTIALLY REDUCED THE STRUCTURAL STRENGTH OF THE WINDSHIELD. THE

1953 SKYLARK CONVERTIBLE BY PLAYTOY. MASTERED BY CARLO BRIANZA, THIS MODEL HAS IMPRESSIVE DETAIL, INCLUDING TINY PHOTO-ETCHED INSIGNIA AND DELICATE WIRE WHEELS. NO P3. (AUTHOR COLLECTION)

FLAWLESS GRILLE OF THIS DESIGN STUDIO NO DS-17 IS HEAVILY PLATED. (AUTHOR COLLECTION)

barred grillework of that year's Buick is rendered with great skill in Motor City USA's white metal replica of the Century 2 door hard-top coupe, convertible, and Skylark convertible.

Initially available as part of the more detailed Design Studios line, the Century hard-top and convertible were reissued in the late 1990s with slightly fewer details (fewer interior pieces and external badges) as both a USA Models and an American Models offering. Motor City USA's other Buick for model year 1954 is the Skylark (see sidebar).

Less common and less detailed but still of interest to avid collectors is Marty Martino's '54 Skylark. A builder during the early period of handbuilt model production, Martino Model's (USA) edition was produced in both a top down and closed version. A simply detailed model, I was told that it is related in some way to a Solido die-cast version. There is a resemblance to the profile of that maker's 1957 Eldorado with its cutout wheel wells, but there

1954 CENTURY CONVERTIBLE. AMERICAN MODELS AM-2. (AUTHOR COLLECTION)

MOST RARE OF MOTOR CITY USA'S 1954 SKYLARK CONVERTIBLES IS THIS TOP UP VERSION. MC-40. (COURTESY B GORMAN)

PROFILE – 1954 BUICK SKYLARK BY MOTOR CITY USA

ADMIRABLE IN ITS USA MODELS AND AMERICAN MODELS FORM WITH CAREFUL ASSEMBLY AND ATTRACTIVE PRICING (AROUND $135), THE MODEL IS A TERRIFIC ADDITION TO ANY COLLECTION. HOWEVER, THE FULLY OUTFITTED, TOP OF THE LINE MOTOR CITY USA 1954 SKYLARK (MC-40) IS A REVELATION.

ISSUED IN SEVERAL COLORS AS AN OPEN MODEL WITH A FEW TOP UP VERSIONS AVAILABLE INITIALLY, THE BUILDERS AT MOTOR CITY USA WERE MASTERFUL IN PRODUCING THIS ONE. THE MCUSA SKYLARK IS AS CLOSE TO AN EXACT 1:43 SCALE REPLICA OF THE ORIGINAL VEHICLE AS IT IS POSSIBLE TO GET IN THE MEDIUM OF WHITE METAL. PROPORTIONS, DETAIL, MATERIALS, AND BUILD QUALITY ARE PEERLESS. THE SHINY NICKEL-PLATED WHITE GRILLE IS AN EXCEPTIONAL PIECE OF CRAFTSMANSHIP.

THE PRECISION OF THE ORIGINAL PATTERN IS IMPRESSIVE, AS IS THE ACCURACY OF DETAIL. THIS IS MADE POSSIBLE THROUGH THE SKILLFUL USE OF PHOTO-ETCHING, PRIMARILY FOR SCRIPT, INTERIOR METAL AND THE DELICATE DEEP DISH WIRE WHEELS. THE METICULOUSLY RENDERED WIRE WHEELS ARE SET OFF BY A REFLECTIVE BASKET (RED ON MY MODEL) THAT ENHANCES THEIR APPEARANCE.

THIS REPLICA IS COMMONLY REGARDED AS ONE OF THE AMERICAN BUILDER'S GREATEST ACHIEVEMENTS. (AUTHOR COLLECTION)

the comparison ends. Of note is that some examples suffer from warping of the body with a pronounced sagging at the middle. This phenomenon is also common to many humans I know who were issued at the same time.

CADILLAC-LaSALLE 6

GENERAL MOTORS' PREMIUM MARQUE BOWED IN IN 1902 WITH 3 UNITS sold that year. From its early days Cadillac was a prestigious automobile known for stout engineering. Cadillac drivetrains were used for passenger buses and saw service in tanks in World War II. Cadillac was a survivor of the Depression and witnessed the demise of competitors such as Pierce-Arrow and, eventually, its main rival, Packard.

In 1949 Cadillac introduced the overhead valve V-8 engine and sold its millionth model, a Coupe de Ville. During the 1950s it continued to win international car races and to gain sales in prosperous North America. By the end of the decade the Cadillac Division was regularly selling 200,000 cars a year and outselling its Lincoln and Imperial competitors by huge margins, not to mention mid-priced makes of DeSoto, Hudson, Chrysler,

SOME FEATURED CADILLAC MODELS

YEAR	MODEL	MANUFACTURER
1930	V16	SOLIDO
1930	V16	ELEGANCE
1933	V16	MATCHBOX
1933	V16	WESTERN
1934	LASALLE	BROOKLIN
1934	LASALLE	WESTERN
1937	LASALLE	MINI MARQUE '43
1937	LASALLE	ELC
1938	SIXTY SPECIAL	BROOKLIN
1938	V16	REXTOYS

YEAR	MODEL	MANUFACTURER
1939	LASALLE	BROOKLIN MODELS
1940	V16	BROOKLIN MODELS
1940	LASALLE	AMERICANA
1940	LASALLE	VICTORY MODELS
1941	SERIES 62 AND SIXTY SPECIAL	VICTORY MODELS
1947	SERIES 62	PROVENCE MOULAGE
1947	SERIES 62	BROOKLIN MODELS
1947	SERIES 75	CONQUEST MODELS
1947	SERIES 75 AND SIXTY SPECIAL	BRUCE ARNOLD MODELS
1948	SERIES SIXTY SPECIAL	BRUCE ARNOLD MODELS
1948	SERIES SIXTY SPECIAL	MINIMARQUE
1949	SERIES 62	MOTOR CITY USA
1949	SERIES 62	WESTERN MODELS
1950	SEREIS 61	BRUCE ARNOLD MODELS
1950	SERIES 62	AMR
1950	SERIES 62	VITESSE
1950	SERIES 61, 62, 75, 86, AND SIXTY SPECIAL	ELEGANCE
1951	SERIES 61, 62, 75, 86, AND SIXTY SPECIAL	ELEGANCE
1952	SERIES 62	ERTL
1953	ELDORADO	BRUCE ARNOLD MODELS
1954	ELDORADO	MINI MARQUE '43'

and Nash. It had become the most coveted automobile on Earth, befitting its 'standard of the world' title.

Cadillac has been the most frequently modeled General Motors' brand, surpassing the entire Chevrolet line, including the popular modelers' subject – Corvette.

Model-by-model   1927-38

Few 1:43 scale 1920s Cadillac replicas exist except for Enchantment Land Coachbuilder's unique resin cast 1927 LaSalle roadsters by ELC founder, Jerry Rettig.

Once modelers discovered model years 1930-31 Cadillac as

their subject they rapidly moved into high gear. There are several significant replicas of the Cadillac from this period.

Found in toy boxes, closets, bookcases and on model railroad layouts throughout the world in a multitude of different colors and body styles is Solido's 1930-31 Cadillac. This die-cast model was produced by the French maker in the early 1980s and was priced in the $10-20 range. Comprising approximately 20 parts, most detail is stamped into the well-proportioned and scale-accurate body. Like many die-cast models of its time, the Solido Cadillac is midway between a child's toy and a collectible replica. It was marketed primarily as the latter with a perspex case and polystyrene plinth.

Solido made the Cadillac as a 1930 window van and panel van in a dizzying number of versions, and as a 1931 landaulet with open rear passenger area. It is a tribute to the model's

1927 LaSalle roadster that paced that year's Indianapolis 500 race. Jerry Rettig created this and a few other 1927 LaSalle resin scale models that are the only ones of their kind in the world. Note the windshield is in the lowered position. Enchantment Land Coachbuilders. (Courtesy J Rettig)

1927 LaSalle roadster top down in a striking red by Jerry Rettig, Enchantment Land Coachbuilders. (Courtesy J Rettig)

1931 Cadillac Boattail speedster top up by Mini Auto Emporium. MAE-115. (Courtesy C Hardegger)

A pair of 1930 Cadillac V16 Phaeton scale models. Die-cast by defunct builder, Guisival of Spain, and reputed to be 1:45 scale. Model no 756. (Courtesy J Rettig)

patternmaker that Elegance of France based some of its production on the Solido.

Rio of Italy and Franklin Mint rounded out the production with 1930-31 Cadillac Roadsters. In 2005, Altaya/IXO made a terrific die-cast 1930 Cadillac Imperial V16 sedan replica that sold for around $30.

The streamlined 1933 Cadillac phaeton, with its canted radiator shell, was an early Western Models handmade effort in white metal in open and top up versions. Matchbox later produced a die-cast town car, fire service, and paddy wagon, the latter two being quite whimsical in conception.

No senior Cadillac from 1934-37 has been modeled in 1:43 but several LaSalle

ANOTHER UNLIKELY BUT AMUSING SOLIDO SCALE MODEL CELEBRATING NEW YORK CITY IS THIS 1930 CADILLAC V16 WINDOW VAN. NO 4038. (COURTESY J RETTIG)

THESE 1930 LONG-WHEELBASE CADILLAC WINDOWED HEARSE AND AMBULANCE DIE-CAST MODELS ISSUED BY SOLIDO/VEREM ARE REALISTIC AND HAVE QUITE A BIT OF CHARACTER. MODEL NO 306. (COURTESY J RETTIG)

models have. The 1934 LaSalle was seen by many people to be one of the most attractively styled motorcars of its time. Evidently several builders felt the same way. Nostalgic Miniatures of the USA produced a white metal handbuilt version in the 1970s as a coupe and convertible.

Brooklin Models created a very accurate 1934 LaSalle 2 door coupe released in 2001. It is one of the author's favorite models from the popular builder because it packs so much detail into a low-priced handbuilt. As well, Brooklin's patternmaker has

A COUPLE OF UNLIKELY 1930 CADILLAC V16 SCALE MODELS ARE SOLIDO MODELS' PANEL VAN IN CADBURY CHOCOLATE CO LIVERY AND A WINDOW VAN DRESSED UP AS A POLICE CAR. SOLIDO DIE-CAST MODELS NO 4060. (COURTESY J RETTIG)

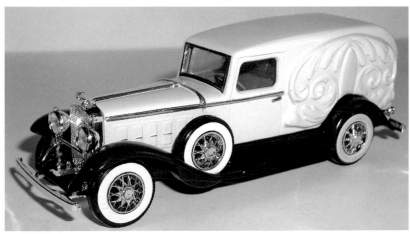

AN UNUSUALLY CHEERFUL AND WELL-DETAILED WHITE AND RED ART-CARVED 1930 CADILLAC HEARSE FROM THE INVENTIVE AND ACTIVE MIND OF JERRY RETTIG. ENCHANTMENT LAND COACHBUILDERS. (COURTESY J RETTIG)

A BIT OF A THROWBACK TO ITS VICTORIAN HORSE-DRAWN ANCESTORS, THIS QUASI-OPEN 1931 CADILLAC 'LANDAULET' WITH ITS UNIQUE HEAVY-FRAMED SPLIT WINDSHIELD WAS RELEASED BY SOLIDO MODELS AS A DIE-CAST REPLICA. NO 4085. (COURTESY J RETTIG)

THIS RICHLY FINISHED REPLICA OF CADILLAC'S 1930 FLEETWOOD 'FLEETCREST' V16 TOWN BROUGHAM FOR 7 PASSENGERS, IN A DEEP MERLOT AND BLACK COMBINATION, IS FROM ELEGANCE MODELS. HANDCRAFTED IN RESIN, BUILDER CLAUDE THIBIVILLIERS BASED HIS DESIGN ON THE AFOREMENTIONED SOLIDO DIE-CAST MODELS. NO 504B. (AUTHOR COLLECTION)

AN ENORMOUS VEHICLE POSSESSED BY CELEBRITIES, INDUSTRIALISTS, AND OTHER GENTRY, FEW 1930 CADILLAC V16 TOWN CARS WERE ALIKE. VERY FEW IDENTICAL ELEGANCE MODELS WERE ISSUED AS WELL. THIS RED AND BLACK VERSION, ISSUED IN THE LATE 1980s IS NO 504. (AUTHOR COLLECTION)

captured the rakish long looks of the original automobile with great accuracy.

Finished in a blue gray with major components such as bumpers, headlights, rumble seat step plates, and radiator shell in polished chrome, the little model looks more expensive than its original $85 issue price. It has the usual features of later Brooklin Models, namely details such as the running board pattern cast into the body and painted, major brightwork in chrome, and a simple interior with accurately shaped seats and dashboard. To coin a phrase from a popular British toy builder, Brooklin Models' '34 LaSalle is 'spot on'!

Cadillac V16 Imperial Sedan 1930

LEFT FROM TOP: MORE COMMON THAN THE TOWN CAR BUT HARDLY COMMONPLACE WAS THE 5200LB 1930 CADILLAC V16 IMPERIAL SEDAN. IN 2006 ALTAYA/IXO RELEASED THIS PEERLESS SCALE MODEL. AT ITS ISSUE PRICE OF AROUND $30 IT IS A SUPERB REPLICA. (AUTHOR COLLECTION); FRANKLIN MINT MADE THIS WELL-DETAILED DIE-CAST REPLICA OF CADILLAC'S 1931 V8 CONVERTIBLE COUPE. NO LC-2; A RARE AND EXQUISITE 1931 CADILLAC FLEETWOOD V16 COUPE IN CREAM AND MAROON. RESIN CAST BY CLAUDE THIBIVILLIER'S ELEGANCE MODELS, THIS WELL-FINISHED SCALE MODEL IS NO 4035. (COURTESY J RETTIG)

Another terrific scale model of the '34 LaSalle is Durham Classics' convertible. Sold in different colors with top down, top up, rumble seat closed or open, and as a pace car, this moderately-detailed, white metal replica is well-finished and proportionately accurate. Collectors appear to like it because examples sell at auction for more than its $125 issue price.

The 1937 LaSalle was a beautiful automobile that paced the Indianapolis 500 race of that year. Mini Marque '43' created a flawless replica of this convertible as a pace car and stock convertible. One of the last models produced by the company in 2002, the LaSalle has fine details such as photo-etched chevron trim on each front fender, an intricate grille, clear reflective headlight lenses, and fully detailed interior. This model came in a variety of authentic colors and a few were outfitted with a top. Enchantment Land Coachbuilders also thought the 1937-38 LaSalle made a good subject for a replica. In addition to its Indianapolis 500 pace car, ELC produced a number of intriguing resin-bodied LaSalle service vehicles in an assortment of liveries and colors. Hardly any two are alike, including the fabulous art-carved LaSalle hearse.

The chronological history of 1:43 scale Cadillac replicas resumes for the 1938 model year with Rextoys' 1980s production of several thousand die-cast V16 models in five body styles (2 door convertible, 4 door convertible sedan, 2 door coupe, 4 door sedan, town car) and 12 variations in several colors. Rextoys' Cadillac replicas have little brightwork but are nicely finished.

Rounding out 1938 is Brooklin Models' lovely Series Sixty Special 4 door sedan and open phaeton (750 of the latter were issued as 'factory specials'), handbuilt in white metal. Brooklin's replica captures to perfection the 'small' Cadillac of its day with proper proportions, stellar craftsmanship, and much detail carved into the body. The painstakingly scribed grille is literally the model's centerpiece and breathtaking to behold.

1931 CADILLAC V16 DIE-CAST MODELS FROM RIO OF ITALY. FAIRLY COMMON TODAY, THESE MODELS HAVE GOOD PROPORTIONS AND ARE QUITE AFFORDABLE. NO 77. (COURTESY J RETTIG)

1933 CADILLAC V16 TOWN CAR FROM DANBURY MINT. ISSUED IN SHINY PEWTER, SOME HOBBYISTS – SUCH AS JERRY RETTIG – CHOSE TO PAINT THE MODEL TO ALTER ITS APPEARANCE. (COURTESY J RETTIG)

POPULAR WITH BUILDERS, THE LAVISH V16 FLEETWOOD TOWN CAR BROUGHAM SEEN HERE IS MATCHBOX MODELS' DIE-CAST REPLICA NO Y-34. A 1933 MODEL, STYLISTS WERE BEGINNING TO EXERT MORE INFLUENCE OVER AUTOMOBILE DESIGN, IN THIS CASE, THE ROUNDED RADIATOR SHELL AND PONTOON-LIKE FENDERS ARE MAKING THEIR FIRST APPEARANCE. (COURTESY J RETTIG)

THE FIRST MODERATELY DETAILED HANDBUILT 1930S CADILLAC MODELS WERE THESE 1933 V16 CARS ISSUED IN TOP UP AND OPEN PHAETON BODY STYLES BY PROLIFIC BUILDER, WESTERN SCALE MODELS. EXPERTLY RENDERED, THESE SUBSTANTIAL WHITE METAL MODELS DEBUTED IN THE EARLY 1980S. WHAT DISTINGUISHES THEM FROM LATER MODELS FROM THE SAME BUILDER IS THE SOMEWHAT MATTE-LIKE FINISH OF THE BRIGHTWORK AND MOLDED HEADLIGHT PATTERN. HEAVILY PLATED CHROME BRIGHTWORK AND SEPARATE RESIN, PLASTIC OR ENAMEL HEADLIGHT LENSES APPEARED LATER. WMS-28. (COURTESY J RETTIG)

BECAUSE OF ITS ROBUST CONSTRUCTION AND LEGENDARY DEPENDABILITY, CADILLAC WAS A POPULAR BASE FOR PROFESSIONAL MOTORCARS, NOTABLY AMBULANCE AND FUNERAL CARS. EVEN FIRE RESCUE VEHICLES WERE PRODUCED SUCH AS THE PAIR OF 1933 VERSIONS MODELED HERE BY MATCHBOX. NO VFE-03. (COURTESY J RETTIG)

LaSalle's 1934 coupe was first produced as a handbuilt white metal scale model by Nostalgic Miniatures, which issued this no 231, circa 1975. Molded almost entirely in one piece, the builder relied heavily on expert painting to bring out the details of the pattern. (Courtesy J Rettig)

1934 LaSalle top up by Durham Classics. DC-30. (Author collection)

LaSalle's streamlined 1934 coupe is one of the most pleasing automobile designs to emerge from the era. Priced at $1595, the Fleetwood bodied beauty was quite the car. Brooklin Models chose a smoky dark blue metallic for its handbuilt white metal replica issued in August 2000. BRK-84. (Author collection)

This example of Nostalgic Miniatures' 1934 LaSalle roadster shows more detail than the builder's coupe, notably the amber headlight lenses and separate door handles. No 682. (Courtesy J Rettig)

1937 LaSalle convertible coupe with custom body by Sodomka, reputedly built for King George VI of England. Miva Models (Czechoslovakia) issued this unusual white metal handmade version and then disappeared from the modeling scene. No 1. (Author collection)

1934 LaSalle Indy 500 open pace car from Durham Classics. This white metal replica is nicely finished and better proportioned than the Nostalgic Miniatures version of 25 years earlier. DC-30. (Courtesy J Rettig)

1937 LaSalle open convertible coupe with many details, including full rear fender skirts, from Enchantment Land Coachbuilders. (Courtesy J Rettig)

The first builder to produce a handbuilt 1937 LaSalle was Jerry Rettig's Enchantment Land Coachbuilders, which issued a few of these pace cars. (Courtesy J Rettig)

Mini Marque '43 1937 LaSalle pace car. Interior detail is quite complete with separate chromed door pulls and window winders, gearshift with knob, and instrument panel parts. Missing are the numbers on the gauges. No RP-14. (Author collection)

The Sodomka 1937 LaSalle had rear-hinged doors and an elongated body. Miva Models no 1. (Author collection)

The 1937 LaSalle paced that year's Indianapolis 500, making it the second year in the marque's short history to be so honored. Mini Marque '43 issued this flawless handbuilt white metal open convertible late in its existence. No RP-14. (Author collection)

Designer Bill Mitchell's gorgeous 1938 Sixty Special is a milestone design. Many examples of the car still exist despite low initial production of 3695 units. Brooklin Models issued a similar number of white metal replicas in an attractive gray-green hue. Here is the sedan BRK-86 and phaeton BRK-FS-5. (Author collection)

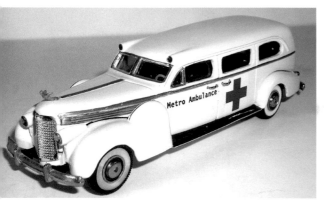

1938 LaSalle long-wheelbase ambulance as envisioned by Jerry Rettig. Resin scale model from Enchantment Land Coachbuilders. (Courtesy J Rettig)

A pair of 1940 Cadillac V-16 scale models, a formal sedan and town car die-cast by Rextoys in the 1980s. Model nos 3 and 2. (Courtesy J Rettig)

1938 Sixty Special in the livery of the Palace Hotel with Omen figure. 1 of 200 pieces made by Brooklin Models in 2001 for the San Francisco Bay Brooklin Club. BRK-86X. (Author collection)

1938 LaSalle Limousine style funeral car and art-carved hearse handmade in resin by Enchantment Land Coachbuilders. (Courtesy J Rettig)

Model-by-model   1939-42

For the 1939 model year, Brooklin Models made a scale-accurate and beautifully patterned LaSalle 2 door Touring Sedan and Series 50 5-window coupe, released in 2003 and 2006 respectively. Apparently rendered by the same patternmaker as Brooklin's Sixty Special, the LaSalle has accurate proportions, sculpted details, and a finely formed grille with LaSalle script. The white metal hood ornament on this replica is particularly delicate. The mid-green of the sedan is somewhat unusual for a replica and appears a little bland in photographs. The color is more effective seen in person and contrasts nicely with the typical dark solid colors of many vehicles from the period.

Prominent scale models of 1940s Cadillac and LaSalle vehicles begin with Mikansue's LaSalle 4 door sedan and Brooklin's early but excellent V16 convertible coupe. As part of

1940 Cadillac V16 die-cast replicas by Rextoys. The coupe is as issued by the maker. The convertible has been well detailed by Jerry Rettig. Model nos 5 and 6. (Courtesy J Rettig)

ECLIPSED IN SALES VOLUME BY BUICK AND CHALLENGED BY CADILLAC'S SIXTY SPECIAL, THE LOVELY 1939 LASALLE WAS IN ITS NEXT TO LAST YEAR. THESE SCARCE COUPE AND CONVERTIBLE REPLICAS ARE BY ENCHANTMENT LAND COACHBUILDERS. (COURTESY J RETTIG)

THIS VIEW OF A JOHN ROBERTS CRAFTED LASALLE SHOWS THE MODEL'S SIMPLE BUT QUITE ACCURATE INTERIOR. (AUTHOR COLLECTION)

Mikansue's Americana series, its sedan is quite well done. Not having an actual vehicle to measure or behold from different angles, the patternmaker has managed to quite accurately capture the model's proportions from old photographs. Sold primarily as a white metal kit, Mikansue's is a simple replica with little detailing that benefits greatly from skilful painting and the application of bright chrome foil.

Appearing a few years after the Mikansue LaSalle, Brooklin's V16 convertible is quite common on the secondary market, and though it has few parts it is superbly rendered with great proportions and details sculpted into the model. It too dresses up well with chrome foil and polishing of the non-plated grille.

Mini Auto Emporium's white metal handbuilt 1940 Series Sixty sedan and convertible is less common. This white metal scale model has an elaborate and heavy appearing front clip that is festooned with accessory lighting and grille protector.

Enchantment Land Coachbuilders made a handful or two of 1940 LaSalle service cars as ambulances and hearses. With greatly stretched wheelbases, these replicas are impressive for their size and uniqueness. Such is patternmaker's Jerry Rettig's talent that the LaSalle's lineage is difficult to determine, perhaps a combination of Rextoys Cadillac and early Mikansue.

Finally, for 1940, Victory Models produced a nicely detailed resin LaSalle convertible. About 100 of these carefully sculpted replicas were issued in gray or maroon. A full Victory model, they came with a removable top and a convertible boot.

The high water mark Cadillac styling year of 1941 is aptly rendered in Victory Models' stunning assortment of S62 sedanet, convertible, convertible sedan, and Series Sixty sedan, all handbuilt in resin with white metal base. These low-production models are very accurate, have a high level of detail and were

1939 LASALLE BY BROOKLIN MODELS. THE 2 DOOR SEDAN WAS OUTSOLD 15 TO 1 BY THE 4 DOOR MODEL'S 15,000 BUYERS. A NICE MODEL WITH A CAREFULLY HAND-SCORED GRILLE, THE BUILDER ISSUED THIS REPLICA IN LIGHT GREEN ONLY. BRK-98 (COURTESY D MATHYSSEN)

available in a variety of authentic colors and paint combinations. Build quality and paint finishing is superb. Victory Models ensured that these models would be available in a range of hues and shades across the color spectrum.

No 1942 Cadillac 1:43 scale replicas exist.

A ONE-OF-A-KIND 1939 LaSalle 4 DOOR CONVERTIBLE SEDAN MADE BY JOHN ROBERTS FROM A BROOKLIN MODEL. NOTE THE RESIN HEADLIGHT LENSES REPLACING THE USUAL WHITE METAL LENSES. (AUTHOR COLLECTION)

AN EARLY WHITE METAL 1940 LaSalle S52 4 DOOR SEDAN FROM MIKANSUE'S AMERICANA LINE, THIS EXAMPLE HAS BEEN WELL PAINTED AND DETAILED TO A HIGH STANDARD. IN THE AUTHOR'S OPINION, THIS IS MIKANSUE'S MOST ACCURATE MODEL OF A NORTH AMERICAN CAR. No 5. (COURTESY J RETTIG)

ONLY ONE OF THESE 1939 LaSalle 4 DOOR SEDAN REPLICAS WAS MADE BY JOHN ROBERTS FROM A BROOKLIN MODELS 2 DOOR SEDAN. (AUTHOR COLLECTION)

USING MIKANSUE'S SEDAN AS A STARTING POINT, JERRY RETTIG CREATED THIS 1940 LaSalle CONVERTIBLE SEDAN WHICH WAS LaSalle'S LEAST COMMON BODY STYLE. (COURTESY J RETTIG)

1939 LaSalle 5 WINDOW COUPE, GM'S LOWEST PRICED LaSalle AT $1200. BROOKLIN MADE THIS WHITE METAL MODEL IN MAROON. (AUTHOR COLLECTION)

400 SCALE MODELS OF THESE 1940 V16 CONVERTIBLE COUPES IN A STRIKING LIPSTICK RED WITH SIDE-MOUNTS WERE MADE IN 1983 FOR THE CANADIAN TOY COLLECTORS SOCIETY EDITION. BRK-14. (COURTESY D MATHYSSEN)

ANOTHER JERRY RETTIG INSPIRED PROFESSIONAL CAR, THIS TIME A 1940 LASALLE LIMOUSINE HEARSE IN MAROON. (COURTESY J RETTIG)

VICTORY MODELS' 1940 LASALLE S52 CONVERTIBLE VM-10. (COURTESY D LARSEN)

1940 LASALLE S52 CONVERTIBLE BY VICTORY MODELS. CAREFULLY CRAFTED IN RESIN, THIS HANDBUILT MODEL IN OXBLOOD MAROON CAME WITH A TOP AND CONVERTIBLE BOOT SO THAT IT MAY BE DISPLAYED OPEN OR CLOSED. VM-10. (AUTHOR COLLECTION)

1941 S62 CONVERTIBLE COUPE IN OCEANO BLUE WITH SIMULATED OXBLOOD LEATHER INTERIOR. PRODUCED BY VICTORY MODELS IN 2002, THIS GORGEOUS LIMITED EDITION RESIN AND WHITE METAL REPLICA RETAILED FOR $175. VM-1A. (AUTHOR COLLECTION)

1940 CADILLAC V16 CONVERTIBLE COUPE FROM BROOKLIN MODELS. THE BRITISH BUILDER ISSUED THIS SUPERBLY RENDERED WHITE METAL MODEL IN 1983. BRK-14. (AUTHOR COLLECTION)

THE 1940 SIXTY SPECIAL HAD PANACHE. THIS MINI AUTO EMPORIUM WHITE METAL SCALE MODEL FROM THE 1980s IS FESTOONED WITH GRILLE BARS AND DRIVING LIGHTS. IT IS QUITE A RARE PIECE AND ALSO CAME IN A SCARCE CONVERTIBLE VERSION. MAE NO 117. (COURTESY J RETTIG)

1941 CADILLAC S62 CONVERTIBLE SEDAN IN FAIROAKS GREEN METALLIC. VICTORY MODELS USED GENUINE CADILLAC COLORS FROM THAT YEAR. VM-4. (AUTHOR COLLECTION)

1941 WAS THE LAST YEAR THAT CADILLAC OFFERED BOTH A 2 DOOR AND 4 DOOR CONVERTIBLE. THE 4 DOOR CONVERTIBLE SEDAN OR 'PHAETON' SOLD ONLY 400 UNITS, WHICH WAS A FAR CRY FROM THE 3100 2 DOOR CONVERTIBLE SERIES 62 MODELS THAT CADILLAC MADE. VICTORY MODELS VM-1A WITH DETACHABLE TOP UP AND VM-4. (AUTHOR COLLECTION)

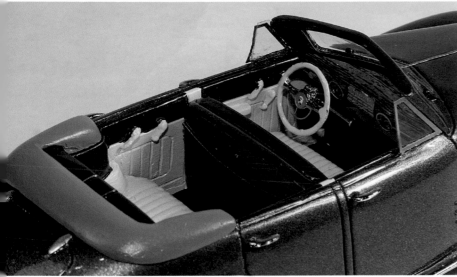

THE INTERIOR OF VICTORY MODELS' 1941 CADILLAC S62 HAS QUITE A BIT OF DETAIL, PARTICULARLY THE IMPRESSIVE WOOD GRAINED DASHBOARD WITH FULL INSTRUMENTS, MULTI-PIECE STEERING COLUMN AND WHEEL WITH CHROME GEAR SELECTOR AND AUTHENTIC CENTER HUB MEDALLION. VM-4. (AUTHOR COLLECTION)

A SUPERBLY PROPORTIONED AND WELL DETAILED 1:43 SCALE REPLICA OF THE 1941 S61 CLUB COUPE. ISSUED BY VICTORY MODELS IN 2002. VM-8. (AUTHOR COLLECTION)

IN 1941 CADILLAC MADE A COUPE AND A FASTBACK SEDANET THAT IT CALLED A 'CLUB COUPE'. IT WAS AVAILABLE AS A STANDARD OR DE LUXE MODEL WITH FENDER SKIRTS. DEPICTED HERE ARE VICTORY MODELS' 1941 CADILLAC CLUB COUPE REPLICAS IN DUSTY GRAY/RIVERMIST GRAY AND ELCENTRO GREEN/FAIROAKS GREEN. WM-8. (AUTHOR COLLECTION)

1941 CADILLAC SIXTY SPECIAL. REPLICA BY VICTORY MODELS FROM 2001-02. IN GUNMETAL GRAY AND BERKLEY GRAY. VM-3. (AUTHOR COLLECTION)

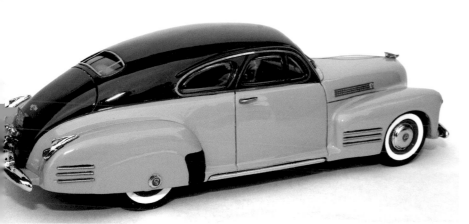

THE FLOWING LINES OF CADILLAC'S SERIES 61 SEDANET SHOW HOW MUCH INFLUENCE STYLISTS HAD BY 1941. VICTORY MODELS VM-8. (AUTHOR COLLECTION)

1941 CADILLAC SIXTY SPECIAL. REPLICA BY VICTORY MODELS FROM 2001-02. IN GUNMETAL GRAY AND BERKLEY GRAY. VM-3. (AUTHOR COLLECTION)

Model-by-model   1946-47

Following World War II, buyers could not get enough of Cadillac's 1946-47 models. For the patient scale model collector, this is not the case because many builders have modeled this desirable automobile and replicas are available.

Several European builders issued resin and white metal sedanets, sedans, limousines and convertibles. Tron (Italy), Provence Moulage (France), Milestone Miniatures (UK), and VF (Germany) made scale models in some or all of the body styles mentioned. Many of these models have great similarity in pattern with variation in finishing and materials.

Later, Brooklin Models released a sedanet of its own. An excellent handbuilt white metal model, Brooklin's S62 was sold as a cream-on-red number at a low issue price of $95. 999 units were also sold as a Factory Special in silver to commemorate Brooklin Models' 25th anniversary.

Bruce Arnold Models created a fine 1947 Sixty Special and a 1947 Series 75 limousine that was also issued by Conquest Models. A substantial, hard to find model that has a high level of detailing, rich colors, and careful finishing, this lovely replica was reissued in 2007 by Conquest at a price of $250.

Finally, if a person wants an ambulance, hearse, or flower car version of the 1946-47 Cadillac, Enchantment Land Coachbuilders is the only builder of these type of subjects, creating just a few at a time.

Of the foregoing models, Provence Moulage issued a variety of body styles, covering the majority of Cadillac passenger car models produced that year. Made in resin with heavy white metal bases, the

PROVENCE MOULAGE'S 1:43 SCALE 1947 CADILLAC S62 2 DOOR USED POLISHED WHITE METAL BRIGHTWORK AND WAS AN EARLY ADVOCATE OF DELICATE PHOTO-ETCHED METAL, SEEN HERE IN THE REAR WINDOW DETAIL AND FENDER SCRIPT. NO 4. (AUTHOR COLLECTION)

ALMOST ALL AUTOMOBILES IN THE FIRST COUPLE OF YEARS AFTER WWII HAD BLACK WALL TIRES. MOREOVER, THE MAJORITY OF CARS, EVEN LUXURY CADILLAC MODELS, WERE PAINTED ONE COLOR. THIS DARK RED 1947 S62 BY PROVENCE MOULAGE IS A REALISTIC RENDITION OF A TYPICAL CADILLAC FROM THAT ERA. NO 4. (AUTHOR COLLECTION)

most common style is the 2 door fastback sedan. It shows up every few months on eBay. The 4 door sedan is far less common. Offered as both a kit and a factory built-up, Provence Moulage's little Cadillac has many parts including resin headlights and delicate photo-etched window frames and windshield wipers. Emblems are 4 color water transfers. The paint on the factory built-ups I have is nicely done, two-tone on some models with clean color separation and using metallic colors. Because of the relative abundance of 1946-48 Cadillac replicas from the many builders, prices of the Provence Moulage models have hovered around the $100 mark, making them a great value purchase.

MORE POPULAR WITH CUSTOMERS BUT LESS COMMONLY MODELED IN 1:43 WAS THE 1947 CADILLAC S62 4 DOOR SEDAN. HERE, A RESIN AND WHITE METAL PROVENCE MOULAGE MODEL SPORTS A TASTEFUL METALLIC BROWN PAINT JOB SET OFF BY ACCURATE WHITEWALL TIRES AND FULL WHEEL COVERS. THIS FACTORY-BUILT SCALE MODEL IS QUITE RARE TODAY. NO 306. (AUTHOR COLLECTION)

THE 1947 CADILLAC CONVERTIBLE INTERIOR FEATURED SMOOTH LEATHER SEATS AND WOOD GRAIN ACCENTS ON THE DASHBOARD, AS WELL AS FULL INSTRUMENTATION. VF MODELS' VERSION HAS A FULLY DETAILED DASH. REV-005. (AUTHOR COLLECTION)

1947 SERIES 62 CADILLAC CONVERTIBLE COUPE. BROOKLIN MODELS ISSUED 200 OF THESE SPECIAL REPLICAS IN 1999 FOR THE NATIONAL CADILLAC CLUB, SANTA CLARA CHAPTER. BRK-74X. (COURTESY D MATHYSSEN)

1947 CADILLAC S62 OPEN CONVERTIBLE. A VERY ATTRACTIVE REPLICA FROM VF MODELS OF GERMANY. REV-005. (AUTHOR COLLECTION)

ONE OF 300 1:43 SCALE HANDBUILT WHITE METAL MODELS BROOKLIN PRODUCED IN GRAY WITH BLACK TOP UP FOR THE CANADIAN TOY COLLECTORS SOCIETY IN 1998. BRK-74X. (COURTESY D MATHYSSEN)

Brooklin's 1947 Cadillac is moderately detailed. Modelers like Steve Williams add details such as painted ornaments to add realism to the model. BRK-105. (Courtesy S Williams)

Brooklin Models was the first to issue a white metal version of the 1947 Cadillac, in 2003. BRK-105. (Courtesy D Mathyssen)

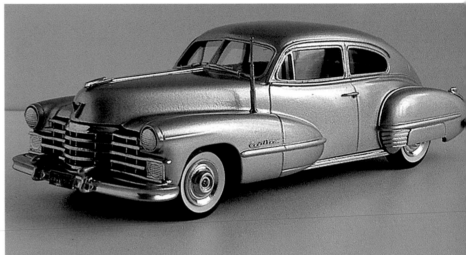

The standard Brooklin Models 1947 Cadillac dresses up nicely with detailing provided here by Steve Williams. (Courtesy S Williams)

1947 Cadillac Series 62 Sedanet 2004 Anniversary Special. 1 of 999 units made by Brooklin in Champagne Metallic. BRK-105X. (Courtesy D Mathyssen)

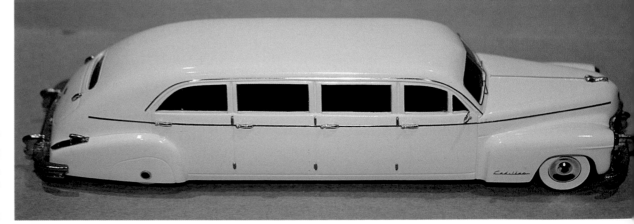

Eight doors graced this magnificent 1947 Cadillac S75 airport limousine by Hess and Eisenhardt. The replica pictured here is one of only two produced by Elegance Models. (Courtesy D Larsen)

1947 CADILLAC S75 7 WINDOW LIMOUSINE DERHAM-STYLE CONVERSION WITH DOOR CREST AND 1947 S75 LIMOUSINE FROM JERRY RETTIG'S ENCHANTMENT LAND COACHBUILDERS. THE FORMER IS A ONE-OF-A-KIND REPLICA. (COURTESY J RETTIG)

A RICH PEARLESCENT DOVE GRAY SEEMS LIKE THE RIGHT COLOR FOR THIS UNUSUAL 1947 CADILLAC LIMOUSINE-STYLE HEARSE (LEFT) BY JERRY RETTIG. NEXT TO IT IS A 1947 CADILLAC LONG-WHEELBASE (S75 CHASSIS) FLOWER CAR WITH SIMULATED WOOD BED COVER AND FENDER SKIRTS. THE BUILDER HAS USED THE HIGHLY ACCURATE PROVENCE MOULAGE CADILLAC AS A BASIS FOR THESE FINE CONVERSIONS. ENCHANTMENT LAND COACHBUILDERS NOS C12 AND C19. (COURTESY J RETTIG)

A FEW COACHBUILDERS SUCH AS MAURICE SCHWARTZ, WHO CRAFTED A 6-DOOR VERSION FOR WESTERN STAR GENE AUTRY, MAY HAVE ATTEMPTED A WOOD BODIED LOOK ON 1946-49 SERIES 75 MODELS. IN THIS CASE JERRY RETTIG HAS TAKEN A PROVENCE MOULAGE LIMOUSINE AND CREATED HIS OWN 'TOWN AND COUNTRY'-LIKE VERSION IN METALLIC GREEN. (COURTESY J RETTIG)

A COMMON SIGHT ON NORTH AMERICAN STREETS IN THE LATE 1940S AND EARLY 1950S WAS THE CADILLAC-BASED AMBULANCE OFTEN IN THE LIVERY OF PRIVATE COMPANIES OR CITY FIRE DEPARTMENTS. HERE IS A 1947 VERSION SKILLFULLY CRAFTED BY JERRY RETTIG WHO HAS CONVERTED A PROVENCE MOULAGE SEDAN INTO THIS LONG-WHEELBASE MILLER METEOR EXAMPLE. ENCHANTMENT LAND COACHBUILDERS NO C13. (COURTESY J RETTIG)

CONQUEST MODELS ISSUED THIS BRUCE ARNOLD PATTERNED REPLICA AS ONE OF ITS LAST MODELS. AN EXTREMELY HEAVY, WELL-DETAILED AND CAREFULLY FINISHED MODEL THAT WAS CAST, PAINTED AND ASSEMBLED BY SMTS, IT WAS PRICED IN THE HIGH $200 RANGE BUT HAS SOLD FOR MORE THAN TWICE THIS PRICE IN 2007. CNQ-30. (AUTHOR COLLECTION)

FOR 1947, CADILLAC MOTOR DIVISION PRODUCED 2405 SERIES 75 AUTOMOBILES, CLEARLY MAKING IT THE PREFERRED VEHICLE OF THE 'CARRIAGE TRADE'. PICTURED IS A HANDBUILT WHITE METAL REPLICA IN ANTOINETTE BLUE FROM CONQUEST MODELS. CNQ-30. (AUTHOR COLLECTION)

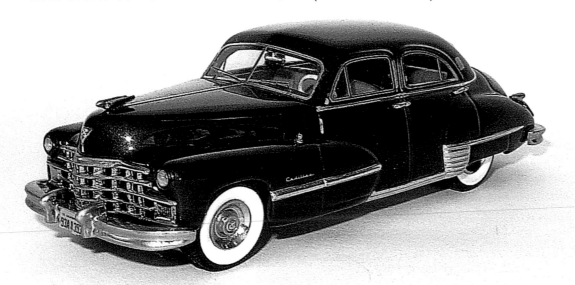

THE CADILLAC SIXTY SPECIAL CARRIED ON ITS TRADITION OF BEING JUST THAT – 'SPECIAL' – IN 1947. THE FLEETWOOD-BODIED MODEL HAD LONGER DOORS AND WHEELBASE AND MORE LUXURIOUS APPOINTMENTS TO JUSTIFY ITS MUCH HIGHER PRICE THAN THE MORE COMMON SERIES 62 SEDAN. BRUCE ARNOLD MODELS BAM-7. (COURTESY A MOSKALEV)

1947 FLEETWOOD SIXTY SPECIAL BY BRUCE ARNOLD MODELS. HANDCRAFTED IN WHITE METAL, THIS IS THE ONLY 1:43 SCALE REPLICA OF THE MODEL. FEWER THAN 200 EXAMPLES WERE MADE IN ITS 2004 PRODUCTION RUN. BAM-7. (COURTESY A MOSKALEV)

INTERIOR OF BRUCE ARNOLD MODELS' 1947 FLEETWOOD SIXTY SPECIAL. BAM-7. (COURTESY BRUCE ARNOLD MODELS MODEL MUSEUM COLLECTION)

Model-by-model

Historians point to the P-38 aircraft-inspired 1948 Cadillac as the birthplace of the finned rear fender, or 'fins' as they became known in the 1950s. The first 1:43 replica made of that year's car is Brooklin Models' sedanet. A few thousand units of this model were produced in black. Later the casting was lightly reworked and more chrome details added to produce a lovely Ardsley Green model.

THE HARBINGER OF EARLY '50S CADILLAC DESIGN WAS THE BREATHTAKING P-38 INSPIRED DESIGN FROM HARLEY EARL'S STUDIOS OF 1948. BROOKLIN MODELS CHOSE THE SERIES 62 SEDANET BODY STYLE AS THE SUBJECT FOR THIS 1992 RELEASE, SEEN HERE IN THE STANDARD DARK BLUE COLOR. BRK-40A. (COURTESY D MATHYSSEN)

CADILLAC REPRISED ITS SUCCESSFUL SIXTY SPECIAL IN 1948. THIS MODEL HAD A 4IN LONGER WHEELBASE THAN THE POPULAR SERIES 62 AS WELL AS A MORE LUXURIOUS INTERIOR AND SUBTLE EXTERIOR CHROME EMBELLISHMENTS. DESPITE BEING ALMOST A THIRD MORE EXPENSIVE THAN THE SERIES 62, CADILLAC FOUND 6561 EAGER BUYERS. PROTOTYPE BY BRUCE ARNOLD. (COURTESY BRUCE ARNOLD MODELS MODEL MUSEUM COLLECTION)

BROOKLIN MODELS' WHITE METAL 1948 CADILLAC SEDANET WAS REISSUED IN 2000 AS A SERIES 61 WITH MORE CHROME DETAILS. BRK-40A. (COURTESY D MATHYSSEN)

THIS 1948 SIXTY SPECIAL FINISHED IN A METALLIC MAROON IS A PROTOTYPE CREATED BY BRUCE ARNOLD. (COURTESY BRUCE ARNOLD MODELS MODEL MUSEUM COLLECTION)

1948 SIXTY SPECIAL SEDAN BY BRUCE ARNOLD FOR HIS MODEL MUSEUM COLLECTION. THIS SCALE MODEL PROTOTYPE FEATURES THE DISTINCTIVE REAR ROOF PILLAR CHROME SLASHES RESERVED FOR THE CADILLAC'S PREMIERE PASSENGER CAR.

'48 CADILLAC BY BROOKLIN, DETAILED BY STEVE WILLIAMS. (COURTESY S WILLIAMS)

(COURTESY BRUCE ARNOLD MODELS MODEL MUSEUM COLLECTION)

1948 FLEETWOOD SIXTY SPECIAL BY MINI MARQUE NO GRB-42. (COURTESY MINI MARQUE)

MINI MARQUE'S 1948 FLEETWOOD SIXTY SPECIAL WAS RELEASED IN 4 COLORS IN 2007. WITH ONLY 50 PIECES PRODUCED, THIS ARDSLEY GREEN NUMBER IS A RARE ITEM. NO GRB-42. (COURTESY MINI MARQUE)

HANDBUILT IN WHITE METAL, THE MINI MARQUE 1948 SIXTY SPECIAL REPLICA HAS MANY WONDERFUL DETAILS, SUCH AS THE FINELY SCULPTED TRUNK LID HANDLE SEEN HERE. (COURTESY MINI MARQUE)

THE CAR OF MOVIE STARS, THE 1949 CADILLAC S62 CONVERTIBLE WAS A HIGHLY COVETED MACHINE. DIE-CAST PRODUCER, YATMING MADE THOUSANDS OF THIS SURPRISINGLY ACCURATE MODEL, HERE WITH MINOR DETAILING BY JERRY RETTIG. THIS LITTLE REPLICA HAS EXCELLENT PROPORTIONS, TRULY IS 1:43 SCALE, AND CAN BE ACQUIRED FOR A FEW DOLLARS. (COURTESY J RETTIG)

1949 CADILLAC CONVERTIBLE IN WHITE METAL FROM WESTERN MODELS. RELEASED IN THE 1990s FOR AROUND $150, THE BUILDER EMPLOYED MODERN TECHNIQUES SUCH AS PHOTO-ETCHING FOR WIPERS AND EMBLEMS, AND OLDER METHODS SUCH AS FLAT BLACK PAINT INSIDE THE GRILLE AND TRANSLUCENT ENAMEL-PAINTED HEADLIGHTS TO PRODUCE THIS PLEASING REPLICA. WMS 68X. (COURTESY J RETTIG)

CADILLAC SHARED THE 'PILLARLESS CONVERTIBLE COUPE' DESIGN WITH BUICK AND OLDSMOBILE. INTRODUCED IN THE MIDDLE OF THE 1949 MODEL YEAR, THIS GROUNDBREAKING BODY STYLE WOULD CATCH ON QUICKLY WITH THE PUBLIC, BE WIDELY ADOPTED BY COMPETITORS AND REMAIN A GENERAL MOTORS DESIGN STAPLE UNTIL 1974. HANDBUILT WHITE METAL REPLICA BY WESTERN MODELS. WMS-68. (COURTESY J RETTIG)

MOTOR CITY USA PRODUCED HANDBUILT WHITE METAL REPLICAS OF THE 1949 CADILLAC IN 2 DOOR HARD-TOP, CONVERTIBLE, AND SEDANET BODY STYLES. A FEW HUNDRED TOTAL MODELS WERE ISSUED AT AROUND $250 EACH. THEY ARE VERY RARE AND WILL FETCH MULTIPLES OF THEIR ORIGINAL PRICE WHEN THEY INFREQUENTLY APPEAR FOR SALE TODAY. MC-20, 21, AND 19. (AUTHOR COLLECTION)

In mid-2007, not one but two builders issued scale models of the 1948 Sixty Special. First out of the gate was Bruce Arnold Models' resin-bodied replica with white metal parts available in Madeira Maroon and Vista Gray Metallic with two-toned interior (BAM-8). Retailing for $399, this model was being issued in tiny numbers, hand made by Bruce himself, often being built when ordered.

Mini Marque also released 200 total pieces of its '48 Fleetwood Sixty Special in Ardsley Green, Beldon Blue, Madeira Maroon and black (nos GRB 41-44). For $275 collectors received a white metal model handmade in England – the maker's first Cadillac since the new owners resurrected the company.

Handbuilt white metal 1949 Cadillac convertible and 2 door hard-top replicas from Western Models were produced until the firm's closure in 2007. That year Western introduced a very nicely proportioned 1949 sedanet in the $150 range.

Motor City USA also produced a 1949 convertible, 2 door hard-top, and sedanet. Issued in authentic colors, MCUSA's replica has the builder's usual attention to detail including interior door handles, instruments with actual increments on the dial faces and painted surfaces that somehow capture the look and

A HIGH DEGREE OF DETAIL DISTINGUISHES PREMIERE HANDBUILT MODELS FROM LESSER SCALE MODELS. IT IS HARD TO BELIEVE THAT THIS REALISTIC-LOOKING '49 CADILLAC INTERIOR IS 1/43RD THE SIZE OF THE ACTUAL AUTOMOBILE. MOTOR CITY USA NO MC-21. (AUTHOR COLLECTION)

A GLOSSY MADEIRA MAROON AND TAN LEATHER INTERIOR COMBINATION IS REPRESENTED IN MOTOR CITY USA'S VERSION OF THE 1949 SERIES 62 OPEN CONVERTIBLE. MC-21. (AUTHOR COLLECTION)

THE 1949 HARD-TOP CADILLAC CONVERTIBLE COUPE WAS AVAILABLE IN SEVERAL COLOR COMBINATIONS WITH MOST MODELS TWO-TONE. THIS MOTOR CITY USA REPLICA WAS AVAILABLE IN FRENCH GRAY WITH DARK GRAY ROOF. MC-20. (AUTHOR COLLECTION)

IN 1949 CADILLAC USED A NEW COMMERCIAL CHASSIS. 1861 SMOOTH RIDING CADILLAC SERVICE VEHICLES WERE MADE ON THE NEW CHASSIS. AFTER 2003, MOTOR CITY USA RELEASED SEVERAL RESIN-BODIED 1949 CADILLAC COMMERCIAL VEHICLES, SUCH AS THIS LIMOUSINE-STYLE HEARSE. (AUTHOR COLLECTION)

1949 CADILLAC SERIES 62 SEDANET IN A RICH CYPRESS GREEN. IT TOOK THE AUTHOR SEVERAL YEARS TO ACQUIRE THIS RARE MOTOR CITY USA MODEL NO 19. (AUTHOR COLLECTION)

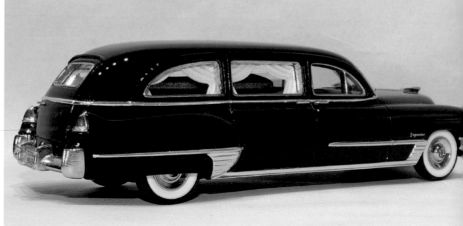

1949 CADILLAC SUPERIOR LIMOUSINE-STYLE HEARSE FROM MOTOR CITY USA. IN ADDITION TO FLAWLESS ASSEMBLY AND FINISHING, IT IS ATTENTION TO DETAIL, SUCH AS THE REALISTIC DRAPERIES, THAT PUT REPLICAS FROM THIS RESPECTED BUILDER IN A CLASS OF THEIR OWN. (AUTHOR COLLECTION)

THE LEGEND GOES THAT HARLEY EARL AND BILLIE MITCHELL TOOK THEIR DESIGNERS OUT TO VIEW THE LOCKHEED P-38 FIGHTER, AND THAT THIS PLANE'S DESIGN INSPIRED THE REAR TREATMENT OF THE 1948 CADILLAC. WHETHER THIS STORY IS TRUE OR NOT, THE DISTINCTIVE REAR FENDER AND TAILLIGHT TREATMENT REMAINED MUCH LIKE THAT SEEN HERE UNTIL THE END OF 1956. 1949 S62 SEDANET BY MOTOR CITY USA MC-19. (AUTHOR COLLECTION)

feel of the original materials. Add to this seemingly indestructible build quality, flawless finishing and a very low production run of fewer than 250 of each unit produced, and it is apparent why these models – less than a decade after their initial release – often sell at twice their original $250 issue price.

From the die-cast world, the only notable 1949 model is the Yat Ming/Road Champs convertible that is an accurate replica at an astonishing price of around $5.

Model-by-model — 1950-54

A styling change to Cadillac in 1950 introduced a more aggressive front appearance with infamous 'Dagmar' bumper adornments. Several builders have made 1950-53 Cadillac 1:43 scale models.

Much like the 1930-31 Solido Cadillac that spawned so many handbuilt variations, die-cast producers Vitesse (Portugal) and Ertl (USA) produced thousands of early '50s Cadillac models that were nice as toys, and with some massaging from the hands of a few craftspeople became inspired works of art.

Made in the early 1980s, Vitesse's Cadillacs were a 1950 convertible and a hard-top. Ertl's model was a 1952 S62 sedan. Dinky/Matchbox (UK) and Sun Star (China) released a 1953 Eldorado convertible based on Vitesse's 1953 version. All of these die-cast models were available on the aftermarket and some, notably Yat Ming, Road Champs, and Sun Star were still in some stores at the time of this book's printing.

The sophisticated one-piece bumper and grille of Vitesse's 1950-51 Cadillac reappeared (double plated) on a number of exquisite handbuilt resin and white metal replicas from Elegance Models.

AMR (France) created a beautifully detailed white metal 1950

CADILLAC-BASED SUPERIOR SERVICE CAR MODELED BY MOTOR CITY USA. (COURTESY MOTOR CITY USA)

1949 CADILLAC SUPERIOR LANDAU-STYLE LIMOUSINE FROM MOTOR CITY USA'S SUNSET COACH LINE. (COURTESY MOTOR CITY USA)

MOTOR CITY USA OFFERED A VARIETY OF LIVERIES FOR ITS 1949 CADILLAC AMBULANCES. A FEW HUNDRED WERE ISSUED IN TOTAL AT A PRICE OF $275, AND DISAPPEARED INTO THE HANDS OF COLLECTORS, MAKING THEM VIRTUALLY UNOBTAINABLE. (COURTESY MOTOR CITY USA)

2 door hard-top and convertible. These models came as a model kit and as a factory built-up. Comprising many parts, including the photo-etched variety of which AMR was a pioneering adopter, the model has a high degree of accuracy and tends to be a cut above many models issued during the early 1980s.

Late in 2007, Bruce Arnold Models introduced a new replica of the 1950 'Baby Cadillac' Series 61 sedan (BAM-10). This

POPULAR WITH THE MOTORING PUBLIC AND SCALE MODEL BUILDERS ARE CADILLACS FROM THE EARLY 1950s. A FASCINATING – ALBEIT UNLIKELY SUBJECT – IS THIS CADILLAC S61 2 DOOR HARD-TOP COUPE OUTFITTED AS A FIRE CHIEF'S CAR. DIE-CAST BY VITESSE IN THE EARLY 1980s, IT SHOWS THE TOY PRODUCER'S TECHNICAL EXPERTISE AND THE NEED TO STIMULATE DEMAND FOR PRODUCT BY CREATING A MULTITUDE OF VARIATIONS. VITESSE NO 284. (COURTESY J RETTIG)

THIS RED '51 COUPE DE VILLE DIE-CAST MODEL BY VITESSE HAS BEEN DETAILED; THE '53 ELDORADO CONVERTIBLE BESIDE IT HAS NOT. PAINTING THE CONVERTIBLE'S CHROME STEERING WHEEL AND ADDING BLACK TO THE BACK OF ITS GRILLE WOULD BE TWO STEPS TO IMPROVING THE ACCURACY OF THE CONVERTIBLE'S APPEARANCE. VITESSE NOS 21 AND 281. (COURTESY J RETTIG)

1950 S62 HARD-TOP COUPE AND CONVERTIBLE HANDBUILT WHITE METAL REPLICAS FROM ANDRE-MARIE RUF (AMR). THESE ARE THE FIRST TRULY ACCURATE MODELS OF A FIFTIES CADILLAC TO BE INTRODUCED IN THE LATE 1970S. THESE INTRICATE HANDBUILT MODELS WERE ALSO ISSUED AS KITS. AMR 04 AND 09. (COURTESY J RETTIG)

1950 CADILLAC 2 DOOR HARD-TOP COUPE BY AMR. NO 04. (COURTESY D LARSEN)

AMR'S 1950 CADILLAC AS BUILT BY ACCOMPLISHED PATTERNMAKER AND BUILDER, DICK ARMBRUSTER, WHO ADDED DELICATE PHOTO-ETCHED WIRE WHEELS AND MANY OTHER DETAILS, INCLUDING HIS SIGNATURE FENDER-MOUNTED RADIO AERIAL. AMR-308. (AUTHOR COLLECTION)

FOR 1950 THE SEDANET HAD DISAPPEARED FROM THE CADILLAC LINE-UP AND ALL 2 DOOR COUPES WERE OF THE NEW PILLARLESS DESIGN. FRANCE'S CLAUDE THIBIVILLIERS ADORED THE 1950-52 CADILLAC. FROM 1984 THROUGH THE 1990S HE CREATED ALMOST EVERY POSSIBLE VARIATION ON THE CADILLAC. PICTURED IS ELEGANCE MODELS' NO 109. (AUTHOR COLLECTION)

THE 1950 SERIES 62 COUPE WEIGHED 7LB LESS THAN 2 TONS. HERE IS ELEGANCE MODELS' NO109 WITH CHROME FOIL APPLIED TO THE UPPER PORTIONS BY THE AUTHOR. (AUTHOR COLLECTION)

CADILLAC DIVISION'S SMALLEST AND LOWEST PRICED 1950 MODEL SHARED ITS BODY WITH THE BUICK SUPER. HOWEVER, THE S61'S APPEARANCE WAS ALL CADILLAC. SLIGHTLY MORE MANEUVRABLE IN TIGHT QUARTERS, IT FIT IN SMALLER GARAGES AND HAD HIGH RESALE VALUE BECAUSE, AFTER ALL, IT WAS A CADILLAC! ELEGANCE MODELS' NO 198. (AUTHOR COLLECTION)

HEADS TURNED WHEN A 1950 S62 CONVERTIBLE CRUISED DOWN THE STREET. AN IMPRESSIVE AUTOMOBILE, ESPECIALLY WITH CONTINENTAL KIT, CLOSE TO 7000 BUYERS SHELLED OUT THE $3654 REQUIRED TO OWN ONE. ELEGANCE MODELS' NO 139. (AUTHOR COLLECTION)

1951 CADILLAC MODELS CHANGED SLIGHTLY WITH THE ADDITION OF AN 'EGG CRATE' PATTERN ON THE LOWER BUMPER ENDS. PICTURED ARE SCALE MODELS OF THE S62 CONVERTIBLE. CLOCKWISE FROM LOWER LEFT: ELEGANCE MODELS' NO 118, NO 118 BIS, TOP UP NO 118. (AUTHOR COLLECTION)

resin-bodied replica debuted in a rich Triumph Blue Metallic with gray interior or Vista Gray Metallic. With an exclusive price of just under $400, very few units were likely to be produced. From the builder: "Fully finished from the 'sombrero' wheel covers to the twin fog lamps mounted in the grille, a separate chrome rear view mirror and antenna are also part of the exterior package. Other chrome-plated parts include bumpers, windshield wipers, door handles, grille and wheels. All other trim is expertly applied chrome foil. Badges and emblems are reproduced with full-color decals and every interior detail is represented from the pattern on the seats and doors to the readable dash gauges. Stalks, winders, handles and an inside rear-view mirror are also present."

Sun Models (UK) added to the selection of early 1950s Cadillac replicas by re-mastering Ertl's die-cast S62 into an S75 long-wheelbased limousine.

THESE 1950 S61 SEDAN REPLICAS BY ELEGANCE ARE WELL DETAILED. BRIGHTWORK IS ACTUALLY THIN STRIPS OF PLATED POLYSTYRENE AS OPPOSED TO THE MORE COMMON CHROME FOIL. ELEGANCE MODELS' NO 198. (AUTHOR COLLECTION)

1950 SIXTY SPECIAL BY ELEGANCE MODELS. BUILDER, CLAUDE THIBIVILLIERS, OFFERED A VARIETY OF AUTHENTIC COLORS FOR HIS CADILLAC REPLICAS. THIS IS A SHINY METALLIC, 'FIESTA IVORY'. NO 111. (AUTHOR COLLECTION)

THE FLEETWOOD SIXTY SPECIAL RETAINED ITS STATUS IN 1950 AS THE TOP OF THE LINE 'SELF-DRIVEN' CADILLAC. 13,755 BUYERS WOULD PAY A PREMIUM TO OWN THE LARGER CAR VS 41,890 S62 OWNERS. ELEGANCE MODELS' NO 111. (AUTHOR COLLECTION)

1950 SIXTY SPECIAL. ELEGANCE MODELS' NO 111. (AUTHOR COLLECTION)

1951 CADILLAC PHILIP WRIGHT-DESIGNED COACHCRAFT CUSTOM STATION WAGON ON SERIES 62 CHASSIS. ELEGANCE MODELS' NO 131. (AUTHOR COLLECTION)

1951 CADILLAC COACHCRAFT STATION WAGON WITH LUGGAGE RACK AND CONTINENTAL KIT. ELEGANCE MODELS' NO 131. (AUTHOR COLLECTION)

1951 CADILLAC STATION WAGON OBTAINED FROM ELEGANCE MODELS CLAUDE THIBIVILLIER'S PRIVATE COLLECTION. NO 131. (AUTHOR COLLECTION)

METICULOUS ATTENTION TO DETAIL, AS EVIDENCED BY THE PRECISELY APPLIED ROOF-MOUNTED CHROME LUGGAGE RUB STRIPS, IS AN ELEGANCE MODELS HALLMARK. ELEGANCE NO 131. (AUTHOR COLLECTION)

A LATE ISSUE FROM ELEGANCE MODELS, THIS 1951 CADILLAC STATION WAGON HAS THE FULL COLOR HOOD EMBLEM AND ABUNDANT CHROME. NO 131. (AUTHOR COLLECTION)

THE DERHAM COACH CO OF ROSEMONT, PENNSYLVANIA, CREATED MANY FINE CADILLAC-BASED LIMOUSINES CHARACTERIZED BY A DISTINCTIVE ENCLOSED PASSENGER COMPARTMENT. HERE ARE A PAIR OF 1950 DERHAM CADILLAC SCALE MODELS FROM ELEGANCE. MODEL NOS 124 AND 108B. (AUTHOR COLLECTION)

THIS PHOTO OF A NICELY FINISHED 1950 S75 BY ELEGANCE MODELS SHOWS PATTERNED BROADCLOTH UPHOLSTERY. NO 108. (AUTHOR COLLECTION)

1950 CADILLAC FORMAL LIMOUSINE WITH ENCLOSED REAR WINDOW BY DERHAM COACH. THIS RESIN HANDBUILT MODEL HAS A FAUX VINYL ROOF. ISSUED IN 1984, IT IS ELEGANCE MODELS' NO 108B. (AUTHOR COLLECTION)

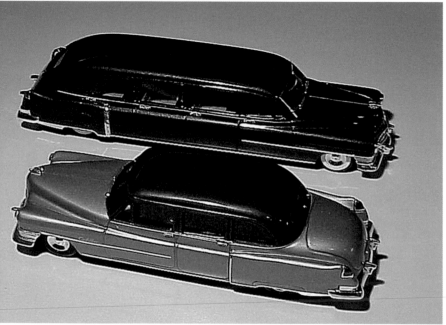

HESS AND EISENHARDT BUILT AN 8 DOOR AIRPORT LIMOUSINE (BACKGROUND) ON THE 1950 S86 COMMERCIAL CHASSIS. ELEGANCE MODELS' NO 137. IN THE FOREGROUND IS A 1950 S75 HANDBUILT RESIN MODEL, NO 108 FROM ELEGANCE MODELS. (COURTESY D LARSEN)

TWENTY OF THESE UNUSUAL 6 DOOR 1951 CADILLAC LIMOUSINES WERE MADE FOR SAUDI POTENTATE, IBN SEOUD, TO TRANSPORT HIS HAREM. NOTE THE MIRRORED WINDOWS THAT WERE USED TO CONCEAL THE PASSENGERS. IT IS SAID THAT THE INTERIOR DIVISION GLASS WAS ALSO MIRRORED TO PREVENT THE DRIVER AND FOOTMAN FROM SEEING THE SHEIK'S WIVES. ELEGANCE MODELS' NO 117. (AUTHOR COLLECTION)

1950 CADILLAC LIMOUSINE-STYLE HEARSE AND LANDAU HEARSE BY ELEGANCE MODELS. NOS 124 AND 116. (AUTHOR COLLECTION)

CADILLACS WERE POPULAR AS FLOWER CARS. HERE IS A PAIR OF MILLER METEOR CONVERSIONS MODELED BY ELEGANCE OF FRANCE IN 1986. NO 107. (AUTHOR COLLECTION)

SOME OF THE FIRST REPLICAS OF THE 1950 CADILLAC FROM ELEGANCE WERE THESE AMBULANCES THAT WERE CRAFTED IN 1983. THE WHITE VERSION IS A MILLER METEOR AND THE RED NEW YORK FIRE DEPARTMENT, A SUPERIOR. NOS 102 AND 103. (AUTHOR COLLECTION)

ROTH CADILLAC COMMISSIONED ELEGANCE MODELS TO PRODUCE THIS SCARCE PROMOTIONAL 1950 CADILLAC PARTS CAR. (COURTESY RAY PASZKIEWICZ, JR COLLECTION)

BUILT ON A 122IN WHEELBASE SHARED WITH LESSER BUICK AND OLDSMOBILE MODELS, THE 1950 CADILLAC S61 HAD 14,619 BUYERS. BRUCE ARNOLD MODELS BAM-10. (COURTESY BRUCE ARNOLD MODELS MODEL MUSEUM COLLECTION)

PROFILE – 1952 CADILLAC EXECUTIVE SPEEDSTER BY ELEGANCE MODELS

DURING THE KOREAN WAR, GM DESIGN CHIEF, HARLEY EARL, COMMISSIONED A SPECIAL 1952 CADILLAC ROADSTER FOR HAROLD R 'BILL' BOYER, WHO WAS IN CHARGE OF TANK PRODUCTION FOR THE COMPANY. TO PRODUCE THIS ONE-OF-A-KIND MODEL, THE DESIGNERS

TOOK A 1951 S62 COUPE AND REDUCED ITS WHEELBASE BY 10IN AND OVERALL HEIGHT BY 6IN. DROPPED INTO THE ENGINE BAY WAS A SPECIAL 230HP ENGINE SIMILAR TO THE 1953 ELDORADO, AN IMPRESSIVE TOP THAT DISAPPEARED UNDER A LID BETWEEN THE CABIN AND TRUNK LID (SHADES OF THE '53 ELDORADO AS WELL), AND AN AIRCRAFT-INSPIRED INSTRUMENT PANEL WITH GAUGES FOR MANIFOLD PRESSURE, TACHOMETER, OIL TEMPERATURE, AND CLOCK.

ELEGANCE MODELS' CLAUDE THIBIVILLIERS CREATED THREE REPLICAS OF THIS MODEL, WHICH HE DUBBED THE 'EXECUTIVE SPEEDSTER'. PICTURED IS ONE FROM THE AUTHOR'S COLLECTION, ACQUIRED FROM MONSIEUR THIBIVILLIERS IN 2006. IT IS TRUE TO THE ORIGINAL MODEL IN EVERY DETAIL, INCLUDING THE AFOREMENTIONED GAUGES AND WONDERFUL WIRE WHEELS. AN IMPRESSIVE SCALE MODEL. (AUTHOR COLLECTION)

CADILLAC MOTOR DIVISION'S 50TH ANNIVERSARY WAS IN 1952. DESPITE RESTRICTIONS DUE TO THE KOREAN CONFLICT, CADILLAC MANAGED TO FIND 42,625 BUYERS FOR ITS MOST POPULAR MODEL, THE SERIES 62 SEDAN. ERTL MODELS MANUFACTURED SEVERAL THOUSAND OF THESE FINE DIE-CAST TOYS THROUGHOUT THE 1980s. No 2541. (COURTESY J RETTIG)

CADILLAC SERIES 75 LIMOUSINE. BASED UPON ERTL'S WELL-PROPORTIONED DIE-CAST SEDAN, ROD WARD'S SUN MOTORS COMPANY OF ENGLAND CREATED THIS RESIN AND WHITE METAL 1:43 SCALE MODEL NO 123. (AUTHOR COLLECTION)

The only handmade 1953 Cadillac replicas are from Bruce Arnold Models (USA). They are a highly-detailed Sixty Special sedan, Eldorado convertible, and a custom 'Aretha' convertible.

1954's face-lift of the Cadillac saw a lower profile with a longer appearance. Mini Marque '43' renders this well in its intricate handbuilt white metal convertible – the first 1:43 scale model of a 1954 Cadillac. It has glossy paintwork and delicate photo-etched replica Kelsey-Hayes wire wheels (see sidebar).

In 2007 the new Mini Marque company took the '54 Eldorado and customized it into the 'Piano Key Cadillac' complete with black and white piano key upholstery and chrome mini baby grand pianos on each fender. A tour de force that celebrated a "certain famous celebrity", this $275 replica was beloved by collectors who value the more offbeat subjects.

PROFILE – 1953 CADILLAC SIXTY SPECIAL BY BRUCE ARNOLD MODELS

THE SECOND MODEL BY BRUCE ARNOLD WAS THE 1953 SIXTY SPECIAL. THIS FULLY FINISHED AND COMPLETELY DETAILED MODEL HAD SEVERAL SMALL BUT NOTICEABLE DETAIL IMPROVEMENTS WHEN COMPARED TO THE FIRST RELEASE ELDORADO. CADILLAC USED VERY SUBTLE CUES TO DISTINGUISH DIFFERENT LINES IN THE EARLY '50S; THE SERIES SIXTY SPECIAL HAD A FOUR INCH LONGER WHEELBASE THAN THE SERIES 62 (ONE DESIGNATION WAS SPELLED, THE OTHER NUMBERED) WITH THE 'BIGGER' CAR IDENTIFIED BY WIDER ROCKER PANEL MOLDINGS ON THE REAR FENDERS AND EIGHT SMALL VERTICAL CHROME HASH MARKS BEHIND THE VERTICAL SCOOP. FLEETWOOD BODIES HAD GOLD HOOD AND TRUNK 'VEES', AND A SMALL GOLD FLEETWOOD SCRIPT ON THE REAR DECK.

BAM MODELED ALL THOSE FEATURES PRECISELY, ALONG WITH VIRTUALLY EVERY OTHER DETAIL ON THE CAR. EVEN THE TRUNK LOCK CYLINDER HAS BEEN CAREFULLY PAINTED SILVER. THERE WAS A LOT OF PAINSTAKING HANDWORK ON THIS MODEL, WITH THE HOOD STRIPE, FENDER SPEARS, ROCKER PANEL MOLDINGS, AND WINDOW SURROUNDS ALL CAST IN CRISP RELIEF AND EXPERTLY 'PLATED' WITH CHROME FOIL. TINTED FOIL WAS USED FOR THE GOLD 'VEES', WHILE THE CADILLAC BADGE, 'FLEETWOOD' SCRIPT, AND THE SERIES SIXTY HASH MARKS WERE DONE WITH DECALS THAT WERE APPLIED BEFORE THE FINAL CLEAR GLOSS COAT.

THE BUMPERS, ACCURATE 'SOMBRERO' WHEELS, BEAUTIFULLY DONE 'SEE-THROUGH' EGG-CRATE GRILLE, HEADLIGHT BEZELS AND EYEBROWS, TAILLIGHT HOUSINGS, VERTICAL SCOOP ON THE REAR FENDERS, AND OTHER SMALL DETAILS (INCLUDING THE TINY DOOR HANDLES) ARE SEPARATE CHROME-PLATED METAL CASTINGS.

CRAFTSMANSHIP WAS FIRST-RATE THROUGHOUT; THERE'S NOT A FLAW OR BLEMISH OF ANY KIND. HEADLIGHTS HAVE SEPARATE CLEAR LENSES WHILE TAILLIGHT LENSES HAVE BEEN CAREFULLY PAINTED WITH TRANSLUCENT RED.

INTERIOR DETAILS INCLUDED AUTHENTIC UPHOLSTERY PATTERNS IN TWO SHADES FOR THE SEATS, WITH THE CORRECT BLUE AND BLUE-GRAY COLORS AND METALLIC SILVER ON THE DOOR PANELS. THE SILVER SECTION CORRECTLY ALIGNS WITH THE CHROME CENTRAL PORTION OF THE DASHBOARD, TOO. THE GLARE SHIELD IS THE CORRECT BLUE COLOR AND THE SPEEDOMETER FACE HAS BEEN PAINTED; LEGIBLE INSTRUMENTS WERE STILL IN THE FUTURE. THE STEERING WHEEL WAS ESPECIALLY WELL DONE WITH A BLUE AND WHITE RIM, CHROME HORN RING, AND TRANSLUCENT RED CENTER. OF COURSE, THE INNER HANDLES AND CRANKS ARE SEPARATE PLATED PIECES.

ALL OF THESE DETAILS WOULDN'T AMOUNT TO MUCH IF THE BASICS WEREN'T UP TO SCRATCH, BUT BAM'S CADILLAC COMPARED VERY WELL WITH

THE BEST EUROPEAN HANDBUILT MODELS OF THE TIME. ITS BODY CASTING WAS VERY CLEAN AND SMOOTH, WITH GOOD CRISP PANEL LINES AND A MIRROR-SMOOTH EXTERIOR FINISH IN AUTHENTIC COLORS, SUCH AS THIS EXAMPLE'S COBALT BLUE OVER PASTORAL BLUE. LINES AND PROPORTIONS MATCH PHOTOS OF THE ACTUAL MOTORCAR, AND ALL DETAILS ARE RIGHT ON THE MONEY. THE SAME GOES FOR MAJOR DIMENSIONS; THIS MODEL IS 1:43 SCALE, PERIOD. ALL IN ALL, BRUCE ARNOLD MODELS' 1953 SIXTY SPECIAL IS AN EXCELLENT HANDBUILT WHITE METAL MODEL. WHILE IT WASN'T CHEAP AT $269, PAINSTAKING HANDWORK NEVER WAS, AND YOU GET A LOT OF THAT WITH THIS MODEL. (THIS REVIEW USES EXCERPTS, WITH PERMISSION, FROM AN ARTICLE BY WAYNE MOYER THAT APPEARED IN *MODEL CAR HUB* IN 1999. PHOTOS COURTESY BRUCE ARNOLD MODELS MODEL MUSEUM COLLECTION)

IN 1953 THE DRAMATIC AND EXTREMELY EXPENSIVE ELDORADO DEBUTED. AT ALMOST TWICE THE PRICE OF THE S62 CONVERTIBLE, A CUSTOMER COULD HAVE A CUT-DOWN WINDSHIELD, CURVY 'DARRIN DIP' TYPE DOORS, FULLY ENCLOSED TOP, CUSTOM TRIM, WIRE WHEELS, AND A DISTINCTIVE BADGE. 532 BUYERS PURCHASED THE NEWEST MEMBER OF THE CADILLAC FAMILY. HERE, THE S62 AND ELDORADO ARE CONTRASTED IN SCALE MODELS FROM VITESSE. NOS 282 AND 280. (COURTESY J RETTIG)

FOR 1953, THE 'MID-SIZED' CADILLAC (BETWEEN THE S62 AND S75) WAS THE SIXTY SPECIAL, WHICH CADILLAC DUBBED ITS LARGEST 'OWNER DRIVEN' SEDAN. BRUCE ARNOLD MODELS NO 2 IN THE AUTHENTIC COLORS OF GLOSS GREEN OVER EMERALD GREEN. (AUTHOR COLLECTION)

BUILDER, BRUCE ARNOLD CHOSE THE 1953 ELDORADO CONVERTIBLE AS THE SUBJECT FOR HIS FIRST HANDBUILT WHITE METAL REPLICA. ONE OF *MOBILIA MAGAZINES*' TOP 10 COLLECTIBLES FOR 1999, A TOTAL OF 200 WERE MADE, WITH 50 EACH IN RED, WHITE, BLACK, AND POWDER BLUE. THESE MODELS WERE INTRODUCED AT A PRICE OF $239. PICTURED IS A SPECIALLY DETAILED PROTOTYPE. NO BAM-1. (AUTHOR COLLECTION)

THIS IS WHAT HANDBUILT REPLICAS ARE ALL ABOUT – UNIQUENESS. BRUCE ARNOLD CREATED ONLY ONE OF THESE OPEN SIXTY SPECIAL TOWN CARS. IT SOLD QUICKLY AT AN ON-LINE AUCTION TO A RESPECTED CADILLAC MODEL COLLECTOR. VISIBLE HERE ARE FEATURES SUCH AS REAR 'SUICIDE DOOR' AND CHROME 'BASKET HANDLE' ROOF BAR. (COURTESY MODEL MUSEUM COLLECTION, BRUCE ARNOLD MODELS)

BRUCE ARNOLD MODELS' TOWN CAR HAS A DETAILED DRIVER'S DIVISION WINDOW AND HIGHLY-DETAILED INTERIOR. (COURTESY MODEL MUSEUM COLLECTION, BRUCE ARNOLD MODELS)

THE CUSTOM 1953 SIXTY SPECIAL TOWN CAR HAD SEPARATE SOFT-TOPS FOR BOTH DRIVER AND PASSENGER COMPARTMENTS. BRUCE ARNOLD MODELS' ONE-OF-A-KIND MODEL. (COURTESY MODEL MUSEUM COLLECTION, BRUCE ARNOLD MODELS)

FOR 1953, GM UNVEILED THE ORLEANS MOTORAMA CONCEPT CAR; A PREVIEW OF WHAT WOULD BECOME A POPULAR BODY STYLE, THE 4 DOOR HARD-TOP. THIS WAS THE FIRST TO FEATURE 'SUICIDE' DOORS, PRECEDING THE FAMOUS PRODUCTION 1957 ELDORADO BROUGHAM BY FOUR YEARS. TO MAKE IT, FISHER BODY LENGTHENED A COUPE deVILLE BODY AND MOUNTED IT ON THE 130IN WHEELBASE 60 SPECIAL CHASSIS. PICTURED HERE IS AN EXTREMELY LOW PRODUCTION 1:43 SCALE REPLICA FROM BRUCE ARNOLD MODELS. (COURTESY MODEL MUSEUM COLLECTION, BRUCE ARNOLD MODELS)

FROM THE $849 ORLEANS MODEL DESCRIPTION: "IT IS COMPLETE FROM ITS MANY EMBLEMS AND BADGES TO THE BEIGE 'PADDED' ROOF. SEPARATE CHROME PARTS INCLUDE WINDSHIELD WIPERS, INSIDE AND OUTSIDE DOOR HANDLES, ANTENNA AND AN INSIDE REAR VIEW MIRROR. DASH GAUGES ARE ALL FAITHFULLY REPRODUCED WITH FULLY READABLE DECALS. EVERY OTHER INTERIOR DETAIL IS REPRESENTED FROM THE PATTERN ON THE SEATS AND DOORS TO THE SHIFTER AND TURN SIGNAL STALKS."
(COURTESY MODEL MUSEUM COLLECTION, BRUCE ARNOLD MODELS)

THIS VERSION OF ARNOLD'S '53 ORLEANS ISSUED IN 2007 IS FINISHED IN DAMASCUS GRAY, THE COLOR OF THE MODEL THAT WAS DISPLAYED IN NEW YORK'S PRESTIGIOUS WALDORF ASTORIA HOTEL. AN ALTERNATE COLOR WAS TURKISH COPPER.
(COURTESY MODEL MUSEUM COLLECTION, BRUCE ARNOLD MODELS).

AN EXAMPLE OF THE DETAIL DEMANDED IN THESE FINE REPLICAS IS THE ORLEANS DECAL ARTWORK.
(COURTESY MODEL MUSEUM COLLECTION, BRUCE ARNOLD MODELS)

1954 CADILLAC FLEETWOOD SERIES SIXTY SPECIAL IN ARLINGTON GREEN METALLIC FROM BRUCE ARNOLD MODELS. BAM-6.
(COURTESY MODEL MUSEUM COLLECTION, BRUCE ARNOLD MODELS)

TOURING ON GM'S MOTORAMA CIRCUIT IN 1954 WAS THE ALUMINIUM-TOPPED CADILLAC EL CAMINO. THOUGH ITS NAME WOULD SURFACE ON A CHEVROLET IN THE LATE 1950s, OTHER FEATURES – SUCH AS THE REAR FENDER AND TAILLIGHT TREATMENT – WOULD APPEAR A YEAR LATER ON THE ELDORADO. THIS MODEL IS A WHITE METAL REPLICA HANDBUILT FOR GREAT AMERICAN DREAM MACHINES. GADM NO 7.
(COURTESY J RETTIG)

PROFILE – 1954 CADILLAC ELDORADO BY MINI MARQUE '43'

CADILLAC MOTOR DIVISION'S ELDORADO FOR 1954 WAS STILL REGARDED AS A 'SPECIAL' MODEL, BUT HAD FEWER FEATURES TO DISTINGUISH IT FROM THE SERIES 62 MODEL. LESS COSTLY THAN THE 1953 VERSION, 2150 ELDORADO UNITS FOUND BUYERS. MINI MARQUE '43'S SPLENDID 1954 ELDORADO (MMQ-24) WAS AVAILABLE UP UNTIL THE PASSING, IN 2002, OF THE COMPANY'S FOUNDER, RICHARD BRIGGS. BUILT IN NUMBERS OF ONLY A FEW HUNDRED, THE MOST COMMON VERSION – THE OPEN CONVERTIBLE – HAS APPEARED PERHAPS TWICE A YEAR ON EBAY. THIS IS FOLLOWED BY THE LESS COMMON TOP UP VERSION AND, LATE IN THE MODEL RUN, MINI MARQUE '43' ADDED A MORE EXPENSIVE MODEL EQUIPPED WITH CONTINENTAL KIT IN BOTH OPEN AND CLOSED STYLES. THE BUILDER'S WEBSITE ALSO LISTED AN S62 HARD-TOP WITH CONTINENTAL KIT THAT THE AUTHOR HAS NOT SEEN. VERY FEW, IF ANY, OF THESE MODELS WERE ISSUED.

MINI MARQUE'S CADILLAC IS AN EXCELLENT REPLICA THAT HAS SOME HIGH END FEATURES SUCH AS A PHOTO-ETCHED GRILLE WITH BLACK BACKGROUND, AND HEADLIGHT LENSES SET INTO CORRECT FLUTED CHROME TRIM RINGS THAT TRACE THE SCULPTING OF THE BODY. THE BUILDER USES, TO GOOD EFFECT, PAINT AND TRANSFERS TO MIMIC THE HEAVILY-CHROMED REAR FENDER TREATMENT. THE INTERIOR IS CAREFULLY DETAILED WITH DOOR HANDLES, POWER WINDOW BUTTONS, CHROMED STEERING WHEEL HORN RING, AND AN ACCURATELY MOLDED AND DETAILED DASH. INTERIOR UPHOLSTERY IS TWO-TONE BUT LOOKS A LITTLE PLASTIC-LIKE. THE HIGHLIGHT OF THIS MODEL IS THE FABULOUS PHOTO-ETCHED WIRE WHEELS. THESE EXTREMELY DELICATE PIECES ELEVATE THE OVERALL ACCURACY AND VALUE OF THE MODEL. THE DEMAND FOR MINI MARQUE '43'S 1954 ELDORADO HAS KEPT PACE WITH MOST OF THE BUILDER'S 1950S OFFERINGS, WHICH IS TO SAY, TRADING STEADILY AT PRICES 60-100 PER CENT OF THE ORIGINAL $180 OR SO. (AUTHOR COLLECTION)

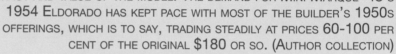

CHEVROLET AND GMC LIGHT TRUCKS 7

GENERAL MOTORS HAS BEEN A LEADING PRODUCER OF LIGHT TRUCKS SINCE 1902 when Rapid Trucks founder, Max Grabowsky, sold his first truck to the American Garment Co of Detroit, and William Durant's subsequent 1908 acquisition of Rapid. The first trucks to appear with the 'GMC' emblem rolled off the line in 1911. GMC trucks did the company proud during WWI with the ¾ ton GMC Model 16 being the US Army's primary mechanized ambulance as well as a troop carrier. Throughout the 1920s and early 1930s, GMC built many mid- to heavy-duty trucks and buses that sometimes employed components from Buick and Cadillac. Eventually, its light duty products – such as pickups and panel delivery models – became shared with Chevrolet.

Chevrolet's focus during the early days was on passenger automobile production. Chevrolet's first truck appeared in 1918. It was the no 490 ½ ton light delivery chassis cowl that required the buyer to add the appropriate cab and box. It was not until 1931 that Chevrolet produced a pickup, panel, sedan delivery, and canopy body style made entirely in the General Motors factory.

In 1937, customers saw a greater convergence with Chevrolet

SOME FEATURED GENERAL MOTORS LIGHT TRUCK MODELS

YEAR	MODEL	MANUFACTURER
1936	CHEVROLET/GMC SUBURBAN	ELC
1937	GMC PANEL VAN	ERTL/MATCHBOX
1941	CHEVROLET PANEL VAN	DURHAM CLASSICS
1948	CHEVROLET COE	ERTL/MATCHBOX
1949	PONTIAC PICKUP	R & J
1950	CHEVROLET/GMC PANEL VAN	ERTL
1953	CHEVROLET PICKUP	DURHAM CLASSICS
1953	PONTIAC SEDAN DELIVERY/PICKUP	BROOKLIN MODELS

1953 CHEVROLET ½TON PICKUP BY DURHAM CLASSICS. DC-28. (AUTHOR COLLECTION)

and GMC light duty designs emerging from the same Art and Color Studio. From this point on, the Suburban, panel delivery and pickup models would have only minor styling differences to suggest whether they were a GMC or Chevrolet.

Model-by-model   1929-47

1:43 scale models of pre-1937 General Motors light trucks are quite rare. Hallmark Card Stores sold a 1929 Chevrolet fire truck Christmas tree ornament and DGM (UK) made a 1934 panel van. Ashton Models (USA) made some early 1930s Chevrolets that could possibly be converted into a truck. Elegance issued a scarce Cadillac 1930 fire truck and Nostalgic Miniatures released a white metal 1936 Panel Van as well. Perhaps the best bet for a truck model of this vintage would be from Jerry Rettig's Enchantment Land Coachbuilders. Jerry has made a number of variations of the 1936 Chevrolet Panel Truck, including a terrifically detailed Suburban.

The first mass-produced 1937 light truck is a nice die-cast panel van made in 1987 by Matchbox for its Models of Yesteryear series. Available in a variety of liveries, including Jim Beam, US Post Office, Coca-Cola and as an ambulance, the little Matchbox

A NICE MODEL OF A 1929 CHEVROLET PUMPER THAT IS ACTUALLY A CHRISTMAS ORNAMENT BY HALLMARK. (COURTESY J RETTIG)

AN UNUSUAL 1931 CADILLAC PUMPER TRUCK BY ELEGANCE MODELS. NO 36. (COURTESY C HARDEGGER)

A VERY LIMITED PRODUCTION HANDBUILT REPLICA 1936 CHEVROLET SUBURBAN BY ENCHANTMENT LAND COACHBUILDERS. (COURTESY J RETTIG)

1938 GMC RESCUE YFE-10 BY MATCHBOX. (COURTESY J RETTIG)

A POPULAR AND INEXPENSIVE DIE-CAST SCALE MODEL OF THE 1938 CHEVROLET PANEL VAN WAS MADE BY ERTL. NO 2824. (COURTESY J RETTIG)

1936 CHEVROLET PANEL VAN, NOSTALGIC MINIATURES 248 (COURTESY J RETTIG)

1941 CHEVROLET FROM MATCHBOX. NO YTC-01M. (COURTESY J RETTIG)

is quite faithful to the original, albeit a little shy of details such as windshield wipers, windshield trim, and brand emblems. Door handles and trim moldings are in relief as is typical of inexpensive die-cast models. Thousands of copies were made so the little die-cast truck should be available on the secondary market. Thirty different vendors were listing the model when the eBay auction site was checked in June 2007.

The distinctive 1941 Chevrolet pickup has been modeled as a die-cast by Matchbox Collectibles and Gearbox. It has nice proportions and an opening hood to reveal an engine as well as opening driver and passenger doors. The Gearbox version was still being produced at the time of writing and is quite a bargain at $10-15 retail.

In the handbuilt white metal field, Durham Classics released a Dick Armbruster mastered 1941 Chevrolet panel truck. Many variations of this replica were available from around 1992. Later in the 1990s a windowed Suburban Carryall became available. There were some interesting and amusing versions created by the builder, including a railcar model complete with O scale train wheels and a length of track, a Niagara Falls Tours model with passenger luggage stacked on the top, and a touring band model with band leader Acker Bilk carrying his clarinet and sporting his trademark goatee. In the early 2000s a final variation of the panel delivery was issued. Known as a 'canopy express', this model has open sides and rear to display and access the vendor's wares. In the Temple's Market edition, of which 300 were issued, the openings reveal baskets of brightly colored fruits and vegetables.

Unlike the automobiles produced by GM, the appearance of Chevrolet and GMC trucks changed little during 1948-54. There have been about half-a-dozen nice scale replicas of the makers' trucks from this era.

Model-by-model   1948-54

One of the first truck replicas from 1948-54 is neither a GMC nor Chevrolet. The 1949 Pontiac was modeled in scale by R&J Miniatures/SAMS (UK) as a somewhat whimsical pickup or flatbed truck. Handbuilt in white metal, the little truck came in a wide variety of liveries and configurations, sometimes with figures, packing crates and clipboards.

A substantial model built during the early 1990s using traditional techniques such as scraping through the paint to reveal the five raised 'silver streaks', the R&J pickup has a good level of detail, including clear headlight lenses set into chrome bezels, separate chromed door handles, radio aerial and 'Chief' hood mascot. The front clip has a one-piece grille surround that would benefit from a blackwashed background or the superb photo-etching that the builder later adopted for its splendid 1959 Oldsmobile. Despite having superior detail to the competing Brooklin and Durham Classics models of the period, the R&J Pontiac has tended to hover around the $100 mark and is still available at a few stockists. There is a reputed 1952 Pontiac pickup model from the same maker as referenced in Jerry Rettig's

DURHAM CLASSICS ISSUED SEVERAL DIFFERENT VERSIONS OF THE 1941 CHEVROLET PANEL VAN; THIS ONE HAS LABATTS' BREWERY LIVERY. DC-12. (COURTESY J RETTIG)

1941 CHEVROLET PANEL VAN IN FRESNO BEE NEWSPAPER LIVERY. DC-12. (COURTESY COLLECTORS ANTIQUES)

BALLY'S CASINO COMMISSIONED DURHAM CLASSICS TO PRODUCE THIS 1941 CHEVROLET PANEL DELIVERY WITH UNUSUAL FENDER SKIRTS. DC-12. (COURTESY COLLECTORS ANTIQUES)

A VARIATION ON THE 1941 CHEVROLET PANEL VAN WAS DURHAM CLASSICS' CANOPY EXPRESS. DC-35. (COURTESY DURHAM CLASSICS)

1941 CHEVROLET PANEL TRUCK CANOPY EXPRESS PRODUCE TRUCK. NUMBER 50 OF 300 CREATED BY DURHAM CLASSICS. DC-35. (COURTESY S WILLIAMS)

1941 CHEVROLET PANEL TRUCK DURHAM CLASSICS. DC-35. (COURTESY S WILLIAMS)

THE CANOPY EXPRESS 1941 CHEVROLET WAS MADE AVAILABLE WITH A SCREEN. DC-35A. (COURTESY DURHAM CLASSICS)

A FULLY DRESSED NEW YORK TIMES CANOPY EXPRESS '41 CHEVROLET HAS QUITE A BIT OF DETAIL. DC-35. (COURTESY DURHAM CLASSICS)

1941 SUBURBAN CARRYALL IN A FUN NIAGARA FALLS TOUR COMPANY LIVERY COMPLETE WITH LUGGAGE. DC-17. (COURTESY WWW.ARTCRAFTMODEL.DE)

DURHAM CLASSICS CREATED THIS SET, WHICH INCLUDES MUSICIAN/BAND LEADER, ACKER BILK, WHOSE HIT SONG *STRANGER ON THE SHORE*, TOPPED THE CHARTS FOR SEVERAL WEEKS IN 1961. THIS OMEN FIGURE VERSION IS OF BILK 20 YEARS EARLIER. DC-17. (AUTHOR COLLECTION)

American Wheels: A Reference, and a few 1952 sedan delivery models were made that are scarce today.

Another car-truck combination was Record Models' 1950 Chevrolet ute. Molded in resin, it is a very good model. It shares

1941 CHEVROLET OUTFITTED AS A CHICAGO FIRE DEPT RESCUE VEHICLE FOR THE ANNUAL STRICTLY 43RD SHOW. DC-19. (COURTESY DURHAM CLASSICS)

many characteristics with Record's other 1950 Chevrolet body styles discussed in the Chevrolet chapter.

Brooklin Models produced a 1953 sedan delivery and pickup starting in 1989 and well into the 1990s. This was a time of prodigious growth at the Bath, England based builder with collectors clubs and small companies wanting to celebrate their identity by commissioning special models. At least 26 variations with special colors and liveries were created starting with the standard model in orange and blue Gulf Oil guise and culminating with a 1995 Code 3 version from Germany that was in Coca-Cola livery with a giant Coke bottle aboard. During this time, an intriguing wrecker/tow truck was also created, and Brooklin brought out a special video set that described the process of handcrafting Brooklins. Based on records kept by Brooklin Models clubs, 7000 to 10,000 models of this little Pontiac found homes, making it a huge seller by handbuilt model standards.

As for the Brooklin scale model of the 1953 sedan delivery

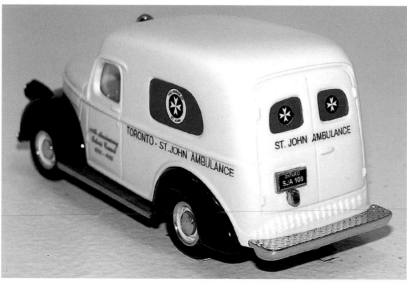

THIS MODEL CELEBRATES ST. JOHN'S AMBULANCE SERVICE'S CENTENNIAL. DURHAM CLASSICS' DC-19. (COURTESY COLLECTORS ANTIQUES)

1941 CHEVROLET RAISEDR OOF AMBULANCE. DURHAM CLASSICS' DC-19. (COURTESY COLLECTORS ANTIQUES)

SUITABLE FOR AN 'O' GAUGE MODEL RAILROAD LAYOUT – 1941 SUBURBAN IN CANADIAN NATIONAL RAILWAY GUISE. DURHAM CLASSICS' DC-17. (COURTESY COLLECTORS ANTIQUES)

THE TRACK CAME WITH THE DURHAM CLASSICS REPLICA. (COURTESY COLLECTORS ANTIQUES)

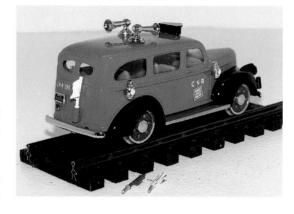

A HIGH LEVEL OF DETAIL IS EVIDENT IN THIS PHOTOGRAPH OF R&J MINIATURES' 1949 PONTIAC PICKUP. IN ADDITION TO THE NUMEROUS CHROMED PARTS AND AERIAL IS A DRIVER. NO RJM001. (AUTHOR COLLECTION)

R&J MINIATURES ISSUED SEVERAL VERSIONS OF THIS PICKUP IN DIFFERENT LIVERIES AND WITH DIFFERENT DETAILS. USUALLY ONLY 70 OR SO WERE PRODUCED IN EACH LIVERY, AND EACH CAME WITH A SIGNED CERTIFICATE ATTESTING THIS. NO RJM001. (AUTHOR COLLECTION)

and pickup, it is much like the majority of replicas issued by the builder during that period, with good proportions that capture the 'verticality' of the vehicle. The rather low greenhouse exaggerates this a little with its comparatively narrow windows in those pre-wraparound windshield days. The patternmaker has taken great care to capture the curves and straight edges of the original motorcar, and has performed much sculpting of the body to reveal details such as the silver streaks and side moldings. The interior is simple with detail confined primarily to getting the correct shape of the dashboard and outlining of major components.

Paint is uniformly applied and solid enamel colors are used. The bumpers and grille are massive pieces and are well executed in shiny white metal. The model has few glued on parts besides the one-piece white metal headlights and rather hefty hood

DPM STUDIOS' 1952 CHEVROLET UTILITY IS A MILLER BEER TRUCK THAT FEATURES AUTHENTIC SIGNAGE, A VERY LARGE BEER KEG, AND TWO-DOZEN CAPPED BOTTLES IN THE PICKUP BED. THE MODEL IS MOUNTED ON A CLEAR ACRYLIC STAND. (AUTHOR COLLECTION)

1953 PONTIAC SEDAN DELIVERY FROM BROOKLIN MODELS. BRK-31. (COURTESY COLLECTORS ANTIQUES)

1953 PONTIAC SEDAN DELIVERY IN POPULAR GULF OIL LIVERY. BROOKLIN MODELS' NO 31. (COURTESY COLLECTORS ANTIQUES)

BROOKLIN MODELS' 1953 PONTIAC SEDAN DELIVERY WAS ISSUED IN SEVERAL COLORS AND THE AUTHENTIC LIVERY OF MANY COMPANIES. BRK-31. (COURTESY COLLECTORS ANTIQUES)

1953 PONTIAC WITH APPROPRIATE SIGNAGE AND COLORS FOR CANADA'S FIRST NATIONAL AIRLINE. MADE FOR CANADIAN TOY COLLECTORS SOCIETY (CTCS). BRK-31. (COURTESY D MATHYSSEN)

1953 PONTIAC PICKUP BY BROOKLIN MODELS. A HANDBUILT WHITE METAL MODEL THAT CAME WITH A VIDEO. BRK-31X. (COURTESY D MATHYSSEN)

750 PONTIAC PICKUPS WITH CANOPY WERE CREATED BY BROOKLIN MODELS FOR A 1992 TOY SHOW IN MILAN. BRK-31X. (COURTESY D MATHYSSEN)

THE WESSEX TOY COLLECTORS CLUB HAD BROOKLIN PRODUCE 250 '53 PONTIAC PICKUP KEG TRUCKS. BRK-31X. (COURTESY D MATHYSSEN)

THE REDRUTH MODEL GARAGE COMMISSIONED 750 OF THESE PONTIAC PICKUPS WITH TOWING APPARATUS FROM MODEL BUILDER, BROOKLIN. BRK-31Z. (COURTESY D MATHYSSEN)

mascot that somewhat resembles the original. A substantial white metal replica, this is a model that benefits from detailing.

Yatming produced a nicely proportioned and detailed die-cast of the 1950 GMC 150 pickup that is available at a ridiculously low price of around $10. Road Champs offered a similar model of the 1953 Chevrolet pickup for a similar price, and even Hallmark's tree ornament of the 1953 GMC is well done with a side-mounted spare tire and, of course, an evergreen tree in the bed.

Thousands of 1:43 scale die-cast models and banks of the 1950 GMC and Chevrolet panel truck were produced in China for Ertl in the 1980s. Though these models are a little plain, some clever detailing improves their accuracy and they fit right into most collections.

Though it is more in the category of a mid- to heavy-duty truck, Ertl's 1950 Chevrolet COE is an excellently proportioned die-cast scale model that enhances any Chevrolet or GMC truck collection because it shares so many styling cues with its smaller brethren. Place it next to Yatming's or Durham Classics' 1950-53 pickup and see the family resemblance.

Finally, the pinnacle of handbuilt model building for Chevrolet trucks is Durham Classics' superb replica of the 1953 Series 3600 pickup (see sidebar for comments about this model). The builder offered a fascinating number of variations on this model. In single rear-wheeled form it came stock with and without bed cover, as a service station truck with oil drums, engine, muffler, and toolbox in the bed, or with a snowplough and bags of sand. In dual-wheeled configuration, Durham's Chevrolet was available as a tow truck/wrecker and as a tanker (for milk or gasoline). All in all, Durham Classics' Chevrolet pickup is a superb example of the realism that handbuilt replicas can achieve.

THE ONLY 1:43 SCALE MODEL OF A GENERAL MOTORS 1950S PANEL DELIVERY IS THIS ERTL DIE-CAST, NO 2825. MODELER, JERRY RETTIG, HAS ADDED CHROME FOIL AROUND THE WINDSHIELD. (COURTESY J RETTIG)

ERTL MADE A GMC VARIANT OF THE PANEL DELIVERY, THIS ONE A 1951 MODEL. NO 2826. (COURTESY J RETTIG)

1953 CHEVROLET 3100 PICKUP DIE-CAST FROM ROAD CHAMPS. (COURTESY J RETTIG)

1953 GMC ½TON PICKUP. A HALLMARK CHRISTMAS ORNAMENT. (COURTESY J RETTIG)

1953 CHEVROLET PICKUP WITH CHROME GRILLE AND BUMPERS. DURHAM CLASSICS' DC-28. (COURTESY A MOSKALEV)

USA MODELS' 1953 GOOD HUMOR TRUCK. NO USA-45. (COURTESY D LARSEN)

NOTE THE EXTENSIVE FAUX WOODWORK ON THIS CAMPBELL-BODIED REPLICA BY JERRY RETTIG. (COURTESY J RETTIG)

DURHAM CLASSICS' 1953 CHEVROLET PICKUP WAS AVAILABLE IN MANY LIVERIES. HERE IS AN IMPERIAL OIL ESSO GAS STATION VEHICLE. DC-28. (COURTESY COLLECTORS ANTIQUES)

ELC 1953 CHEVROLET UTILITY/ SUBURBAN STYLE WITH A CAMPBELL WOOD BODY, BASED ON THE CHEVY 3100 CHASSIS. HANDBUILT IN RESIN. (COURTESY J RETTIG)

A LOAD OF TYPICAL SERVICE STATION MATERIALS IN THE BED ADDS TO THE REALISM OF THIS '53 CHEVROLET TRUCK. DURHAM CLASSICS' DC-28. (COURTESY COLLECTORS ANTIQUES)

1953 CHEVROLET TOW TRUCK BY DURHAM CLASSICS. (COURTESY COLLECTORS ANTIQUES)

THE TOW BOOM AND NUMEROUS DETAILS ON DURHAM CLASSICS' '53 CHEVROLET ADD TO ITS REALISM. (COURTESY COLLECTORS ANTIQUES)

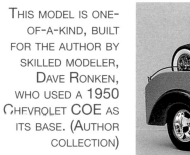

THOSE WHO LIVED IN MANY PARTS OF CANADA IN THE 1950S WILL RECOGNIZE THE PURPOSE OF THE SNOW SHOVEL AND SAND BAGS IN THIS B/A (BRITISH AMERICAN) GAS STATION TRUCK FROM DURHAM CLASSICS. DC-28. (COURTESY DURHAM CLASSICS AUTOMOTIVE MINIATURES)

THIS MODEL IS ONE-OF-A-KIND, BUILT FOR THE AUTHOR BY SKILLED MODELER, DAVE RONKEN, WHO USED A 1950 CHEVROLET COE AS ITS BASE. (AUTHOR COLLECTION)

THE LOAD IN THE BACK OF THE 1950 CHEVROLET COE IS A COUPLE OF DOZEN SPARE WHEELS FROM DIE-CAST TOYS. (AUTHOR COLLECTION)

MATCHBOX PRODUCED ITS 1948 GMC COE IN A VARIETY OF LIVERIES. (COURTESY S WILLIAMS)

PROFILE – 1953 CHEVROLET PICKUP BY DURHAM CLASSICS AUTOMOTIVE MINIATURES

CHEVROLET'S ICONIC PICKUP FROM THE PERIOD 1948-54 IS AN ATTRACTIVE MODEL THAT HAS A STRONG FOLLOWING AMONGST COLLECTORS. DURHAM CLASSICS' LITTLE CHEVY TRUCK (DC-28) HAS A SIMILAR GROUP OF DEVOTEES AMONGST SCALE MODEL ENTHUSIASTS. ONE OF THE REASONS FOR THIS IS THAT IT IS SUCH A CLEAN MODEL WITH AN IMPRESSIVE CASTING THAT CLOSELY RESEMBLES THE ACTUAL CAR. ONLY MODERATELY DETAILED, THIS HANDBUILT WHITE METAL MODEL IS A HEAVY PIECE WITH GLOSSY PAINT AND RELATIVELY FEW – THOUGH WELL-DESIGNED – PARTS THAT HAVE CLOSE TOLERANCES. IT IS NOT UNUSUAL TO HAVE MODELS WHERE PARTS DO NOT FIT WELL, AND THIS CAREFULLY CRAFTED MODEL IS THE EXCEPTION. THE NICELY DETAILED CHASSIS WITH SPARE TIRE, INTERIOR TUB, BODY AND BUMPERS, FIT PERFECTLY TOGETHER.

AS FOR FAITHFULNESS TO THE ORIGINAL SUBJECT, NOT A CURVE, MOLDING, OR SHUT LINE IS OUT OF PLACE. A SKILLED PATTERNMAKER CREATED THIS MODEL. COLORS ARE AUTHENTIC AND DURHAM CLASSICS MADE SEVERAL VARIATIONS IN DIFFERENT LIVERIES TO SATISFY MOST APPETITES.
(AUTHOR COLLECTION)

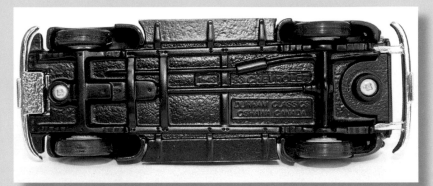

BUILDERS 8

ACCORDING TO THE DEFINITIVE REFERENCE, *AMERICAN WHEELS* BY JERRY Rettig, there have been at least 186 builders of 1:43 scale resin or white metal handmade models of American cars. Of these, 171 or more no longer produce models. Some of these builders were once quite prolific, whilst others produced only a few models before ceasing production.

The work of defunct builders often carries on as master patterns and parts change hands, and models reappear under new banners. Examples of this are Record/JPS and Zaugg/Tin Wizard. Former resin models become white metal and so on.

Because handbuilt models are produced in relatively small quantities with few new models released annually, the business is more about a love for beautiful things than it is about making huge profits. Thus even the largest builders tend to be family operations or have a loyal but small cadre of skilled employees, making this a unique business.

In this section I will identify builders of General Motors scale model cars and trucks, both past and present, that have made an impact on the hobby and whose models may one day find their way into the reader's collection.

ALTAYA/IXO

A maker of die-cast models, this Spanish concern produces a wide range of European and a few classic North American subjects such as '33 Auburn boat-tail speedster, '35 Duesenberg SSJ roadster, '37 Cord 812 convertible, '39 Graham and '39 Lincoln Continental convertible. Altaya also has a very nice 1930 Cadillac Imperial V16 limousine pictured in this book. Of uniformly good quality and using traditional methods such as silver paint to highlight brightwork, the company produces accurate models for about $25.

AMR

A prolific French builder of exquisite model cars and a pioneer in the use of photo-etching, AMR's identity is inextricably tied to its late founder Andre Marie Ruf; AMR produced very few models of American cars. Those that were produced are very nice: a 1950 Cadillac Series 62 convertible (no 308), hard-top coupe (no 1), 1967-68 Coupe de Ville hard-top (no 37), and convertible (no 4).

ABC BRIANZA

Carlo Brianza created finely detailed scale models, mostly of European subjects. He mastered the patterns for four 1:43 scale American automobiles. Playtoy Models of Belgium issued the first three Brianza replicas from 1981 to 1984: '57 Cadillac Eldorado convertible (no 1), '48 Chrysler Town & Country (no 2), and '53

1937 LASALLE SODOMKA BY MIVA MODELS. (AUTHOR COLLECTION)

Buick Skylark (no 3), These models are all crafted from resin and are known for their delicacy, fine proportions and superb detail.

Brianza created one last American model before his death in 1994. This was a 1954 Pontiac convertible (no 22) and was distributed by ABC Models. His work continues to this day in Northern Italy where the company of ABC Brianza is run by his wife Ella, son Andrea, and daughter Laura.

BROOKLIN MODELS

The Bath, England-based firm is the undisputed high volume provider of fine, reasonably priced, handbuilt, white metal 1:43 scale car models. At the time of publication, Brooklin Models was issuing a new North American model approximately every month, producing more than a thousand models in each range, and enjoying a worldwide following of collectors with model clubs in several countries.

Brooklin Models' far-sighted owner,

GENERAL MOTORS COMPANY MODELS FROM BROOKLIN MODELS

NUMBER	YEAR	MARQUE/MODEL	COMMENTS
BRK 4	1937	CHEVROLET MASTER COUPE	
BRK 10	1949	BUICK 2 DOOR FASTBACK SEDAN	
BRK 10X	1949	BUICK ROADMASTER TOP DOWN CONVERTIBLE	LIMITED PRODUCTION OF 250
BRK 14	1940	CADILLAC V16 CONVERTIBLE COUPE TOP UP	
BRK 14X	1940	CADILLAC V16 CONVERTIBLE COUPE TOP DOWN	1 OF 400 FOR CTCS 1983
BRK 20	1953	BUICK SKYLARK CONVERTIBLE	
BRK 31	1953	PONTIAC SEDAN DELIVERY	
BRK 39	1953	OLDSMOBILE FIESTA CONVERTIBLE	
BRK 40A	1948	CADILLAC SERIES 61 SEDANET COUPE	
BRK 45	1948	BUICK ROADMASTER CONVERTIBLE	
BRK 50	1948	CHEVROLET FLEETLINE AERO 2 DOOR FASTBACK SEDAN	
BRK 68	1954	CHEVROLET BEL AIR 2 DOOR HARD-TOP	
BRK 73	1949	OLDSMOBILE 98 2 DOOR HARD-TOP	
BRK 74	1947	CADILLAC SERIES 62 CONVERTIBLE TOP DOWN	
BRK 74X	1947	CADILLAC SERIES 62 CONVERTIBLE TOP UP	CTCS 1998, 1 OF 300
BRK 84	1934	LaSALLE 350 COUPE	
BRK 86	1938	CADILLAC SERIES 60 SPECIAL SEDAN	
BRK 95	1948	BUICK ROADMASTER STATION WAGON	
BRK 98	1939	LaSALLE 2-DOOR TOURING SEDAN	
BRK 105X	1947	CADILLAC SERIES 62 SEDANET	30TH ANNIVERSARY EDITION
BRK 114	1949	OLDSMOBILE 88 CLUB COUPE	
BRK 122	1939	LaSALLE SERIES 50 5 WINDOW COUPE	
BRK 132	1954	CHEVROLET 210 HANDYMAN STATION WAGON	
BRK 133	1934	BUICK 96-S COUPE	
BRK 136	1947	CHEVROLET STYLEMASTER SEDAN DELIVERY	
FS 5	1938	CADILLAC SERIES 60 SPECIAL CONVERTIBLE SEDAN	1 OF 750
IPV 11	1949	OLDSMOBILE 88 ROCKET CALIFORNIA HIGHWAY PATROL	
IPV 26	1947	CHEVROLET STYLEMASTER DELIVERY DALLAS POLICE	

(COURTESY D MATHYSSEN)

Nigel Parker, has established a policy of providing excellent customer service and a practice of bringing out different body styles based on previous patterns. The skill and artistry of highly respected patternmaker, Ian Pickering, has been employed to transform the 1939 LaSalle 2 door Touring Sedan into a 2 door, 5 window coupe, the 1938 Cadillac Sixty Special sedan into a phaeton, and 1954 Chevrolet 2 door hard-top into a Handyman station wagon.

BRUCE ARNOLD MODELS (BAM)

Bruce Arnold is an avid collector of 1:43 scale models and a man of many talents. He was leader of the rock band Orpheus, songwriter for Hootie and the Blowfish, and a regular contributor and feature writer for *Model Auto Review*.

In 1998, Bruce began manufacturing models of his own design and pattern. In 1999, Cadillac Motor Division commissioned a special edition for its worldwide 'Cadillac Collection 2000' promotion and Cadillac continued to merchandise Bruce Arnold Models' replicas. Since then, Bruce

GENERAL MOTORS COMPANY MODELS FROM BRUCE ARNOLD MODELS

NUMBER	YEAR	MARQUE/MODEL	COMMENTS
BAM-1	1953	CADILLAC ELDORADO CONVERTIBLE	TOP DOWN & TOP UP
BAM-2	1953	CADILLAC SIXTY SPECIAL 4 DOOR SEDAN	
BAM-3	1952	PONTIAC CHIEFTAIN STATION WAGON	
BAM-4	1960	CADILLAC S75	
BAM+6	1954	CADILLAC SIXTY SPECIAL 4 DOOR HARDTOP SEDAN	
BAM-7	1947	CADILLAC SIXTY SPECIAL	4 DOOR SEDAN
BAM-8	1948	CADILLAC SIXTY SPECIAL	
BAM-10	1951	CADILLAC S62 4 DOOR SEDAN	
BAM-CS1	1953	CADILLAC CONVERTIBLE	'ARETHA' VERSION
CNQ-30	1947	CADILLAC FLEETWOOD SEVENTY-FIVE LIMOUSINE	
MMC-1	1953	CADILLAC NEW ORLEANS CONCEPT CAR. INTRODUCED AT $895	

has issued a number of handbuilt Cadillac models for which he produced the patterns. In addition to models sold under his own label, Bruce Arnold patterned the much sought after 1947 Cadillac Fleetwood Seventy-Five Limousine for Conquest Models. In 2007 BAM issued a 1948 Cadillac Sixty Special, 1951 Cadillac S62 sedan, and 1954 Cadillac Sixty Special.

CONQUEST MADISON MODELS

Started in Holland, in 1987, by model enthusiast Henk van Asten, Conquest has done an admirable job of modeling what I call 'second wave' models. Namely, after many other

1954 PONTIAC AND 1948 PONTIAC BY CONQUEST MODELS. (AUTHOR COLLECTION)

1953 CADILLAC SIXTY SPECIAL BY BRUCE ARNOLD MODELS. (AUTHOR COLLECTION)

makers virtually flooded the collectors market with '55 and '57 Chevrolets, Conquest would quietly release a '54 Pontiac Star Chief or '50 Oldsmobile 98, scale models not seen before but much appreciated by collectors anxious for something unique. In all, the company has produced more than sixty-two distinct models of North American cars and trucks.

In 2005, American, Dave 'Buz' Kirkel purchased the masters from Henk and started reissuing small numbers of Conquest

and Madison models, often in different authentic colors than the original. Still built by SMTS, these new editions are of a high standard. With Buz's careful attention to customer service, and his practice of releasing small amounts of models at a time, generally 18-24 in each color at $225 and six black at $235, there continues to be a healthy market of devoted Conquest followers.

DURHAM CLASSICS

Founded by Julian and Margaret Stewart, this Canadian company produced models from the 1980s to 2003. As of this book's printing, Durham Classics continues to sell models on eBay and a few remain in stockists' inventories. Margaret Stewart comments: "We are presently working on '55 Ford Panel Vans and will soon be reissuing some of our previous models in new liveries. We receive many email enquiries regarding our models, and there is considerable interest in Durham Classics, as many collectors have never heard of us. We are also completing many of the part assembled models that we have and these will be available with the newer liveries."

Working from a few excellent Dick Armbruster patterns of a 1941 Chevrolet convertible, 2 door coupe, and a 1941 Chevrolet Suburban, the builder has been successful at providing variations on its models in many different colors and liveries.

Durham Classics has other GM models in its repertoire. Durham's models typically are built sturdily with great heft and deep glossy paint. Model proportions and assembly quality are top

Ｇ ENERAL MOTORS COMPANY MODELS FROM CONQUEST MADISON

NUMBER	YEAR	MARQUE/MODEL	COMMENTS
CNQ 1	1954	OLDSMOBILE STARFIRE 98 CONVERTIBLE	1987
CNQ 5	1954	OLDSMOBILE 98 HOLIDAY 2 DOOR HARD-TOP	1990
CNQ 8	1954	PONTIAC STAR CHIEF CONVERTIBLE	1991
CNQ 14	1948	PONTIAC TORPEDO EIGHT DE LUXE CONVERTIBLE TOP DOWN	1993
CNQ 14A	1948	PONTIAC TORPEDO EIGHT DE LUXE CONVERTIBLE TOP UP	1993
CNQ 17	1954	PONTIAC STAR CHIEF CUSTOM CATALINA 2 DOOR HARD-TOP	1994, 2006
CNQ 23	1947	OLDSMOBILE SERIES 76 DYNAMIC CRUISER 2 DOOR CLUB SEDAN	1995, 2006
CNQ 26	1952	BUICK SUPER RIVIERA 2 DOOR HARD-TOP	1995, 2006
CNQ 27	1948	PONTIAC STREAMLINER EIGHT DE LUXE STATION WAGON	1996, 2006
CNQ 30	1947	CADILLAC FLEETWOOD S75 LIMOUSINE	1999
CNQ 35	1952	BUICK ROADMASTER STATION WAGON	1999, 2006
CNQ 37	1947	CHEVROLET STYLEMASTER 4 DOOR SEDAN	2000, 2006
MAD 7	1937	CHEVROLET MASTER DE LUXE 4 DOOR SEDAN	1992
MAD 9	1950	OLDSMOBILE FUTURAMIC 2 DOOR CLUB COUPE	1994
MAD 12	1947	OLDSMOBILE S66 4 DOOR SEDAN	1994
MAD 16	1952	BUICK SUPER CONVERTIBLE	1996, 2005
MAD 17	1950	OLDSMOBILE FUTURAMIC 98 CONVERTIBLE	1996

(COURTESY WWW.ARTCRAFTMODEL.DE)

GENERAL MOTORS COMPANY MODELS FROM DURHAM CLASSICS

NUMBER	YEAR	MARQUE/MODEL	COMMENTS
DC-5	1941	CHEVROLET COUPE	VARIOUS VERSIONS
DC-10	1939	CHEVROLET CONVERTIBLE	TOP DOWN & TOP UP
DC-11	1941	CHEVROLET UTILITY PICKUP	VARIOUS VERSION INCL. PAINTER'S CAR
DC-12	1941	CHEVROLET PANEL DELIVERY	NUMEROUS LIVERIES
DC-16	1953	CHEVROLET ¾TON PICKUP	
DC-17	1941	CHEVROLET SUBURBAN CARRY ALL	VARIOUS VERSIONS INCL. BAND LEADER BUS
DC-19	1941	CHEVROLET RAISED ROOF AMBULANCE	U.S. ARMY, CHICAGO FD AMBULANCE
DC-26	1953	CHEVROLET PICKUP ¾ TON WITH DUAL WHEELS	VARIOUS VERSIONS INCL. TOW TRUCK
DC-27	1938	OLDSMOBILE 4 DOOR SEDAN	VARIOUS COLORS & TRIM LEVELS
DC-28	1953	CHEVROLET ½TON PICKUP	VARIOUS VERSIONS
DC-29	1953	CHEVROLET TANK TRUCK WITH DUAL WHEELS	VARIOUS LIVERIES
DC-30	1934	LASALLE CONVERTIBLE	TOP UP & TOP DOWN
DC-35	1941	CHEVROLET CANOPY EXPRESS	
DC 35A	1941	CHEVROLET CANOPY EXPRESS SCREENSIDE DELIVERY	

1930 CADILLAC TOWN CAR BY ELEGANCE. (AUTHOR COLLECTION)

rate. In later replicas, details such as chrome door handles were added to keep pace with Brooklin and higher end collectibles.

ELEGANCE MODELS

From 1983 to 1998, the French artisan builder Claude Thibivilliers, who formerly provided his expertise to Dinky Meccano France, made some of the most exquisite, jewel-like handbuilt models available. Today, there are collectors who covet Thibivilliers' work so much that they will pay many hundreds of dollars to claim a piece of model building history. To what does one attribute this devoted following?

Counting myself as a devotee, I see several factors. The models, while not as detailed as many of today's, have a purity to them that is a little hard to describe. Perhaps it is the finishing that is without peer. Paintwork is very rich and lustrous, and there are absolutely no flaws to be found, period. One has the impression of each item being a lovingly handcrafted sculpture, in resin. Beyond this, Thibivillier's output was quite small, with many one-of-a-kind models. This ensures exclusivity.

Elegance Models production can be classified into three periods:

• The early period – recreation of the classics: Monsieur Thibivilliers saw the opportunity to take the products of die-cast manufacturers' Rio and Solido as a basis for extensive modifications to create a range of vehicles beyond the toymakers' dreams. During this time he crafted numerous resin body styles and liveries based upon 1932 Duesenberg, 1928 Lincoln, 1927 Packard, 1940 Packard, 1948 Chrysler and 1931 Cadillac.

• The middle period – Cadillacs of the fifties: The builder started with the simple idea of creating a flawless pattern for a 1950 Cadillac. He then extended this idea to produce a myriad of body styles and liveries capturing the public imagination.

From 1983 to 1998 Elegance produced the following body styles for the 1950 Cadillac: S62 convertible (top up and top down); S61/62 2 door hard-top coupe, S61 B-bodied 4 door sedan; S60 Special 4 door sedan; S75 limousine; S86 Meteor and Superior funeral car, ambulance, flower car, and sedan delivery; Coachcraft station wagon; Hess and Eisenhardt six and eight door limousines; 'Sugar Ray' S62 convertible; and Derham-bodied limousines. (Claude has never told me why he omitted the Series 62 sedan from his repertoire.)

Then Monsieur Thibivilliers varied the mix by introducing a 1951 front clip that doubled the model possibilities. Finally, he improved upon Solido's 1957 Eldorado by creating his own resin version, some with vinyl roof.

• The late period – 1970 and 1976: Cadillac models in a vast range of body styles, including many customs. This time period is beyond the scope of this publication.

GENERAL MOTORS COMPANY MODELS FROM ELEGANCE MODELS

NUMBER	YEAR	MARQUE/MODEL	COMMENTS
30	1932	CADILLAC V 16 CABRIOLET 2 PASSENGERS WITH TRUNK & ENCLOSED TOP	1980
31	1932	CADILLAC V 16 TOWN CAR WITH TRUNK	1980
32	1932	CADILLAC V 16 CABRIOLET WITH TRUNK TOP DOWN	1981
33	1932	CADILLAC V 16 DUAL COWL PHAETON	1981
34	1932	CADILLAC V 16 FLEETWOOD TOWN CAR	1980
35	1932	CADILLAC V 16 DUAL COWL PHAETON TOP UP	1981
36	1932	CADILLAC V 16 FIRE RESCUE TRUCK DETROIT FD	1981
69A	1931	CADILLAC V 16 FLEETWOOD 3 WINDOW COUPE	1982
69B	1931	CADILLAC V 16 FLEETWOOD 3 WINDOW COUPE TRANSKIT	1982
70	1932	CADILLAC V 16 LWB AMBULANCE 'PRIVATE'	1982
71	1932	CADILLAC V 16 LWB AMBULANCE 'DETROIT FD'	1982
72	1932	CADILLAC V 16 LWB LANDAU HEARSE	1982
73	1932	CADILLAC V 16 LWB DECORATIVE PANEL HEARSE	1982
101	1932	CADILLAC V 16 LWB ART DECO PANEL HEARSE	1983
102	1950	CADILLAC S86 AMBULANCE CIVILIAN WHITE	1983
103	1950	CADILLAC S86 AMBULANCE "NEW YORK FD"	1983
104	1950	CADILLAC S86 AMBULANCE "US AIR FORCE MEDICAL SERVICE"	1983
105	1950	CADILLAC S86 LANDAU HEARSE	1983
106	1950	CADILLAC S86 HEARSE WITH SILVER LAURELS	1983
107	1950	CADILLAC S86 FLOWER CAR WHITE OR BLACK	1984
108A	1950	CADILLAC S75 LIMOUSINE	1984
108B	1950	CADILLAC S75 LIMOUSINE BY DERHAM	1984
108C	1950	CADILLAC S75 LIMOUSINE BY DERHAM ALL WHITE 1 OF 50	1986
109	1950	CADILLAC S62 2 DOOR HARD-TOP COUPE	1984
111	1950	CADILLAC SIXTY SPECIAL 4 DOOR SEDAN	1985
114	1950	CADILLAC S86 LWB SEDAN DELIVERY "CALENDRE" PARIS STORE	1986
115A	1950	CADILLAC S86 LWB AMBULANCE "NEW YORK FD" (STRETCHED VERSION)	1987
115B	1950	CADILLAC S86 LWB AMBULANCE CIVILIAN WHITE (STRETCHED VERSION)	1987
116	1950	CADILLAC S86 LWB LANDAU HEARSE (STRETCHED VERSION)	1988
117	1951	CADILLAC IBN SEOUD 6 DOOR MIRRORED LIMOUSINE	1986
118	1951	CADILLAC S62 CONVERTIBLE	1987
118B	1951	CADILLAC S62 CONVERTIBLE "SUGAR RAY ROBINSON"	1987
120	1950	CADILLAC S62 CONVERTIBLE	1987
123	1950	CADILLAC S86 FLOWER CAR "METEOR" (STRETCHED VERSION)	1988
124	1950	CADILLAC S86 LIMOUSINE HEARSE (STRETCHED VERSION)	1988
125	1950	CADILLAC S86 SERVICE CAR SILVER LAURELS (STRETCHED VERSION)	1988
126	1950	CADILLAC S86 AMBULANCE "US AIR FORCE MEDICAL SERVICE" (STRETCHED VERSION)	1988
131	1951	CADILLAC S62 COACHCRAFT STATION WAGON	1988
133	1951	CADILLAC S86 SERVICE WAGON "ROTH CADILLAC"	1988
134	1951	CADILLAC S86 LANDAU HEARSE WITH LEATHER ROOF	1988
135	1951	CADILLAC S75 LIMOUSINE BY DERHAM	
137	1951	CADILLAC HESS & EISENHARDT 8 DOOR LIMOUSINE	1988
197	1951	CADILLAC S86 RAISED ROOF AMBULANCE "DETROIT FD"	
198	1950	CADILLAC S61 4 DOOR SEDAN	
503	1931	CADILLAC FLEETWOOD TOWN BROUGHAM	
504	1931	CADILLAC FLEETWOOD TOWN BROUGHAM VINYL ROOF	
504B	1931	CADILLAC FLEETWOOD TOWN BROUGHAM WITH TRUNK	

Public production and sales of Elegance models ceased in the late 1990s. Very few are available in the aftermarket.

In 2006, Claude Thibivilliers wrote me with news that he was issuing one last model, a limited edition 1959 Series 75 limousine, Reference Number 200. I now have one of six of this handmade model in my collection.

ENCHANTMENT LAND COACHBUILDERS (ELC)

Can there be anyone who is more passionate about little North American car and truck models than Enchantment Land Coachbuilders' Jerry Rettig? Unlikely. In addition to being the author of the comprehensive listing of die-cast and handbuilt 1:43 scale replicas, *American Wheels, a Reference*, Jerry has created hundreds of models of Buicks, Chryslers, Cadillacs and Packards of the 1940s and 1930s as well as a number of other cars. Working in his American desert studio, Jerry will rework die-cast models or produce body variations on familiar models such as limousines, ambulances and funeral cars just for the joy of creating.

Made from resin, ELC models are exclusive, with some models numbering fewer than 10 items. They typically sell for $125-$150 and have quite a following of collectors.

GOLDVARG

Sergio and Mariana Goldvarg had a vision to bring affordable handbuilt models of American cars of the 1940s and 1950s to

GENERAL MOTORS COMPANY MODELS FROM ENCHANTMENT LAND COACHBUILDERS

Number	Year	Marque/model	Comments
B-5	1947	Buick Landaulet Hearse	Flxible
B-6	1947	Buick Limousine Hearse	Flxible
B-7	1947	Buick Ambulance	
B-8	1947	Buick Ambulance	Fire Service livery
B-10A	1949	Buick Convertible	Top down
B-10B	1949	Buick Riviera 2 door hardtop	
B-10S	1939	Buick Roadmaster convertible sedan	Top down
B-11	1941	Buick Club Coupe	
B-12	1941	Buick Station Wagon	
B-13	1941	Buick 4 door touring sedan	
B-14	1941	Buick Flxible Service Hearse	
C-10	1931	Cadillac Roadster	Top down Indy 500 pace car
C-12	1947	Cadillac Meteor Limousine Hearse	
C-13	1947	Cadillac Meteor Ambulance LWB	
C-14	1947	Cadillac S75 Formal Limousine	
C-15	1947	Cadillac Meteor Ambulance LWB	Fire Service livery
C-19	1947	Cadillac Flower Car LWB	
C-24	1953	Chevrolet Campbell utility station wagon	
L-4	1938	LaSalle Art carved Hearse	S&S
L-5	1938	LaSalle Limousine Hearse	S&S
L-6	1938	LaSalle Ambulance LWB	
L-7	1938	LaSalle Ambulance LWB	Fire Service livery
L-10	1927	LaSalle Model 303 Roadster Top down	Indy 500 Pace Car
L-11	1937	LaSalle convertible Top down	Indy 500 Pace Car
L-13	1940	LaSalle Limousine Hearse	

1934 CHEVROLET panel van by DGM. (COURTESY J RETTIG)

collectors throughout the world from their native Argentina. From the early 1990s until the end of that decade they did just that.

Goldvarg's merchandising was creative and fun. White metal models from the Goldvarg Collection were packed in a distinctive red and gold box. Each model came with a pamphlet of period appropriate line art, "Rex Morgan-like" comic characters cheerfully extolling the availability of classic cars as rendered by Goldvarg. Each model had a hangtag signed personally by Sergio.

The actual models were very sturdy, and like early handbuilt models, a little impressionistic, which is to say proportions were not always faithful to the original subject. Still, as production continued, accuracy improved and the last few replicas such as the 1958 Oldsmobile were quite good. Unfortunately the economics of Argentine currency fluctuations prevailed and Goldvarg did not produce the last 7 of its planned 16 models. Who knows how nice the 1954 Chevrolet 4 door sedan and 1949 Cadillac Series 62 4 door sedan could have been?

Goldvarg's 1946 Chevrolet Stylemaster 4 door sedan is shown in the Chevrolet chapter.

model, a 1951 Buick Le Sabre, was issued in 1987, an excellent, fully-finished white-metal model, as good as anything available at the time and priced at about $150.00. Each replica came with a photocopy of the Le Sabre booklet handed out at the GM Auto Shows. A new 'Great American Dream Machine' appeared every few months for a while but then the intervals began to stretch out. The models were cast and painted in England with Alderman performing much of the final assembly and detail work, himself. As modeling technology improved, the models became more and more detailed, requiring more time to complete. After the twelfth model (the Chrysler C-200) from Great American Dream Machines, Phil ceased production.

This seemed to increase the demand for GADM models. Paul Burt was one of the many collectors seeking GADM's Lincoln Futura. The story goes that Paul had seen one at Al's Hobbies in Chicago in 1992, but didn't buy it because the price of $200.00 seemed too high. He later returned to the store and the Futura was gone. During the next four years Paul managed to find and acquire several GADM models except for the coveted Futura.

GREAT AMERICAN DREAM MACHINES

Great American Dream Machines (GADM) models were the work of a Brooklyn hobby shop owner, Phil Alderman. GADM's first

1940 BUICK Y-JOB. (COURTESY GREAT AMERICAN DREAM MACHINES)

1946 CHEVROLET BY GOLDVARG COLLECTION. (AUTHOR COLLECTION)

Eventually Paul Burt approached Phil Alderman directly and surprisingly wound up buying not just a Futura model but also the whole enterprise of Great American Dream Machines. Most of the original GADM models have been re-issued and several new models, such as the Buick Wildcat II, have been added. They are made in very limited numbers, with only about 25 examples of each car every other year.

HIGHWAY TRAVELERS

Highway Travelers were made by Illustra Models of Great Britain for Paul Patterson, a model dealer from New York State.

Paul has brought out a handful of high-end models of unusual subjects such as 1954 Hudson Italia, 1951 Frazer, 1961 Plymouth, 1962 Studebaker, and 1992 Cadillac Allante. Usually around 100 pieces of each model were issued.

The last model from Highway Travelers was the 1954 Pontiac Bonneville Special General Motors Concept Car. Highway Travelers' models have superbly accurate patterns and great detail. They are truly to be cherished and command prices greater than their issue price of just under $200. Paul Patterson has retained the masters and re-released the Studebaker in 2004. He stated in 2006 that future re-releases were dependent upon sufficient demand to make production economically viable.

MIKANSUE (AMERICANA)

One of the first builders of models based on North American cars was Mike and Sue Richardson's company, Mikansue that began as a retail and mail-order shop specializing in 1:43 scale models and later, kits. The Richardson's are recognized experts in the field of British die-cast models and authors of the definitive *Dinky Toys and Modeled Miniatures*.

Around 1973, they began to produce their own line of white metal kits. The Americana line was a subset of Mikansue and consisted only of kits of American cars but Mikansue did offer a building service by Linjak Scale Models. The charge was £5-6.65 in addition to the cost of the kit (about £5).

Gene Parrill, pioneer in the handbuilt models field, comments about Mikansue models: "They were good, however, they were not up to today's standard by any means. They would usually have, maybe, nine white metal pieces, besides the wheels and tires, in each kit (body, chassis, two front seats, back seat, steering wheel, steering post, front and rear bumpers). Door handles, chrome trim, windshield wipers, etc. were molded into the body and were tough to paint.

"Since they were in England, the masters were made using photos and company dimensions so in a lot of cases, the model looked like the American car but was missing the 'essence' or personality of the car. Still, they were the only game in town for a lot of American cars."

In its Americana line, Mikansue produced the 1940 LaSalle S50 4 door sedan (no 5) and 1950 Chevrolet Styleline 4 door sedan (no 13).

MILESTONE MINIATURES

Milestone Miniatures of England is owned by Graham and Bernice DuCros. Their son Darren is the main model builder. The company produces handbuilt models that it sells through stockists and its own website. It also undertakes contract work and commissions for other companies and collectors such as K&D Automobilia and Toys For Collectors (TFC). Milestone Miniatures makes several ranges of scale models such as a superb collection of Jaguar models, Gems and Cobwebs; the Brooklands Series (produced in conjunction with the Brooklands Museum Trust); the Milestone range of classic English cars, and the 43rd Avenue range of classic American cars which includes several late fifties to mid-sixties Chrysler, Chevrolet and Mercury models. Its first model of a 1940s North American car was a 1947 Cadillac S62 2 door sedan that appears to be a white metal version of Tron's resin model.

In 2007, the company introduced an original replica of a McLaughlin-Buick Royal used by car King Edward VIII. With only 100 made, the black 1936 Buick S90 formal 4 door sedan is rare.

MINI AUTO EMPORIUM (MAE)

Based in Ontario, Canada, Mini Auto Emporium made a dozen different models of North American cars during the 1980s. Its products were made of heavy white metal and, initially, like Brooklin's models were simple with few parts, but also like Brooklin, they became more detailed as time passed. MAE's most common model is a simple 1959 Cadillac that is seen quite frequently on eBay and has sold in the $50-75 range.

Much more scarce are MAE's 1931 and 1940 Cadillac models that have quite a bit of white metal detailing in the front end and are sought after by collectors because they are so unique. The 1939 McLaughlin-Buick Royal Tour Car mentioned elsewhere in this book is in the author's opinion, the company's best model. Jacqui and Mike Macnally owned MAE.

Jacqui Macnally comments: "We emigrated to Canada in September 1981 and I'm guesstimating that we started MAE in '82 or possibly early '83. It is hard to remember exactly when we started producing our white metal models. I know that the very

GENERAL MOTORS COMPANY MODELS FROM MINI AUTO EMPORIUM

NUMBER	YEAR	MARQUE/MODEL	COMMENTS
107	1939	MCLAUGHLIN-BUICK ROYAL TOUR CAR	TOP DOWN
116	1939	MCLAUGHLIN-BUICK ROYAL TOUR CAR	TOP UP
112	1931	CADILLAC V16 BOATTAIL SPEEDSTER	TOP DOWN
115	1931	CADILLAC V16 BOATTAIL SPEEDSTER	TOP UP
117	1940	CADILLAC SIXTY SPECIAL 4 DOOR SEDAN	
117B	1940	CADILLAC S62 CONVERTIBLE	

first model we made was a 1929 BABS Land Speed Record car. We made it in resin and it had hand-laced wire wheels and real leather straps on the hood with brass buckles that actually worked! It was in 1:43 scale and a limited edition. I honestly can't remember how many we made of those; it was our very first foray in to the world of collector models! They were extremely labor intensive! The first spun cast model was the 1959 Cadillac Eldorado Biarritz Convertible and we offered it in four colors and two versions: top up and top down.

"Mike is a tool and die maker (British) by trade and he made the brass masters for all the models we produced. We also manufactured the tires for the cars using a small molding machine. Mike made the molds for those too."

In researching this book, a photo of the MAE 1939 Buick I sent made its way to Zoe Ovens who sent me this email: "I'm one of the daughters (of Jacqui and Mike Macnally). I would love to see any other pictures that you may have of the vehicles that my parents made. Seeing this Buick is really cool, I can't remember the last time I saw any of the vehicles. I do remember watching my Dad hand painting the flags, lights and hand wiring the wheels for one of the models, also popping the tires from the molds."

MINI MARQUE '43' AND MINI MARQUE

Mini Marque '43' was a prodigious English producer of handbuilt replicas of 1930s Auburn, Cord, Duesenberg and Packard as well as Ford, Lincoln, Edsel, Mercury and a few Cadillacs and Chevrolets. Many of these models are in showcases of non-model collectors who find their accurate evocation of a by-gone era, irresistible.

The company ceased production in 2002 when its passionate founder, the flamboyant Richard Briggs passed away.

GENERAL MOTORS COMPANY MODELS FROM MINI MARQUE '43' AND MINI MARQUE

NUMBER	YEAR	MARQUE/MODEL	COMMENTS
US-24	1954	CADILLAC ELDORADO CONVERTIBLE	
US-92	1937	LASALLE 2 DOOR CONVERTIBLE SEDAN	TOP UP OR TOP DOWN
RP-14	1937	LASALLE CONVERTIBLE	INDY 500 PACE CAR
GRB-42	1948	CADILLAC SIXTY SPECIAL	

1939 MCLAUGHLIN-BUICK ROYAL TOUR CAR BY MINIATURE AUTO EMPORIUM. (AUTHOR COLLECTION)

Mini Marque '43', South View Farm, Halsham, Hull, East Yorkshire, HU12 0BP England
Telephone: (0964) 671116 & 670504   Fax: (0964) 671118

1954 CADILLAC ELDORADO BY MINI MARQUE '43'.
(AUTHOR COLLECTION)

In 2004, Midlantic Models' Steve Overy, Mike Murray, Nick Hagley, Clive Nye, and renowned pattern maker Ian Pickering resurrected Mini Marque. The company has been releasing former and new models, including a 1956 Packard, 1946 Hudson, and amazingly realistic 1934 Packard models. In 2007, the company released a 1954 Cadillac S62 convertible based on celebrity pianist Liberace's customized vehicle and a brand new 1948 Cadillac Sixty Special.

MOTOR CITY USA

Alan Novak is the force behind California-based Motor City USA (MCUSA), which produces some of the most impressive 1:43 scale replicas of North American models on the planet. Since the early 1990s, MCUSA concentrated on late 1930s/early 1960s handbuilt replicas in 1:43 scale. Priced between $100 and $299, they are renowned for their superior proportions, detail, and finishing. In early 2000, MCUSA began to look at the 1:18th scale market and focus on the production of larger scale premium models produced in China. The re-issuing of higher end handbuilt 1:43 scale models has reduced to a trickle and they have not released a new full Motor City replica since the early 2000s.

However, Motor City USA is often full of surprises. In 2004, it created an impressive replica 1:43 scale "Motor City Gold" 1951 Nash, followed by a 1959 Oldsmobile, and 1959 Cadillac S75, each in resin and white metal with commendable proportions and detail and at a very low price of around $100.

Although I have most of MCUSA's models in my collection, it was only when I began assembling the list of models from this builder that I was struck by the realization of what a prolific producer of General Motors replicas Motor City USA has been and what an enormous gap in the hobby there would be if it had not issued these impressive works of art.

NEWBANK MODELS

Newbank Models was a range of 1:43 scale handbuilt white metal models of American Automobiles produced during 2000-2003. It offered primarily three different 1938 Hudson models (Hudson 8 Coupé Victoria, Hudson Convertible, and Hudson 112 Convertible in Indianapolis 500 Pace Car livery) in the Memorial

GENERAL MOTORS COMPANY MODELS FROM MOTOR CITY USA

TOP OF THE LINE

NUMBER	YEAR	MARQUE/MODEL	COMMENTS
MC-7	1953	CHEVROLET BEL AIR 2 DR. HARD-TOP	
MC-8	1953	CHEVROLET BEL AIR CONVERTIBLE	
MC-9	1953	CHEVROLET SEDAN DELIVERY	
MC-19	1949	CADILLAC 2 DR. FASTBACK SEDAN	
MC-20	1949	CADILLAC COUPE DE VILLE	
MC-21	1949	CADILLAC CONVERTIBLE	
MC-26	1949	BUICK RIVIERA 2 DR. HARD-TOP	
MC-27	1949	BUICK RIVIERA TOP DOWN CONVERTIBLE	
MC-40	1954	BUICK SKYLARK CONVERTIBLE	
MC-46	1950	PONTIAC CATALINA CONVERTIBLE	
MC-47	1950	PONTIAC CATALINA HARD-TOP	
MC-60	1948	CHEVROLET FLEETLINE AERO	
MC-61	1948	CHEVROLET FLEETMASTER CONVERTIBLE	
MC-62	1948	CHEVROLET FLEETMASTER CONVERTIBLE PACE CAR	
MC-69	1950	OLDSMOBILE 98 CONVERTIBLE	
MC-70	1950	OLDSMOBILE 98 2 DOOR HARD-TOP	
MC-76	1949	BUICK ROADMASTER STATION WAGON	

1953 CHEVROLET SEDAN DELIVERY BY MOTOR CITY USA.
(COURTESY COLLECTORS ANTIQUES)

Number	Year	Marque/model	Comments
MC-87	1949	Buick Landau Hearse	
MC-91	1949	Cadillac S86 Service Car	
MC-92	1949	Cadillac S86 Landau Hearse	
MC-93	1949	Cadillac S86 Limousine Hearse	
MC-94	1949	Cadillac Ambulance	
MC-97	1949	Buick Flxible Ambulance	
MC-101	1949	Buick Flxible Limousine Style Hearse	

USA Models

Number	Year	Marque/model	Comments
USA-4	1951	Chevrolet Bel Air 2 door Hard-top	
USA-5	1954	Chevrolet Bel Air Four Door Sedan	
USA-21	1951	Chevrolet Bel Air Convertible	
USA-22	1955	Chevrolet 210 Two Door Sedan	
USA-25	1954	Buick Skylark	
USA-27	1937	Chevrolet Deluxe 4 door Sedan	Also in police, fire, and taxi versions
USA-29	1953	Chevrolet Sedan Delivery	Various liveries, including fire, M&Ms
USA-30	1953	Chevrolet Bel Air Convertible	
USA-31	1953	Chevrolet Bel Air 2 door Hard-top	
USA-32	1954	Buick Century Convertible	
USA-33	1954	Buick Century Hard-top	
USA-39	1948	Buick Sedanet	
USA-40	1939	Chevrolet Coupe	
USA-45	1953	Chevrolet "Good Humor" Ice Cream Truck	

American Models

Number	Year	Marque/model	Comments
AM-2	1954	Buick Century Convertible	
AM-3	1954	Buick Century Hard-top	
AM-8	1949	Buick Sedanet	
AM-9	1953	Chevrolet Bel Air Convertible	

Design Studio (Early in Motor City USA's history, top of the line models were named Design Studio. Eventually this name was used for the current rod and custom line.)

Number	Year	Marque/model	Comments
DS-2	1947	Buick Convertible	
DS-5	1948	Buick 2 door Fastback Coupe	
DS-9AMB	1953	Chevrolet Ambulette	By National
DS-16	1954	Chevrolet Bel Air 4 door Sedan	
DS-17	1954	Buick Century 2 door Hard-top	
DS-18	1954	Buick Century Convertible	
DS-19	1951	Chevrolet Bel Air 2 door Hard-top	
DS-104	1953	Cadillac Lincoln Mexican Road Racer	

1948 Buick by USA Models. (Author collection)

Series, which was produced in memory of Ann Newton-Banks the late wife of the founder of Newbank Models, Tony Banks.

The only GM model to be issued by Newbank was a nicely finished top down convertible of the rare and somewhat homely 1942 Oldsmobile B44 convertible coupe. Not a popular scale model because of its plain blackwall tires and slightly overwrought grille, it is one of the very few replicas of a 1942 produced. Newbank Models were last issued at a retail price of £89.00 and because of their subject, rarity, accurate proportions, and high-quality, command more than that price today.

PRECISION MINIATURES

Precision Miniatures of California, USA originated during the 1970s under Gene Parrill and Lloyd Asbury. Its models were popular and of a consistently high caliber. Many carry on today, forming the basis of later Motor City USA releases. Precision Miniatures was also a pioneer, along with AMR in the use of photo-etched parts that took model-making to the next level of accuracy.

The sole General Motors subject modeled by Precision Miniatures was a nicely proportioned, well-detailed, and carefully finished 1953 Corvette.

PROVENCE MOULAGE/PROVENCE MINIATURE AUTOMOBILES

Provence Moulage created its first kits, in the familiar tan polyurethane resin, in 1982. It concentrated on cars with European appeal such as racing cars, primarily producing kits. The company also cast all Tron models. Eventually it acquired the assets of Starter after that company went insolvent and then made "built models" from the Starter molds. Eventually Provence Moulage went bankrupt and ex-employees formed a new company, Provence Miniature Automobiles. It made many

1947 CADILLAC BY PROVENCE MOULAGE. (AUTHOR COLLECTION)

excellent kits of current racing cars and some European show cars but did not produce anything from the old Starter or P.M. molds. PMA too went bankrupt in 2006.

During the 1980s, Provence Moulage issued a great variety of kits, transkits, and handbuilt models based on American cars, including 1950 Buicks in all body styles, Chevrolet concept cars, 1955 Oldsmobile 98 convertible with enormous headlights, 1958 Buick station wagon, and an excellent resin 1947 Cadillac that is highly accurate and uses photo-etched parts. The quality of Provence Moulage models is very high with generally good proportions and clean castings. Factory built-up models or those assembled by skilled modelers are very impressive. Though not abundant, the most commonly seen PM models on the aftermarket are the 1947 Cadillac, 1950 Buick, and 1951 Studebaker.

RECORD MODELS

A French company making resin kits, at first in a hard gray epoxy resin and later in the familiar tan resin with better detail, Record sold a variety of 1950 Chevrolet, 1952 Pontiac, and 1957-58 Cadillac kits and handbuilts during the 1980s in the full range of body styles offered by the original manufacturer. Record's models are quite plain when built straight from the kit, but when detailed with simple chrome foil by a skilled modeler they look very realistic.

GENERAL MOTORS COMPANY MODELS FROM PROVENCE MOULAGE

NUMBER	YEAR	MARQUE/MODEL	COMMENTS
TK21	1950	BUICK 2 DOOR FASTBACK SEDAN	SOLIDO-BASED TRANSKIT
TK23	1950	BUICK 2 DOOR HARD-TOP COUPE	SOLIDO-BASED TRANSKIT
TK24	1950	BUICK STATION WAGON	SOLIDO-BASED TRANSKIT
TK28	1950	BUICK 4 DOOR SEDAN	SOLIDO-BASED TRANSKIT
863	1953	CADILLAC-LINCOLN RACE CAR	
244	1947	CADILLAC S62 2 DOOR FASTBACK SEDAN	
306	1947	CADILLAC S62 4 DOOR SEDAN	
391	1947	CADILLAC S62 CONVERTIBLE TOP DOWN	
TK27	1950	CHEVROLET STATION WAGON	SOLIDO-BASED TRANSKIT
220	1953	CORVETTE ROADSTER TOP DOWN	
334	1953	CORVETTE CORVAIR CONCEPT CAR	
274	1954	NOMAD CONCEPT CAR	

REXTOYS

Rextoys debuted in the 1980s during a time when a growing number of people began to see scale models as being worthy of collecting and perhaps an investment. Seeing the successful efforts of the "mints" to market inexpensive die-cast models priced at several times the cost of production, with unrealistic but craftily photographed opening doors, "steerable" front wheels, and other features, Rextoys sought to create static models that were of good quality and value.

Through the use of rich packaging in the subdued, regal colors of maroon and gold, a full color line art brochure, and some rather well-made scale models, Rextoys was able to generate interest in a product that was priced halfway between die-cast toys and "collectible replicas" turned out by the mints.

I remember being in a hobby shop around 1990 and gazing at the shelves stacked with impossibly long Cadillac models in their distinctive Rextoys boxes. Each Cadillac was in a different body style and color. The little models exuded quality and for around $40 a measure of exclusivity. Today those Cadillac models sell at close to their issue price, the scarcer 1940 Packard often selling at above its original price.

GENERAL MOTORS COMPANY MODELS FROM RECORD MODELS

NUMBER	YEAR	MARQUE/MODEL	COMMENTS
7	1952	CHEVROLET 4 DOOR NOTCHBACK SEDAN	
8	1952	CHEVROLET BEL AIR 2 DOOR HARD-TOP COUPE	
9	1952	CHEVROLET 2 DOOR FASTBACK SEDAN	
12	1952	CHEVROLET 2 DOOR BUSINESS COUPE	
74	1952	CHEVROLET UTE PICK UP	
	1952	CHEVROLET CONVETIBLE TOP DOWN	
79	1950	PONTIAC 2 DOOR HARD-TOP COUPE	
80	1950	PONTIAC CONVERTIBLE TOP DOWN	
81	1950	PONTIAC 4 DOOR FASTBACK SEDAN	
82	1950	PONTIAC 2 DOOR FASTBACK SEDAN	

SAMS/R&J MINIATURES LTD

SAMS was a British company that produced a line of white metal models in the early 1990s which included a 1937 Cord 812 Beverly sedan and an exceptionally well-crafted 1959 Oldsmobile

GENERAL MOTORS COMPANY MODELS FROM REXTOYS

NUMBER	YEAR	MARQUE/MODEL	COMMENTS
1	1938	CADILLAC V16 OPEN FRONT SEDAN	POPE PIUS XII, 2 ATTENDANTS
2	1938	CADILLAC V16 OPEN FRONT SEDAN	2 TONE COLORS
3	1938	CADILLAC V16 FORMAL SEDAN	FAUX VINYL ROOF
4	1938	CADILLAC V16 TOWN SEDAN	
4/1	1938	CADILLAC V16 TOURING SEDAN US ARMY	
4/2	1938	CADILLAC V16 TOURING SEDAN US AIR FORCE	
4/3	1938	CADILLAC V16 TOURING SEDAN US NAVY	
5	1938	CADILLAC V16 2 DOOR COUPE	
6	1938	CADILLAC V16 CONVERTIBLE TOP DOWN	
7	1938	CADILLAC V16 CONVERTIBLE TOP DOWN	"CICCIOLINA EDITION"
12	1938	CADILLAC V16 4 DOOR CONVERTIBLE SEDAN TOP DOWN	
12R	1938	CADILLAC V16 CONVERTIBLE TOP DOWN	F DOOR EDITION

1950 CHEVROLET BY RECORD MODELS. (AUTHOR COLLECTION)

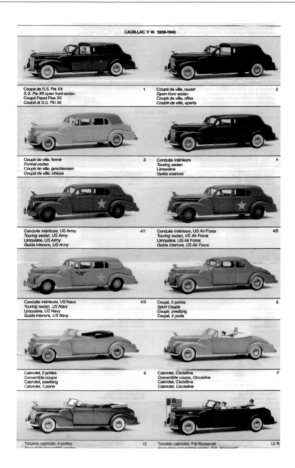

1938 CADILLAC RANGE FROM A REXTOYS BROCHURE. (AUTHOR COLLECTION)

(later made for Motor City USA). Richard Hutchins was the man behind the brand. He had worked with Mini Marque '43 and his initials appear on the base of some of its models. SAMS also produced a 1952 Pontiac sedan delivery that today is extremely scarce.

Jerry Rettig's American Wheels shows the SAMS 1949 Pontiac pickup as being "ex-R&J" which may have been made by Ron Harmon in Detroit for his company, R&J. On both doors of 100 R&J Pontiacs is a decal for SAMS Several versions of the 1949 Pontiac pick up (no 1) with and without canvas covered cargo beds and some outfitted as tow trucks, were handbuilt by R&J Miniatures Ltd.

SUN MOTOR COMPANY

The originator of Sun Models is highly revered enthusiast Rod Ward who is editor of *Model Auto Review*. Rod sells Sun Models and a variety of other models from his on-line store, Modelauto. This English-based builder handmade a small range of white metal and resin American car models during the 1980s, including its first replica, a 1952 Cadillac S75 7 passenger sedan artfully rendered from Ertl's die-cast 62 Series 4 door sedan. This was a sturdy and well-proportioned model that lacks the detail of today's handbuilts. Still, it is a nice model and the only handbuilt model of a 1952 Cadillac.

TRON

Paolo Rampini's Tron Models has been one of the world's leading producers of handbuilt collector model cars in 1:43 scale, since 1975. This productive builder's main interest is in "models of prestigious sports cars current, classic and historical, and Formula 1 cars from the year 1960 until the 1980s" such as models of Ferrari cars from 1947 onwards in both kit and built form. These models are made with white metal and are highly-detailed with engine and hinged opening bonnets.

The 'Tron Club' range are built-up models, well painted and supplied in elegant show case boxes. Tron has produced three sets of American models that occasionally are available on the aftermarket. In addition to the 1956 Dodge Royal Lancer I have owned Tron's Chris Boyer-mastered 1949-50 Oldsmobile convertible (resin), including Indy 500 pace car and club coupe (white metal). These models were fairly plentiful. They are nicely detailed and well-proportioned but are quite small, at around 1:45 scale at most.

Tron's 1947 Cadillac is a delightful model as a fastback and convertible. It has excellent proportions and detailing and is well finished, often with metallic paint.

1949 PONTIAC PICKUP BY R&J. (AUTHOR COLLECTION)

VF MODELAUTOMOBILE

Volker Feldkamp of Germany owns VF Modelautomobile. He handbuilds a variety of 1:43 scale models, many Cadillac models, and distributes them directly through his website. VF's 1949 Cadillac-Fleetwood Series 75 Limousine and 1947 Cadillac S62 convertible are nicely proportioned and well-detailed white metal replicas that appear to be based on Provence Moulage's models from the 1980s.

1947 CADILLAC BY VF. (AUTHOR COLLECTION)

VICTORY MODELS

It seems sometimes that Lalique crystal is more plentiful and accessible than a Victory model. At this point, only Victory's founder, Ray Paszkiewicz Jr. sells Victory Models in the U.S. and there is one dealer known in Europe. That's exclusive! Ray's Victory Models' masters are made from scratch in France by Georges Pont's CCC, using Ray's documentation, photos and drawings. Victory has modeled 1938-1953 cars from Buick, Cadillac-LaSalle, Checker, Chrysler, Packard, and Studebaker as well as a Wrecker/Tow Truck from Diamond T and a transit bus.

A Victory Model is made of resin, usually with a white metal base for the deluxe line, and a resin base for the La Familia line. As a result, models are light, similar to a die-cast model. Similarities to die-cast end there though, because Victory Models are consistently of good proportions, flawlessly painted, assembled with great care and are produced in exceptionally low numbers.

1941 CADILLAC RANGE FROM VICTORY MODELS. (AUTHOR COLLECTION)

Prices range from $159-$240. These beautiful and exclusive models are well worth it.

Ray Paszkiewicz Jr comments: "The third day of my life included a ride home from the hospital with my parents in our 1937 Chevrolet Master De Luxe sedan. As the car accelerated, the whine of the transmission in rhythm with the throaty exhaust must have been music to my ears. It initiated a life-long obsession with everything automotive. It is quite simple; as far back as my memory serves me, there has never been a day that I have not expounded on some facet of the industry or the merits of a fine automobile.

"About the age of eight, I began to cut out auto advertisements from various magazines. I discovered the fantastic *Fortune* magazines of the 1930s at a second-hand bookstore. They were filled with gorgeous Packard, Lincoln, Cadillac and other luxury car ads and my collecting of paper had its beginnings. In 1950, my first visits to auto dealerships began. On a typical Saturday, my friends and I visited every showroom and loaded up with sales brochures. A new Schwinn Hornet helped me travel far and wide in these endeavors. I still have every one.

"Over the years, I added a lot of additional automotive memorabilia, including photos, postcards, data books, signs, trinkets, pin backs, blotters, maps and whatever else I found in my travels. I have collected Dinky toys, slush mold vehicles, all types and kinds of plastic and rubber toys and many different metal cars and trucks. At one time, I had a collection of 700 promotional scale models from 1949 to about 1970.

"In 1978, I began importing 1:43 scale models out of England. The first models were MGs, Triumphs and Austins made by Abingdon Classics. Shortly thereafter I took on Western Models and Brooklin Models, which were made in Canada at that time. I've carried so many different brands of models since those days that it would fill a couple of pages.

"Later in life, I left my day job and turned my obsession into my business. Around 1990, finding a need to create favorite cars from my parent's generation, Victory Models was born. Our first model was the 1941 Cadillac Series 62 Convertible Coupe. It took four different craftsmen to finally mold the body to my satisfaction, but it was well worth the effort. It has been and still is our greatest selling vehicle.

"'Victory' is the appropriate name to convey the spirit of the forties. Victory Models' goal is to recreate the wonderful vehicles built during this decade. During World War II, the United States accomplished industrial feats that proved our strength and resolve to the world. America's production achievements in all phases of the war effort was a tribute to every defense worker on the home front. A time of pride, of Franklin D Roosevelt and Harry S Truman, Winston Churchill, General Douglas MacArthur, fathers and sons, family ties and wonderfully nostalgic automobiles.

"Since our original introduction of the 1941 Cadillac, we have produced more than a dozen different passenger cars, and four commercial vehicles all under the Victory name.

"In 1999, we introduced a new series of cars named 'La Familia' (the family). Years ago, when most families owned one car and Mom stayed home with the kids, the car was referred to as the 'family car'. Mainly, everyday closed models rather than the sporty open models about which Dad probably fantasized. These cars were owned by the middle class and driven to work daily. I know the name sounds European (actually it is Italian), but I like the sound of it and what it represents. This line is priced less than the Victory series.

"I am the sole proprietor of Victory Models, an American company. Our models are totally assembled in France. Our castings are resin. All models are 1:43 scale. We strive for an authentic look in our product. Our goal is to have the customer know he is looking at a Victory piece without seeing the label. It's our look! We match the paint to original paint chips from the auto manufacturer. Our customers appreciate our efforts and there are those who purchase whatever we introduce on standing order."

WESTERN MODELS

Mike and Joyce Stephens founded Western Models. The company produced fine models for three decades under its own banner

General Motors Company models from Victory Models

Number	Year	Marque/model	Comments
VM-1	1941	Cadillac Series 62 Convertible Coupe	Valcour Maroon and Dusty Gray
VM-1A	1941	Cadillac Series 62 Convertible Coupe	Oceano Blue
VM-3	1941	Cadillac 60 Special Sedan	Black, Oceano Blue/Crystal Blue . Gunmetal/Berkeley Gray and Cimarron. Green/Berkeley Green
VM-4	1941	Cadillac Series 62 Convertible Sedan	ElCentro Green Sequoia Cream
VM-8	1941	Cadillac Series 61 Sedanet (fastback)	Valcour Maroon, Dusty Gray/Rivermist. Gray and ElCentro Green/JFairoaks Green
VM-10	1940	LaSalle Series 52 Convertible Coupe	Oxblood Maroon and French Gray

La Familia by Victory

Number	Year	Marque/model	Comments
VL-1	1938	Buick Special 4 door sedan	Botticelli Blue or Titian Maroon

Number	Year	Marque/model	Comments
VL-2	1938	Buick Special Business Coupe	Carot Beige or Raphael Green
VL-3	1940	Buick Super 4 door sedan	English Green or Royal Maroon
VL-4	1938	Buick Special Convertible Coupe open	Homer Gray or Van Dyke Brown
VL-5	1938	Buick Special Convertible Coupe w/top	Homer Gray or Van Dyke Brown
VL-10	1940	Buick Super Convertible Coupe	Bandolier Blue or Sequoia Cream
VL-11	1938	Buick Special Convertible Sedan with side mounts	Titian Maroon or Van Gogh Green

Victory Commercial:

Number	Year	Marque/model	Comments
VC-1	1947	GMC Coach 3506 36 passenger bus	"Public Service Coordinated Transport of New Jersey" Battleship Gray/Light. Gray/White w/Red trim * *
VC-3	1947	GMC Coach 3506 36 passenger bus	"Trenton Transit" Straw w/Green trim 3 billboards decorate sides and front.

GENERAL MOTORS COMPANY MODELS FROM WESTERN MODELS

NUMBER	YEAR	MARQUE/MODEL	COMMENTS
WMS28	1933	CADILLAC V-16 PHAETON	TOP UP AND TOP DOWN
WMS67	1941	BUICK SEDANET	ALSO AVAILABLE IN TWO-TONE (TT)
WMS67P	1941	BUICK SEDANET HIGHWAY PATROL	CALIFORNIA HIGHWAY PATROL TAMPO
WMS68	1949	CADILLAC COUPE DE VILLE	
WMS68X	1949	CADILLAC S62 CONVERTIBLE TOP DOWN	
WMS78	1941	BUICK ROADMASTER CONVERTIBLE TOP UP	
WMS78X	1941	BUICK ROADMASTER CONVERTIBLE OPEN	
WMS84	1941	OLDSMOBILE DYNAMIC CRUISER SEDAN	
WMS96	1941	BUICK STATION WAGON (WOODY)	
WMS103	1941	BUICK SEDAN	
SW13	1953	CORVETTE ROADSTER	TOP UP AND TOP DOWN

1941 OLDSMOBILE BY WESTERN MODELS. (AUTHOR COLLECTION)

tend to range widely and typically match the model's original issue price.

Mike Stephens comments:

"As for model cars, we have produced replicas of both European and American automobiles for many years, including models of lower line cars. Western Models undertakes the complete production process from drawings through origination to final articles. This includes spin casting of different alloys, vacforming, artwork and design."

ZAUGG/EMPIRE

Jurg Zaugg of Switzerland was a pioneer in the production of white metal handbuilt models. Thomas Wolter's Tin Wizard Model Company is still making many of his replicas but no GM models. Zaugg produced several scale models, including a 1951 Chevrolet in multiple body styles such as an ambulance with flashing emergency lights. Slightly smaller than 1:43, this is a nicely finished model that suffered from a windshield frame proportion flaw. It was narrow at the top necessitating smaller roofs and side windows that slanted at an inaccurate angle. Zaugg also made a 1955 Cadillac and 1959 Chevrolet.

and for other companies. In 2007 the Stephens' wound down the business to enjoy a well-earned retirement, a bittersweet event for many hobbyists who will miss their fine products. Offering a broad range of American street models, Western has been particularly careful to issue models in the prosaic but popular 4 door sedan and station wagon body styles.

Western Models are mid-priced, positioned between Brooklin and Motor City USA. Its models are accurate in scale and well detailed with chrome door handles and photo-etched wipers. To keep costs down, emblems are usually decals and interiors are simple.

Western's models are $150 brand new. Aftermarket prices

SUPPLIERS 9

Because of their low sales volume, handbuilt models are sold by only a small number of companies. Shown here are a number of reputable suppliers that are well known to collectors.

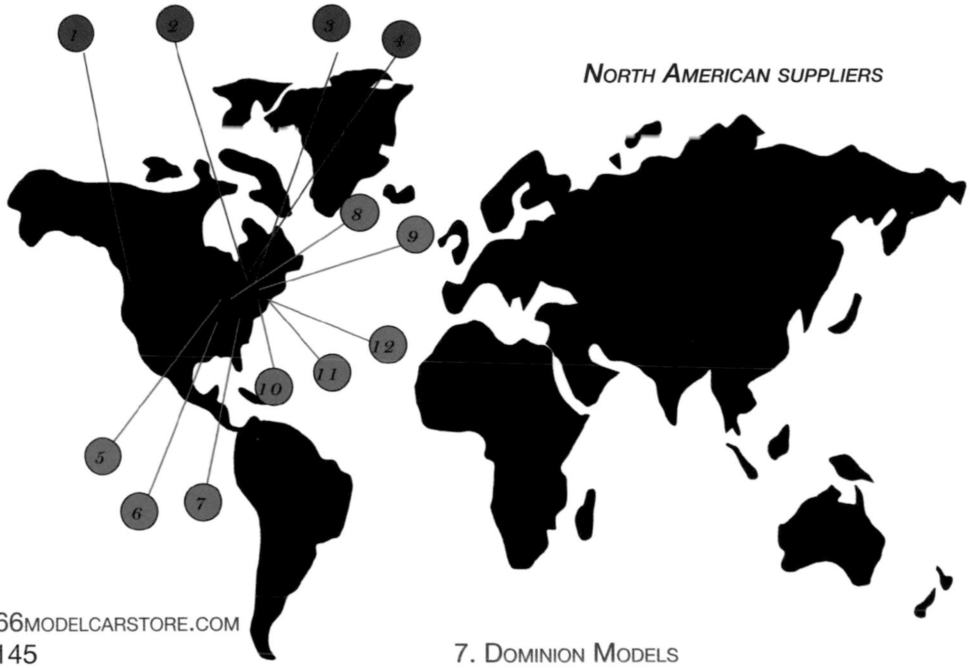

NORTH AMERICAN SUPPLIERS

1. eAutomobilia
2531 Ontario St, Vancouver,
BC V5T 2X7 Canada
Phone: 604-873-6242
Fax: 604-873-6259
info@eautomobilia.com
www.eautomobilia.com

2. Karmodels.com
7252 Vanness, Montreal, Quebec
H1S 1Y7 Canada
Phone: (514) 255-8469
info@karmodels.com
www.karmodels.com

3. Mini Grid Toronto
608 Mt Pleasant Road, Toronto, Ontario
M4S 2M8 Canada
Phone: (416) 488-7663
Fax: (416) 488-4292
www.minigrid.com

4. Bibliauto
1524, Notre-Dame ouest
Montréal, Quebec, Canada
Phone: (514) 938-9399
bibliauto@bellnet.ca
www.bibliauto.com

5. Route66modelcarstore.com
PO Box 145
Western Springs, IL 60558,
USA
Phone: 708-246-1543
Fax: 708-246-1085 buz@
route66modelcarstore.com
www.route66modelcarstore.com

6. Brasilia Press Inc.
PO Box 2023, Elkhart, IN 46515, USA
Fax: (574) 262-8799
www.brasiliapress.com

7. Dominion Models
PO Box 515, Salem, VA 24153, USA
Phone/Fax: 540-375-3750
dominionmodels@aol.com
www.dominionmodels.com

8. Sinclair's Mini-Auto
PO Box 8403, Erie, PA 16505, USA
Phone: 814-838-2274
Fax: 814-838-2274
E-mail: dave@miniauto.com
www.miniauto.com

NORTH AMERICAN SUPPLIERS

9. TOYS FOR COLLECTORS
95 PUBLIC SQUARE, SUITE 511, WATERTOWN, NY
13601, USA
PHONE: 888-445-3322/315-782-4692
FAX: 315-782-8167
E-MAIL: TFCUSA@NORTHWEB.COM
WWW.TFCUSA.COM

10. VICTORY MODELS
PO BOX 156, CLARKSBURG, NJ 08510, USA
PHONE: 732-446-9381
FAX: 732-446-9297
RAYPAZJR@AOL.COM

11. EWACARS
205 US HWY 22, GREEN BROOK NJ 08812,
USA
PHONE: (732) 424 7811
FAX: (732) 424 7814
WWW.EWACARS.COM

12. ACCENT MODELS
PO BOX 295, DENVILLE NJ 07834, USA
PHONE (973) 887-8403
FAX: (973) 887-5088
INFO@ACCENTMODELS.COM
WWW.ACCENTMODELS.COM

EUROPEAN & AUSTRALIAN SUPPLIERS
13. MODEL AUTO LTD
PO BOX SM2, LEEDS LS25 5XA, UK
PHONE: 01977 681966
FAX: 01977 681991
SALES@ZETEO.COM
WWW.ZETEO.COM/MAR

14. J M TOYS LTD
32 ASTON ROAD, WATERLOOVILLE, HAMPSHIRE,
PO7 7XQ, UK
PHONE: 023 9226 2446
FAX: 023 9225 2041
SALES@JMTOYS.NET
WWW.JMTOYS.NET

15. SPACROFT
98 HIGH STREET, TIBSHELF, DERBYS,
DE55 5NU, UK
PHONE: 01773 872780
SPACROFT@AOL.COM
WWW.SPACROFTMODELS.CO.UK

16. SAINT MARTINS MODEL CARS
95 ST MARTINS LANE, LONDON,
WC2N 4AS, UK
TEL: 020 7836 9742
FAX: 020 7240 1219
WWW.STMARTINSMODELCARS.CO.UK

17. GRAND PRIX MODELS
4 THORPE CLOSE, THORPE WAY, BANBURY,
OXFORDSHIRE OX16 4SW, UK
TEL: 01295 278070
FAX: 01295 278072
WWW.GRANDPRIXMODELS.CO.UK

18. AUTOSHOW
ROEGERGASSE 18, A - 1090 VIENNA, AUSTRIA
PHONE: +43-1-31 99 863
AUTOSHOW@AON.AT
WWW.AUTOSHOW.AT

19. CAR43
4 AVENUE PICTET DE ROCHEMONT, CH-1207
GENEVE, SWITZERLAND
PHONE: 0041 (0)22 736 84 90
FAX: 0041 (0)22 736 84 90
CAR43@BLUEWIN.CH
WWW.CAR43.CH

20. SPIEL & HOBBY KUPSCH
KARDINAL-GALEN-STR. 120, D – 47058
DUISBURG, GERMANY
PHONE: +49 203 28 2690
FAX: +49 203 28 8106
PKUPSCH@KUPSCH-GERMANY.COM
WWW.KUPSCH-GERMANY.DE

EUROPEAN & AUSTRALIAN SUPPLIERS

21. MODEL PARADIES
SCHEFFELSTR. 14, 76275 ETTLINGEN, GERMANY
PHONE: +49 (0)7243 / 15959
FAX: +49 (0)7243 / 31720
WWW.ARTCRAFTMODEL.DE
HTTP://STORES.EBAY.COM/ARTCRAFTMODEL-COM

22. MODEL CARS HERITAGE
ST PETERSBURG, RUSSIA
PHONE/FAX: +7 (812) 727 95 72
MCH@SP.RU
WWW.MODELCARSHERITAGE.SPB.RU

AN EXCELLENT SOURCE OF MODELS IS EBAY.COM.
LOOK FOR:

23. BOOSHMAMA
24. 2CV01 (WWW. 2CV01.COM)
25. CHADSWORTH
WWW.STORES.EBAY.COM/
BROOKLINANDBRITISHMODELAUTOCO
26. HOBIE48
27. TOYBOY (HTTP://MEMBERS.AOL.COM/AWTOYBOY/
AWTOYBOY.HTML)
28. MODEL CARS OF THE WORLD
39 BENWERRIN DRIVE, BURWOOD EAST, VICTORIA
3151, AUSTRALIA
PHONE: +61 3 9887 9929
FAX: +61 3 9887 8336
SALES@MODELCARS.COM.AU
WWW.MODELCARS.COM.AU

CONTACT DETAILS
APPENDIX 1

BROOKLIN MODELS LTD
PINESWAY INDUSTRIAL ESTATE
IVO PETERS ROAD, BATH BA2 3QS UK
WEBSITE:WWW.BROOKLINMODELS.CO.UK
PHONE:+44 (0)1225 332400
FACSIMILE:+44 (0)1225 447430
E-MAIL: BROOKLIN_MODELS@TALK21.COM

BRUCE ARNOLD MODELS
BRUCEARNOLD@CS.COM

CONQUEST MADISON
PO BOX 145 WESTERN SPRINGS, IL 60558,
USA
WEBSITE: ROUTE66MODELCARSTORE.COM
PHONE: 708-246-1543
FAX: 708-246-1085
EMAIL: BUZ@ROUTE66MODELCARSTORE.COM

DURHAM CLASSICS AUTOMOTIVE MINIATURES
HTTP://STORES.EBAY.COM/DURHAM-CRE8TOR
EMAIL: DURHAMCRE8TOR@HOTMAIL.COM

ENCHANTMENT LAND COACHBUILDERS
2985 N. WALNUT AVENUE
TUCSON, AZ 85712, USA
E-MAIL: JERRYRETTIG@MSN.COM

GREAT AMERICAN DREAM MACHINES
HTTP://STORES.EBAY.COM/GREAT-AMERICAN-
DREAM-MACHINES

MILESTONE MINIATURES LTD
25 WEST END, REDRUTH
CORNWALL,TR15 2SA UK
PHONE:01209 218356
FAX:01209 217983
EMAIL: GEMSCOBWEBS@FREEUK.COM
WWW.MODELCARS.CO.UK

MINI MARQUE
TELEPHONE: +44 142 472 2007
WWW.MIDLANTICMODELS.COM

MOTOR CITY USA
13400 SATICOY STREET #12
NORTH HOLLYWOOD, CALIFORNIA 91605
E-MAIL: INFO@MOTORCITYUSA.COM
PHONE: 818.503.4835
FAX: 818.503.4580
WWW.MOTORCITYUSA.COM

VICTORY MODELS
LILLIPUT MOTOR CAR CO.
PO BOX 156, CLARKSBURG, NJ 08510,
USA
PHONE: 732-446-9381
FAX: 732-446-9297
RAYPAZJR@AOL.COM

PHOTO CREDITS
APPENDIX 2

Fellow enthusiasts, suppliers, and builders endowed this book with their photographs. Here are the sources of the photos and where appropriate, their contact information and/or websites:

Bruce Arnold
Bruce Arnold Models
Brucearnold@cs.com

John Arnold

Andy Bradshaw
Collectors Antiques
http://stores.ebay.com/Collectors-Gang

Bradley Gorman

Greg Gunn

Christian Hardegger

Bob Hooper
Dominion Models

Dominionmodels@aol.com
www.dominionmodels.com

David Larsen

Deitrich Lohman
www.artcraftmodel.de
http://stores.ebay.com/artcraftmodel-com

Will Martin

Dirk Mathyssen

Alex Moskalev

Alan Novak
Motor City USA
info@motorcityusa.com
www.MotorCityUSA.com

Ray Paszkiewicz Jr
Victory Models
raypazjr@aol.com

Jerry Rettig
Enchantment Land Coachbuilders
E-mail: jerryrettig@msn.com

Dave Ronken

John Roberts
john.roberts@jrcustombuilt.com
www.jrcustombuilt.com

Mike Stephens

Julian and Margaret Stewart
Durham Classics Automotive Miniatures
http://stores.ebay.com/durham-cre8tor
Email: surhamcre8tor@hotmail.com

Steve Williams

Robert M Woolley
Founder, Model Car Journal, Retired

Why not visit Veloce on the web? – www.velocebooks.com
New book news • Special offers • Details of all books in print • Gift vouchers

INDEX